Menu

Greenshell Mussels
Cracked Stone Crab Claws
Balick Salmon on Black Bread
&
New Zealand Baby Lamb Chops
Venison Filet, Mini-brioche
&
Rose Petal Salad - Three Greens
&
Baby Chocolate Cheesecakes
&
Coffee Kir Royale Cognac

The
TIFFANY
GOURMET
Cookbook

JOHN LORING

DOUBLEDAY

New York London Toronto Sydney Auckland

ALSO BY JOHN LORING

Tiffany Parties
The Tiffany Wedding
Tiffany's 150 Years
Tiffany Taste
The New Tiffany Table Settings (with Henry B. Platt)

*DOUBLEDAY and the portrayal of an anchor
with a dolphin are trademarks of Doubleday, a division of
Bantam Doubleday Dell Publishing Group, Inc.*

*Recipes for "Roast Chicken with Herbs" and "Chocolate Soufflé
with Whipped Cream and Chocolate Sauce" reprinted with permission
of Macmillan Publishing Company from* The Edna Lewis Cookbook
*by Edna Lewis and Evangeline Peterson. Copyright © 1972 by
Edna Lewis and Evangeline Peterson. Originally published by
The Bobbs-Merrill Company, Inc.*

Book design by Marysarah Quinn

Library of Congress Cataloging-in-Publication Data
Loring, John.
     The Tiffany gourmet cookbook / John Loring.
        p.   cm.
     Includes index.
     1. Entertaining.   2. Cookery, International.   3. Menus
4. Celebrities.   I. Title.
TX731.L578   1992
642'.4—dc20   *92-9835*
                                                                          CIP

ISBN 0-385-42571-6
Copyright © 1992 by Tiffany & Co.
All Rights Reserved
Printed in Italy
November 1992

10 9 8 7 6 5 4 3 2 1

FIRST EDITION

Contents

Acknowledgments

My debt and its accompanying gratitude to Charlotte Aillaud for her contribution of the French section of this book, as well as for over thirty years of her guidance and encouragement along whichever paths of civilization I have sometimes falteringly managed to follow, are together incalculable.

Great thanks too go to my longtime friend and Milan's inimitable "Best Dressed List" contessa and journalist, Nally Bellati, and to her so-talented husband, photographer Manfredi Bellati, for their contribution of the Italian section of the book.

More thanks are due too to my friend and frequent companion in the "hauteurs" of New York society, Jean Tailer, for her contributions of Long Island, Newport, Saratoga, and Nashville.

My pal, advisor, and "mother confessor," Eleanor Lambert, who contributed the English section as well as secured the participation of a whole phalanx of other not-so-easy-to-reach personalities, deserves for this project, as for most all my projects, a major vote of gratitude mixed with awe and fondness.

The Tiffany Gourmet Cookbook would never have been brought about without the inspired diplomacy, ingenious traffic direction, and superhuman patience of my "coworkers" Yone Akiyama, Rita Eckartt, and Victoria Colyer of Tiffany & Co.'s Design Department, where they frequently offer the Design Director excellent direction as well as tireless assistance.

The "look" of the majority of the photographs of the book owes very much to my friend and permanent collaborator on illustration, Billy Cunningham, and to the collaboration in turn of his assistant, Martin Friedman.

Tiffany's Director of Product Design, John Fling, has my praise for clarifying my vision of the book's graphic direction.

Food expert, editor, and writer Mary Johnson has my relieved gratitude for correcting and adjusting failings or obscurities in the recipes as they were found in the often colorful but not always clear styles of the contributors.

And finally, all the contributors and their staffs deserve thanks as well for the talent and courage such an adventure required.

LEFT: *A late Louis XIV gate-legged oak table holds buffet foods in the author's Paris apartment. In the background, an 18th-century Austrian court portrait hangs above the room's red marble Louis XIV fireplace. The corner chair is Georgian Irish as are the covered silver urns made for the Mayor of Waterford in 1786.*

ABOVE: *A lunch of Baked Dorades with Ripe Black Olives, Capers, and Fresh Lemon; Potato, Celery, Cucumber, and Pickle Salad; and a Minted Summer Fruit Salad are served in antique Angoulême old Paris porcelains. An 18th-century delft bowl holds champagne roses and white flox. The ribbed baluster crystal candlesticks are 18th-century Irish.*

There are settings that stimulate a sense of pride and privilege, and there are settings that simply delight. The best do both. Whatever the case, every successful setting with its transient splendors of food and furnishings and flowers is a self-portrait of the host or hostess; each is a small monument to the convivial, generous, and hospitable facets of the human spirit.

Over the years hundreds of celebrities and stars of society, business, and entertainment have been invited to do "Tiffany Table Settings" either for Tiffany's displays or for publication in Tiffany books. Their company has included such personalities as Brooke (Mrs. Vincent) Astor, Andy Warhol, Mrs. Henry Kissinger, Cary Grant, Mary Martin, the Ronald Reagans, New York Mayor Koch, Earl Blackwell, Angela Lansbury, Bob Hope, H.R.H.

In the author's Paris dining room, an 18th-century Portuguese tile general watches over an oval table set with early 19th-century Angoulême old Paris porcelains, gilded Italian wineglasses, and Tiffany "Hampton" flat silver. Decanters are Tiffany & Co.'s exclusive "Nemours" from Baccarat. In the background an 18th-century delft plate and vase sit atop a Louis XIV oak sideboard.

Princess Chantal of France, Mikhail Baryshnikov, the Robert Mosbachers, Vladimir Horowitz, Estée Lauder, Bill Blass, Diana Vreeland, the Earl and Countess of Rosse, Andrée Putman, Geoffrey Beene, Mrs. Milton Petrie, James Stewart, Diana Rigg, the Baron and Baroness di Portanova, Mario Buatta, Paige Rense, . . . The list is panoramic. Each has intrigued the public with their very personal interpretation of the art of table setting as the art of self-portraiture.

The qualities that make us attractive to our friends are reflected in the food we offer them and in the tables we set to receive them. The same blend of wit, grace, and charm; simplicity or splendor; conservatism or audacity, that distinguishes us, distinguishes our tables.

We bring a richly textured mix of memories, values, expectations, and sometimes the persuasive argument of hunger to the table. All these elements provoke our imaginations in designing a setting or composing a menu.

The personalities in *The Tiffany Gourmet Cookbook* were asked to create their self-portraits through favorite foods and the table furnishings they would use to serve them. The results present a privileged vision of style and imagination, which should awaken and excite the most dormant epicurean urges.

The great Bette Davis once said to me, "I really haven't much to offer people, but one thing I can do is fix them a good meal."

Making my rounds in 1976 as a magazine essayist, I visited a location for photography, near Weston, Connecticut, an eighteenth-century mill turned country house belonging to friends of Miss

Foods on this dinner buffet include, in the foreground, Roast Tenderloin of Pork with Tarragon-Cognac Cream Sauce and Pan-fried Sour Apples, Steamed Cauliflower with Beurre Noisette, Baked Onions with Golden Raisins, Fine Green Beans with Bacon and Shallots, Saddle of Hare in Mustard Sauce, Boiled Pork Shoulder with Green Cabbage, and Potatoes with Bacon and Green Onions. There is also a Salad of Mâche with Fried Quail, Wild Mushrooms, and Bacon. With the exception of the 18th-century blue and white delft plate holding the green beans, all dishes are from Tiffany & Co.'s exclusive collections of French faience. The serving silver is Tiffany's "Hampton."

Davis. They suggested I visit her nearby cottage for lunch on the way back to New York. A bit intimidated by the invitation and knowing my illustrious hostess had no cook, I called late in the morning to point out that the day was uncomfortably hot and perhaps cooking lunch a bother. That, to be honest, was not my only reservation. Visions haunted me of the culinary atrocities served up to Joan Crawford by Bette Davis in *What Ever Happened to Baby Jane?* Anyway, I called. "I've already made you lunch, Mr. Loring" was the reply in that inimitable New England voice. So I went, to an unforgettable meal of cold Fresh Tomato Soup, Roast Pigeon with Peas, Cucumber Salad, and chocolate ice cream and cookies with my film-star friend turned cook.

Bette Davis, who had given so many evenings of entertainment to millions, felt that offering a good

meal was the best expression of friendship within her formidable bag of tricks and charms. I have always agreed with her.

My own bag of tricks and charms was less formidable when sixteen years before that lunch I had arrived in Paris, aged twenty, to begin what turned out to be an eleven-year stay in France. What, I wondered, had a barely more than teenaged American to offer the French, and like Miss Davis I hit on "the good meal as token of friendship" theory.

French cooking was unfamiliar to me, despite a 1954 *grand tour* of Europe led by my mother during which I had absorbed little more knowledge of *la cuisine française* than that snails and frogs legs were both edible and tasty when combined with generous amounts of garlic, butter, and chopped parsley; that the French could trick a teenager with the intricacies

OVERLEAF: *In the author's New York apartment a Portuguese Prune Meringue Tart topped with cinnamon is served before a backdrop of antique tiles from a Lisbon palace. The three white porcelain figures are early 19th-century Portuguese toothpick holders from Vista Alegre. An American art pottery Fulper vase holds yellow calla lilies. Tiffany's "All Purpose" glasses are used to serve Portuguese rosé wine. The plates are 1860s Paris porcelain, and the hexagonal silver candlesticks are from Tiffany's "Frank Lloyd Wright Collection."*

ABOVE: *Mixed French and northern Italian influences are present in this dinner of Sea Scallop, Watercress, Arugula, and Scallion Salad followed by Veal Kidneys Sautéed with Juniper Berries and Gin and garnished with Fried Croutons. The porcelain plates are Tiffany & Co.'s "Tiffany Poppies" and "Princess Chantal" patterns. The flat silver is "Century." The creamware salt and pepper dishes are 18th-century English. The mid-19th-century toothpick holder in the form of a bull is from Caldas in central Portugal.*

RIGHT: *A fondness for Morocco inspired this meal in the author's New York apartment of Roast Capon with Ripe Black Olives, Lemon Zest, and Sweet Italian Sausage; Rice with Scallions, Golden Raisins, and Pignoli; and Fresh Leaf Spinach with Sour Cream and Nutmeg. The colorful brocade cushions, covered "Safi" pottery rice bowl, and the French orientalist painting of a Moroccan boy were all found in Marrakech. The porcelain bowl is Tiffany's "Liseron—Private Stock." Serving pieces include Tiffany's "Hampton." Sprays of speckled orange orchids sit in a 1920s Danish art pottery vase by Hermann Kehler.*

Here one of the author's favorite first courses, Roast Yellow Peppers and Radicchio with Fresh Goat Cheese, is in preparation. The quartered and cleaned vegetables are coated with olive oil and baked, then served with cold fresh goat cheese.

In the dining room of The Red House, built in western Michigan in 1850 by the author's great-great-grandparents, a traditional family dinner is served on Tiffany's "Malmaison" porcelain. The Russian breakfront in the background displays part of The Red House's original dinner service of Mason's No. 1 Ironstone with its colorful Indian tree pattern.

of a traditional *hors d'oeuvres variés* into eating both beets and carrots in quite acceptable salads; and that it was a toss-up whether poached pears or candied orange rinds tasted best with chocolate. Such was the wisdom of fourteen.

However, what I did know at twenty was how to make great home-style American food. From the cooks at my parents' guest ranch in Arizona, I knew a thing or two about Mexican cooking as well. Good American meals, I thought, in this country of *fins gourmets,* would be something to please the French and just possibly something to surprise them.

There were modest triumphs and there were spectacular failures, but the triumphs prevailed, and within two or three years of my arrival, there were few members of *le tout Paris* who would turn down my dinner invitations.

I learned the hard way that maple and horseradish are flavors abhorred by the French. When the famed Parisian architect and social lion, Emile Aillaud, bellowed *"Enfin, le pain au chocolat!"* on tasting my American devil's food cake, I learned that all ethnic foods don't travel.

There were, fortunately, other American recipes

for success. A crown roast of pork with oyster stuffing finally won Monsieur l'Architecte Aillaud's favor, as did a pecan pie made with golden syrup and walnuts (corn syrup and pecans being unavailable). There were my grandmother's cook's stewed chicken in yellow gravy with baking powder biscuits, and my mother's cook's oven-fried chicken with potato pancakes, or Mother's own lamb stew with dumplings, pot roast with heavy cream, or pepper steaks with bourbon. These and a host of other American dishes could go anywhere with success. What praise the French would lavish on a good American apple pie with its lattice top, or old-fashioned pineapple upside down cake, or fresh peach cobbler. In short, I learned that the French, like everyone else, love good plain food, and I also learned that they like it served with beautiful table furnishings.

When I had my first interview with Van Day Truex in 1978, applying for the job as his successor as Design Director of Tiffany & Co., to my astonishment and delight he didn't wish to discuss design at all. He felt he had a pretty good idea of what I thought about that from my essays in a variety of magazines. What he wanted to talk about was food and how to select it, cook it, and present it at the table. "Unless you know a great deal about food and its settings," he said, "you could never be the design director of Tiffany & Co. How could someone hope to design china, crystal, and silver for a Tiffany table setting who doesn't understand what to eat at one?"

Van Day Truex himself was an excellent cook; and, despite his appearance, that tall, elegant bean pole of a gentleman in his "Best Dressed List Hall of Fame" wardrobe loved great meals. He loved to tell of his own early days in Paris in the 1930s as director of the Parsons School of Design in the Place des Vosges when he was faced with offering lunch in his quarters to the Princesse de Polignac. "I confronted my maid with this not-at-all unpleasant predicament but predicament nonetheless and told her that I didn't see what we could offer such an exalted personage in my small flat," he would recall.

"Monsieur Truex," she said to him, "I make a very good Blanquette de Veau à l'Ancienne and that should do very nicely indeed for Madame la Princesse de Polignac, or anyone else high or low. It is a good dish and I make it very, very well."

The *blanquette* was served. The Princesse de Polignac was delighted by both its excellence and Van's grace in serving something appropriate to the occasion. Van learned the power of a good meal gracefully offered; and, the Princesse de Polignac became his greatest supporter throughout his years in Paris.

My road to the office of Design Director of Tiffany & Co. passed as often through the kitchens of the world as through its great houses and museums. It was the profound interest I always had in food and seeing it well cooked and well presented that, more than knowledge of the decorative arts, led Van Day Truex to appoint me his successor as Tiffany's Design Director.

Table furnishings are only props for acting out the daily ceremonies of dining. They bring charm and beauty and glamor, but they can do little of that if the food isn't up to the expectations of the occasion. Food's flavors, textures, colors, and aromas must play their proper roles in the overall production, or all of Tiffany's magnificently colored and patterned china, all the glitteringly cut crystal, and all the masterfully crafted silverwares backed up by exquisite linens and seductive flowers will not transform an event into a great meal.

Artists are traditionally fond of good food and are more often than not pretty good cooks, with much of the imagination they bring to their art extended to their dining habits. Food, like art, makes its primary appeal to the senses. I feel, as Van Day Truex felt, that taste and style in what we eat is connected to the sensual and imaginative forces that govern taste and style in the rooms we arrange and the art we love.

My arrival in Paris in 1960 was the beginning of four years of formal study of art and design at the legendary École des Beaux-Arts, birthplace of the beaux arts architectural style of well-bred and educated pomposity all splendidly overornamented— the style of opera houses, public libraries, train stations, and turn-of-the-century millionaires' mansions. However, the Beaux-Arts was not a temple of culinary culture. The hot meals in its dining hall which then cost a hardly believable eighty old francs, or about sixteen cents, were rude fare served on compartmented metal trays. The students' "favorite" menu was built around grilled pig's tails and ears with pureed potatoes. These were unspeakable and inedible, but occasioned hilariously messy food-fight free-for-alls once every two weeks. *Tiffany Table Settings* was far off in those days when the art of the French table was to be learned outside the sacred walls of the Beaux-Arts.

Exceptional good luck had given me three advantages in the great game of learning about food and other table furnishings: first, I had quickly been adopted by a large and remarkably cultured French family with a Louis XV *hôtel particulier* in Paris and a sprawling country house near Nemours; second, my older brother had a vast Greek summer house perched on the cliffs of Santorini; and third, my mother had a little gem of a summer house and garden of her own in the shadow of the majestic dome of Santa Maria della Salute in the center of Venice. The secrets of French, Italian, and Greek cooking were not to escape me, nor were the pleasures of hunting for table furnishings at the Paris Flea Market, London's Portobello Road or King's Road antique markets, Athens' Monasteraki district, or in the grander emporiums of the merchants of Venice. It's worthy of note that in all those treasure troves of the decorative arts at least fifty percent of the goods offered were made for use at the table, irrefutable evidence of the world's ongoing passion for dining well. Good food served with beautiful

BAKED DORADES WITH RIPE BLACK OLIVES, CAPERS, AND FRESH LEMON
POTATO, CELERY, CUCUMBER, AND PICKLE SALAD
MINTED SUMMER FRUIT SALAD

ROAST TENDERLOIN OF PORK / TARRAGON-COGNAC CREAM SAUCE
PAN-FRIED SOUR APPLES
STEAMED CAULIFLOWER WITH BEURRE NOISETTE
BAKED ONIONS WITH GOLDEN RAISINS
FINE GREEN BEANS WITH BACON AND SHALLOTS
SADDLE OF HARE IN MUSTARD SAUCE
BOILED PORK SHOULDER WITH GREEN CABBAGE
POTATOES WITH BACON AND GREEN ONIONS
SALAD OF MÂCHE WITH FRIED QUAIL, WILD MUSHROOMS, AND BACON

TIGER SHRIMP GRILLED WITH GARLIC
PORK WITH CLAMS
POTATOES WITH ROSEMARY
KALE WITH GARLIC AND OLIVE OIL
ZUCCHINI WITH PEPPER SAUCE
PRUNE MERINGUE TART

ROAST CAPON WITH RIPE BLACK OLIVES, LEMON ZEST, AND SWEET ITALIAN
    SAUSAGE
RICE WITH SCALLIONS, GOLDEN RAISINS, AND PIGNOLI
FRESH LEAF SPINACH WITH SOUR CREAM AND NUTMEG

SEA SCALLOP, WATERCRESS, ARUGULA, AND SCALLION SALAD
VEAL KIDNEYS SAUTÉED WITH JUNIPER BERRIES AND GIN / FRIED CROUTONS

ROAST YELLOW PEPPERS AND RADICCHIO WITH FRESH GOAT CHEESE

BONED RIB ROAST
YORKSHIRE PUDDING
FRIED GREEN GARDEN TOMATOES

CHINA LORING'S GRAHAM CRACKER TORTE
CHINA LORING'S DATE BARS
CHINA LORING'S HOLLAND BUTTER COOKIES
GRANDMA WEBSTER'S MOLASSES CAKE

CHILLED FRESH PEA SOUP
SMOKED SALMON MOUSSE / CUCUMBER AND SOUR CREAM SAUCE
BEET, WALNUT, ONION, AND SAUSAGE OMELETTE

things—how much pleasure that combination ever continues to bring to life.

However, it takes flair and experience to plan and cook a meal or to plan and carry out a table setting successfully.

I had believed as a child, from familiarity with two vast family dinner services—one Spode's Blue Tower, and the other a Mason's Indian Tree pattern known in the history of ceramics as "Mason's No 1"—that all dishes were imported from the English town of Stoke-on-Trent just as all foodstuffs were imported from the local Safeway or A & P supermarket. Both beliefs obviously turned out to be false.

A family move to Arizona in 1945 opened the avenues of ethnic design and ethnic food as I explored the Mexican and American Indian cultures of that strange and then undeveloped country. Eventually I discovered that Mexican silver and colored glass combined with Mexican and Indian ceramics, baskets, and weavings had their own rudely stylized and unsophisticated splendor and could be used as

The family collection of handwritten cookbooks in the author's Red House contains hundreds of recipes for old-fashioned cakes and cookies. Here a children's tea party includes four of the author's mother's favorites: Graham-Cracker Torte; Holland Butter Cookies, Date Bars and Great-Grandma Webster's Molasses Cake, named for Betsy Matilda Hathaway Webster, who lived in The Red House from 1850 to 1912. Dishes include three "Tiffany Private Stock" patterns; "Halcyon," "William IV," and "Coeur Fleurs," as well as 19th-century English stonewares. The Humpty-Dumpty doll was given to the author's mother in 1904.

well (or badly) as the civilized table furnishings of England. My move to Paris some years later opened my eyes to the glories of faience and fine porcelain, just as it opened horizons in gastronomy beyond my American mother's and English father's deliciously homey and satisfying dishes, punctuated with the traditions of their various imported Southern, Mexican, or northern European domestics.

Nonetheless, my Yorkshire-born father's dinners of a Rib Roast of Beef, Yorkshire Pudding, Fried Green Tomatoes, and Boiled Leeks have remained a staple of my culinary vocabulary, as have the excellent cakes and cookies: the Graham Cracker

Tortes of my birthdays, Grandma Webster's Molasses Cake, cinnamon-and-almond-flavored Holland Butter Cookies, and the perfection of Mother's simple Date Bars. And just as everyone's childhood memories of favorite family foods influence their future tastes, so the English potteries, bone china, and ironstone of my youth remain quite acceptable to my eye despite whatever refinements of taste have been acquired in the more elevated fields of continental European and Oriental tablewares.

In thirty years of cooking and designing for the table there have been many moments memorable for their excitement as well as some for their absurdity.

A summer luncheon of Chilled Fresh Pea Soup; Smoked Salmon Mousse with Cucumber and Sour Cream Sauce; Jellied Molded Tarragon Chicken; Beet, Walnut, Onion, and Sausage Omelette; and mixed green salad is served on the back porch of the author's Red House. Dishes are Tiffany & Co.'s Mason Ironstone "Yellow Flowers." The flat silver is Tiffany's "Wave Edge." The engraved wineglasses are from The Red House's original dinner service.

My greatest compliment in the kitchen was paid me by another legendary actress, Lillian Gish, at a dinner I had cooked for a hundred guests on the opening night of the Max Reinhardt exhibition in the mid-1970s at New York's now-vanished Cultural Center. The late art impresario Mario Amaya hosted that dinner for the world of New York art society with the likes of Lotte Lenya, Lady Diana Cooper, Lillian Gish, and other stars of Reinhardt films. After my dinner he introduced me to Miss Gish, challenging her to tell me that the dinner was the best in memory. "I'm not sure," responded the ever-civilized Miss Gish, "that it was the best food I remember, but it was certainly the most acceptable food I've had in a long, long time."

Another New York Cultural Center dinner, this time in celebration of Man Ray, re-creating his legendary Pecci-Blunt White Ball of 1922 on its fiftieth anniversary, required a trip to Paris to lunch with Man Ray in my rue du Dragon flat to discuss not only the dinner and ball but also the poster which he had delegated me to design and print. A pressed chicken with tarragon accompanied by a sour cream, yogurt, and mayonnaise-based cucumber sauce of my invention delighted the great artist-photographer though he refused to believe that I could have made such a thing myself, simple as it was in reality. "Now look here," he said to me, "be good and tell me which neighborhood charcuterie made this. You know I live quite nearby, and I want to be able to order this myself. Anyway, I'm sure this wasn't cooked by you just as I'm sure the portrait of your father over there by the bookcase wasn't painted by Titian."

This convoluted compliment pleased me greatly. My poster of a blue baguette ("Blue food for blue people") on an amorphously shaped canary-yellow background intersected by a giant cadmium orange

Man Ray signature pleased the New York Cultural Center public, who believed it to be an authentic Man Ray design. And I had the unique privilege of cooking an all white dinner of *brandade de morue,* roast veal with cauliflower and salsify, endive salad, and vanilla ice cream with lichee nuts assisted by the legendary muse of Surrealism, Lee Miller (Lady Penrose), then food editor of English *Vogue.* I retain two things from that dinner: the first that color plays an important, even vital, role in food and its presentation (white was not enough); the second a wonderful image of Lee Miller stirring and tasting my *brandade de morue* and exclaiming, "More garlic! More olive oil! More martinis!"

"More" is a term of possibility, of opportunity identified, of promised satisfaction, never to be lost sight of either in the kitchen or in a table setting. "More" is the cry that comes from the generosity of spirit that motivates all great cooks and all great hostesses. In architecture "less" may be desirable, although a quick comparison of Philip Johnson's Glass House and the Petit Trianon might tend to refute this, but at the dinner table more is more. Underseasoned dishes, undernourished guests, and underadorned tables never brought a sense of festivity nor event. Whereas generous portions of good food in beautiful settings never fail to please.

The variety of styles in table furnishings offered in the world is as seemingly endless as the world's variety of foods. Every culture has its uniqueness. The pure-visioned, pared-down refinements and satisfying simplicity, the reined-in physical energy and close-to-the-earth-and-Nature harmony of traditional American design are precisely reflected in good old-fashioned American dishes; the Baroque and operatic stylishness of Italy is mirrored in its lusty and sensual cuisine; and the exquisitely sophisticated and rococo chic of the French is expressed in the dazzling orchestration of foods at once very simple and very complicated served up at their tables.

The same parallel between food and art is surely true of all countries. Russian food as Russian art is both barbaric and splendid. Modern Greek and Turkish food and art lean toward unrefined luxury and somewhat distressing sensual and caloric excess. The "anything goes" eclectic fantasies of Portuguese design have their equal in the deliciously unexpected taste combinations of Portuguese cuisine. The confectionery bent to Austrian food and art is self-evident. The greatest English painters focused their art on handsome portraits of wealthy farmers and charming landscapes of their estates; similarly, English food of roasts, meat or fish pies, stews, unembellished vegetables, and rich puddings, although often excellently prepared and eminently soul-satisfying, is nonetheless the hearty fare of farmers.

All countries design table furnishings to complement their cuisine. The French and Italians triumph in this. The English, whose cares focus so little on refinement in food, have nonetheless produced a remarkable percentage of the world's truly wonderful tablewares. The eighteenth-century mania for tea, coffee, and hot chocolate inspired in Germany rococo splendors of porcelain and silver. These are of consummate refinement but for that very reason seldom integrate successfully into the somewhat boisterous stylishness of contemporary western Europe or America where, unlike central and eastern Europe, the sybaritic custom of afternoon cakes and coffee is long vanished from life's daily ceremonies.

There are also smaller countries that excel in the arts of the table. Little Portugal's porcelains, ceramics, crystal, and silverwares are as finely crafted and as imaginatively designed as any in the world, the result of remarkable native artisan skill and centuries of aesthetic cross-pollination with the large English port wine-dealing community in Pôrto, as well as with Chinese and Indian influences imported from Portugal's colonies of Macao and Goa.

In the early 1960s, the German interior design magazine, *Schöner Wohnung,* published a table setting from an apartment I then had on Paris's Île St.-Louis with a caption cavalierly informing the readers that the table was in a fisherman's cottage on the North Sea and set for a fine dinner of freshly caught eels. Yet the table, which was set with Mexican and Austrian peasant dishes, did not seem so incredible attributed to the fancied Nordic location. The eighteenth-century painted Spanish paneling of the dining room could easily have been mistaken for its Bavarian counterpart and the dishes too could have passed for other Bavarian designs. This is the genius of peasant potteries the world over; they all have a common denominator of rustic charm that gives them world citizenship.

The higher styles of fine tablewares, however, do not have that charmed adaptability. English ironstone and pottery do not comfortably mix with French faience or Italian ceramic which, in fact, don't often successfully mix with each other. Even within cultures different materials can seldom be used together successfully. Faience and ceramic refuse to mix willingly with porcelain no matter how related their patterns, and this is true in France and England and Germany and Italy and Portugal and every other ceramic-producing country. Their surface textures—faience soft and sensual, porcelain hard and brilliant—clash disconcertingly. The same unwillingness to cooperate persists between the warmth and "hominess" of English bone china and the cool sophistication of continental porcelain. And even within the range of continental porcelains, fine German wares with their soft, just off-white colorings and their slightly waxy glazes are never well matched with the pure white color and highly reflective glazes of Limoges wares.

These nuances seem finely drawn at first glance; yet, on closer inspection, they are as dramatic as the obvious differences between national cuisines and vital in understanding the arts of the table.

As can legitimately be suspected, all these marked differences evolved through intention and not through happenstance. Each culture created table furnishings to complement its cooking, with the result that English food and English tablewares are eminently suited to each other; French haute cuisine looks best served on French porcelains, and French peasant or provincial dishes look best served on French faience. Italian food is essentially country food and looks best served in Italian ceramic or faience dishes, which probably explains Italy's restricted fine-porcelain production and its preeminence in the world of pottery.

None of this, however, presents insurmountable obstacles to variety in foods and table settings. No host or hostess is expected to have as large a range of table furnishings as a range of recipes, yet an intelligent assessment of the resources at hand to present food appropriately is basic to success in any table setting.

The Tiffany Gourmet Cookbook travels across America and Europe to visit an eclectic list of prominent personalities, each known for expertise in the preparation and presentation of food, and each with a very personal vision of the art of entertaining at the table. The secrets of each household's kitchens and the often intriguing furnishings collected for their dining tables reflect and complement each other.

Each setting, with its so-personal combination of foods and furnishings, is a telling portrait of its author and a tribute to his or her personal style; not there to be imitated, but to be admired and serve as both guide and inspiration for all those whose lives are uplifted and brightened by the "convivial, generous, and hospitable facets of the human spirit."

Charlotte Aillaud ~ Paris

CONCHITA'S CHEESE SOUFFLÉ (SOUFFLÉ AU FROMAGE CONCHITA)
CONCHITA'S SEAFOOD QUICHE (QUICHE AUX FRUITS DE MER CONCHITA)
FILLETS OF SOLE WITH ARTICHOKE HEARTS
STUFFED VEGETABLES

One block west of Paris's Place St.-Germain-des-Prés, the rue du Dragon begins its short and gently meandering path south to the Croix Rouge where its name changes descriptively to the rue du Cherche Midi.

Behind the eighteenth-century portals that imposingly punctuate an otherwise uneventful procession of boutiques and bistros, the rue du Dragon conceals some of Paris's more delightful *hôtels particuliers*. Of these, the Aillaud house, a small gem of Louis XV architecture just off the boule-

vard St.-Germain, best retains the air of worldly elegance and luxury that made Paris the capital of all things intellectually, emotionally, and physically pleasurable in the midst of the eighteenth century.

In her enchanted pavilion perched between a catalpa-shaded courtyard and a chestnut-shaded formal garden, Charlotte Aillaud, justly described as one of the last true Parisian *femmes du monde*, holds court to a superbly eclectic and ferociously loyal coterie of celebrities of the arts and letters and of society, who are "Madame Aillaud's" family and friends.

The house's stuccoed and *faux* marbled Empire dining room, opening on one side to the Louis XV oak-paneled grand salon and on another to the gardens, is the scene several times a week of formal/informal luncheons where the orchestration of conversation, food, and decor are invariably memorable.

"My Parisian lunches," Charlotte Aillaud explains, "are planned to avoid spending an eternity around the table. Everyone today is busy, but it is both pleasant and essential to meet at lunchtime for a restful moment in a relaxed atmosphere.

"We frequently serve the 'famous'—and justly reputed—Soufflé au Fromage Conchita followed by a Salad of Shrimp, Smoked Salmon, and Mâche in the summer (or Seasonal Stuffed Vegetables on cool days) followed by a green salad and good, simple French cheeses.

"We finish with dessert, Charlotte aux Abricots or sliced fresh pears covered with finely flaked Parmesan cheese.

"A Bordeaux or a light Burgundy happily accompany this type of meal."

Here the large, oval white marble dining-room table is set for lunch with a pale green embroidered Italian tablecloth, Tiffany "Palmette" sterling flat silver, Herend porcelains, and paper-thin Venetian crystal. Four small trompe l'oeil porcelain cabbages echo the real Savoy cabbage used as a centerpiece.

A remarkable multitiered, early nineteenth-century Italian ceramic gueridon filled with a mixture of real and *faux* fruits and vegetables ornaments a corner of the room; while perched atop a marble column an opulent and subtly hued informal bouquet of garden flowers grown and arranged by the hostess animates the overall decor.

Such glorious bouquets are as carefully cultivated, picked, and arranged by Mme. Aillaud as are the guest lists at her luncheons.

"Entertaining," Mme. Aillaud likes to point out, "is never as easy as some overly optimistic hostesses maintain, nor as complicated as claimed by those who receive badly.

"I sometimes dream," she continues, "of a lunch composed only of an admirable platter of cheeses accompanied by a great vintage Bordeaux and a salad with an olive oil dressing. This formula, however, has fewer admirers than I sometimes allow myself to believe."

In wintertime smaller dinners are served in the dining room, which in cold weather shelters potted orange trees and camellias, giving it the air of a winter garden. At these dinners a fire is lit in the room's generously proportioned white marble Empire fireplace the moment guests are seated. Larger dinners are moved to a series of round tables for eight in the adjoining salon, which for dinners is romantically lit by candles in its two ample Louis XV crystal chandeliers and by a pair of majestic twelve-branch candelabra.

On warm summer evenings the magic of a hidden Paris garden with all its splendid secret charm sets the tone of Mme. Aillaud's glittering dinners. These have been attended over the years by a diverse guest list of celebrities which has run from Marie-Laure de Noailles to Peter O'Toole; from Philip Johnson to Françoise Sagan; and on to Marie Bell, Yves Saint Laurent, and Pierre Bergé, Claude Dauphin, Hélène Rochas, Joseph Losey, Marie-Hélène de Rothschild, Ruggero Raimondi, Rudolf Nureyev, Herbert von Karajan, Michel Piccoli, Olivia de Haviland; and, of course, the hostess's celebrated singer sister, Juliette Gréco. The list is virtually endless.

Here the round tables on the garden's white marble terrace are dressed with blue-green linen cloths found in Salzburg during one of the music festivals that Mme. Aillaud religiously attends and set with Tiffany & Co.'s "Villandry" Limoges porcelain and "Palmette" flat silver.

Again there are no flowers on the tables, which are lit by slender five-branch neoclassic silver candelabra.

"I prefer to avoid floral centerpieces on small tables, as they oblige my guests to play at hide-and-seek all evening," the hostess explains. "I prefer some favorite eighteenth-century Chinese cloisonné enameled pots filled with fruits such as prunes and red currants watched over by Chinese porcelain birds. Even such a slight decoration can tell a story."

The guests arrive at twilight. The fountain chatters at the center of the little formal garden, and the roses and mandarin orange trees release their perfumes joined perhaps by a potted jasmine vine in full bloom or masses of tuberoses (one of Charlotte Aillaud's favorite flowers) in tall blue and white

K'ang Hsi vases just inside the open bedroom windows above the garden.

Before dinner, the guests tour the garden drinking iced champagne.

The hostess dislikes the habit of hors d'oeuvres before dinner. "Either they have too strong a flavor," she says, "or else they are insipid and ruin everybody's appetite."

For this dinner, Mme. Aillaud has chosen a menu of Fresh Seafood Quiche (without pastry); Fillets of Sole with Artichoke Hearts, a salad of red lettuce, cherry tomatoes, sliced raw mushrooms, and "blanched" and cooled cauliflower and green beans; fresh white Fontainebleau cheeses in their cheesecloth "dresses"—a rarity which can still be found at the neighborhood cheese merchants; and, for dessert, fruit- and flower-shaped sorbets inside open-worked nougatine baskets from the Bonbonnière de Buci in the nearby Marché de Buci.

Only one wine, a chilled Gamay or Bouzy, will be served at such a summer garden dinner.

"These dinners succeed," Charlotte Aillaud observes, "because they maintain a warm sense of intimacy no matter how celebrated (or 'notorious') the guests.

"Entertaining well is not, contrary to what some believe, a matter of following some 'infallible' rule to the letter. It is at once simpler and more delicate than all that: it is enough to have taste, to have appetite, and above all—*above all*—to avoid boredom in any and all its diverse forms."

Charlotte Aillaud~Nanteau

SPANISH MEATBALLS (ALBONDIGAS)
BRAISED VEAL SHANK (JARRET DE VEAU)
STUFFED CHICKEN
STACKED VEGETABLE OMELETTES (OMELETTES EN PILE)
CONCHITA'S RICE PUDDING (GÂTEAU DE RIZ CONCHITA)
CONCHITA'S CHOCOLATE CAKE (GÂTEAU AU CHOCOLAT CONCHITA)

When weather permits, and in central France it almost always does, the Aillaud family abandon the activity of Paris from early Friday evening until late Sunday night or Monday morning for the relative calm of the postcard-perfect hamlet of Nanteau-sur-Lunain not far from Fontainebleau.

Here at a series of old stone farm buildings lovingly transformed over nearly half a century into a rambling country domain of considerable complexity and beauty, the family and intimate family friends give themselves over to the arts of con-versing, gardening, noncompetitive tennis and card games, cooking, and possibly best of all, enjoying the *cuisine de Nanteau* as the superb house brand of internationalized French country cooking has become known.

A book could easily be written on the hundreds of house favorites augmented over the years by contributions of new friends and new family members. There are Mexican influences from Charlotte Aillaud's late husband, the great French "urbanist" architect Emile Aillaud, who was born into a French

colonial family in Mexico. Italian and even American influences have been added by various other members of the extensive family: and, it is not unusual to detect Greek or North African notes introduced after some particularly happy family summer safari to faraway places.

One need look no further than the dining room's painted Mexican chairs acquired from an exposition at Paris's Galeries Lafayette some thirty-two years ago to find clues of the *cuisine de Nanteau*'s many international secrets.

"If I describe the latest lunch at Nanteau," Mme. Aillaud explains, "I will describe all of them, as to a large degree every one has a strong family resemblance to every other.

"When the meteorologist has the audacity to promise fine weather, our family and our friends express their need for the country with such determination that they leave me no choice but to quit the rue du Dragon for Nanteau.

"The number of guests at weekend tables changes little over the years: at sixteen we are very comfortable; with more than twenty, the situation becomes critical.

"With Conchita, our cook of thirty-five years standing, we choose recipes that can be simmering while we wait for guests lost on their way between Nemours and Fontainebleau and others who cannot seem to resolve their tennis match. Amongst the dishes made regularly, part of the day's menu at

Nanteau are Braised Veal Shank with Olives; Stuffed Chickens with Leeks, Carrots, and Turnips; Boiled Beef; Mexican Red Beans; Albondigas; and Fines Omelettes en Pile, which is simply a great pile of very thin warm or cold vegetable omelettes of all flavors—onion, green pepper, zucchini, eggplant, tomato—which is cut like an American layer cake, giving everyone a taste of each.

"Time-honored household traditions imply a lengthy preparation of these dishes as well as of innumerable desserts.

"On occasion Conchita has allowed close friends who she too has known for decades to join her in cooking, and such departures from the rigid protocol of her kitchen produce some memorable dishes: a Crown Roast of Pork with Oyster Stuffing, Veal with Oranges, Duck Glazed with Grand Marnier and Marmalade, Fish Stew with Capers, Green Olives, and Pink Peppercorns.

"However, it remains an act of considerable daring to venture into Conchita's kitchen. After reigning over her pots for a very long time, her moods, like the climate, are abruptly subject to change and can go in a flash from 'continuing fair weather' to a storm.

"Like the French railroad's 'Wagons-Restaurants,' we serve twice. The bell rings at one o'clock for the children, and again towards two o'clock for the grown-ups.

"To welcome those arriving, a *vin blanc cassis* is served along with some slices of *saucisson au poivre* that are always within reach of guests who fancy such things.

"Through the ten-foot-tall *porte-fenêtres* the meadows and gardens appear to spill into the vast dining room along with the children tripping over the dogs as they rush to show off a newly discovered baby hedgehog.

"On very hot days, small tables for eight are sometimes set on the terrace or on the lawn under the garden's immense chestnut tree, but, for me, the proportion of the great dining-room table is more charming.

"There is always a long tablecloth made from acres of flowered country gingham; and, in the morning, I try to steal flowers from the garden without the garden appearing to miss them. Then, along with the flowers, we make huge bouquets of leaves to fill out the room's summer dress."

A pair of Tiffany's "Strasbourg" flowered ceramic pitchers hold Mme. Aillaud's towering and sumptuous bouquets, which like her gardens bloom in pinks, blues, and white with a firmly intentional avoidance of reds and oranges; although, the palest yellows can occasionally be allowed.

The table is set with simple English transferware plates, Tiffany's simple, unpatterned "Faneuil" flat silver, and an all-purpose glass at each place.

An antique white faience duck and white faience pumpkin and cabbage tureens further ornament the setting.

Covering the entire far wall of the dining room, an intriguing and maniacally detailed map of Nanteau painted as a pastime by Aillaud family members exiled to the country house during the German Occupation of Paris in World War II, makes an unconventional and perfect backdrop for Aillaud family lunches, which are relaxed and joyous, full of originality and improvisation.

Immediately after the main courses, the lunch party will move from the block of farmhouses that includes the dining room to a northern terrace beyond a second block which houses the family living quarters. "Here," Charlotte Aillaud explains, "the many desserts will be served: the wonderful Gâteau de Riz, whose recipe I have always kept for us alone; the Floating Island; the Gâteau au Chocolate; and the Charlottes all bring back the tastes of childhood.

"Of course, here on the terrace, we do have to fight off the wasps who also react enthusiastically to Conchita's desserts, and we chase off the children when they come offering us horrible little bunches of dandelions, but," she adds, "only the country can color certain hours of our lives with such sweetness.

"After dessert and coffee, the light Bordeaux served with the meal invites us each to a nap under the apple trees in the meadow, but before that a sincere ovation salutes Conchita, who condescends at the end of the lunch party to appear like Queen Elizabeth on her balcony."

Françoise Sagan

CONSERVED GOOSE (CONFIT D'OIE)
SALAD OF ASPARAGUS TIPS
BRIOCHE WITH CANDIED FRUITS (BRIOCHE DU SUD-OUEST)

"Françoise Sagan adores her native Lot in southwestern France, its houses, its landscapes, its people, and its cuisine," explains Sagan's lifelong friend Charlotte Aillaud. "She can't resist a Purée de Marrons or Pommes de Terre Sarladaises, or the wild mushrooms that evoke the forests of her childhood.

"Nonetheless, her habitual indifference toward the pleasures of the table is the subject of pleasantries for her entourage, and the press has long ago given up any hope of photographing Françoise Sagan putting a pie in the oven.

"She sometimes prepares improbable Croque Monsieurs for apprehensive friends, but in principle prefers to let Pepita, her cook, take charge of the occasional dinners. At these charming and ever-successful *soirées-buffets,* she serves wonderful dishes (which she herself rarely tastes).

"Sagan's classic French *bourgeois* upbringing gave her the taste for great wines; and, it's with the smile of a true connoisseur that she serves a 1961 Gruaud-Larose or a 1938 Lynch-Bages.

"By habit, Françoise Sagan is so carefree that she seems to be a guest in her own house when she entertains, but she supervises everything to make her guests comfortable and happy with a precision otherwise quite unlike her.

"In short, she loves to spoil her friends; and for her, the French expression *faire la fête* has an excellent ring to it. A large tin of caviar brought from some trip will serve as a pretext for a cheerfully improvised Russian dinner in the small garden that prolongs her salon and allows for long summer *soirées,* or in the dining room where the light-colored bamboo furniture creates a colonial atmosphere.

"Most often Françoise Sagan has no idea just how many of the artists, journalists, authors, or designers invited in a sudden burst of gaiety (or could it also be in an excess of *tristesse?*) will show up. Yet, however many arrive, her admirable ease and flawless tact shed their light of generosity and gaiety on the evening. Everyone is happy around her."

Françoise Sagan has her own comments on pitfalls to be avoided for a successful dinner:

"Above all, never invite either two very amusing people, or two lugubrious ladies: the first will steal the show, the second will bring out the handkerchiefs.

"Avoid guests that are going to congratulate each other (too much honey) or guests that want to hit each other (too much vinegar). Everyone must be able to exteriorize their feelings without high risks.

"Avoid the chronically melancholic; because, if by chance, your party wakes them from their melancholy, they may never leave.

"Avoid gluttons and ascetics.

"Beware of guests with convoluted attitudes who tell mysterious stories and of the indiscreet who are always disturbing."

The last advice:

"In case of either small problems or irreparable *gaffes,* keep a low profile, don't intervene in the hostilities, and slip away to your private apartments to powder your nose."

Here for a happy and friendly dinner in the dining room of her Paris home, Françoise Sagan offers her guests a classic southwestern French dinner of *la cuisine du Lot* of Confit d'Oie (Conserved Goose) garnished with chestnuts, mushrooms, and "Pommes Sarladaises"; Asparagus Salad, and a Brioche with Candied Fruits served with an orange and mandarin sauce.

"Japanese Bird" French faience buffet plates from Tiffany's complement the room's "colonial" atmosphere.

La Baronne Guy de Rothschild

> MONKFISH WITH CREAMED LEEKS
> (LOTTE À LA CRÈME DE POIREAUX)
> PUREED POTATOES WITH SAFFRON
> (PURÉE DE POMMES DE TERRE PARFUMÉE AU SAFRAN)

*P*osed like a great ship on the Seine at the eastern tip of the Île St.-Louis, the Hôtel Lambert, built by Le Vau in 1642, is a palace like no other. Guests privileged to dine here with the Baron and Baroness Guy and Marie-Hélène de Rothschild are transported through time and space in the grand manner of heroes in a fairy tale to a decor in the magically opulent style that has become known quite simply as *Le Style Rothschild*.

The exquisite politeness of the hosts, the spontaneous warmth in their welcome, the elegance of the guests, the profusion of garden roses placed everywhere all contribute to the enchantment.

As in the eighteenth century, tables are set in the different salons according to the number of guests. In the famous Galerie d'Hercule, the long table can seat up to seventy-four.

The Rothschild collections of silver, crystal, and porcelains which include a 481-piece *vert pomme* Sèvres service provide inexhaustible possibilities.

Here for a dinner both intimate and sumptuous, the Salon des Cuirs serves as a showcase for the Rothschild style. The salon's walls are covered with seventeenth-century Flemish paintings on leather depicting *David's Triumphant Entry into Jerusalem* formerly in the dining room of the Rothschilds' Château de Ferrières in Brie.

Marie-Hélène de Rothschild's inlaid mother-of-pearl table is centered by a sixteenth-century Augsburg vermeil statue of Diana, goddess of the hunt. Diana in turn is surrounded by a superb collection of seventeenth-century nautilus shell and silver gilt cups including a swan cup from Augsburg and a dragon cup from Utrecht.

The settings' engraved glasses are French Louis XIV, the silver chargers are seventeenth-century English, and the contemporary art flatware is by celebrated French pop-Surrealist sculptor Claude Lalanne. Candles on the table are held by sixteenth-century Italian rock crystal baluster candlesticks engraved with vines and festoons of fruit.

So much beauty would seem to exclude the idea of food; however, in her inimitable style Marie-Hélène de Rothschild will see to it that the menu is even more elaborate than the decor.

At her table, one of the most innovative in Paris, her guests have discovered the little Soufflés à la Truffe, .the Pigeon à la Miel, and the Sorbet au Fromage Blanc that are among her myriad creations. Here dinner will include her Lotte à la Crème de Poireaux.

Baronne de Rothschild's perfectionism as a hostess coupled with her well-known power of seduction and irresistible smile make all her guests, be they princes or painters, firmly believe that the *joie de vivre* still lives.

"However rich or poor one is," she says, "certain ingredients are essential: a pinch of madness, two dashes of refinement, three grains of effort, and a few heartbeats."

Yves Saint Laurent

Lamb Curry (Curry de Pré Salé)
St. Marcel Cake (Gâteau St. Marcel)/*Vanilla Custard Sauce*
(Crème Anglaise)

*A*ny dinner at couture great Yves Saint Laurent's Paris home satisfies Diaghilev's much-quoted command to his entourage, "Amaze me!" Conceived as works of art, Saint Laurent's evenings with their sense of theater coupled with a taste for perfection are unforgettable.

For Saint Laurent, each meal and its decor is preceded by a flight of imagination, fed by the diversity and quality of the sumptuous objects that surround him and that offer him limitless inspiration.

Yves Saint Laurent is unmoved by society's *vie mondaine* and reserves these treasures of invention, which like his dress designs are frequently informed by a literary or artistic memory, for only a few close friends. His love of intimacy is as great as his fame.

Here at his dining table decked with a favorite decor, an ambiance of gold and rock crystal punctuated by the motif of a sheaf of wheat, symbol for him of all food, he will offer a dinner of whole steamed truffles followed by simple and delicious Curry de Pré Salé and a rich chocolate Gâteau St. Marcel.

The table is ornamented with gilt bronze angels holding huge amethysts and centers on a magnificent vermeil covered rococo shell, ewer, and basin that formerly belonged to the Archduke of Austria.

Comtesse Sheila de Rochambeau

QUAIL EGG NESTS (NIDS D'OEUF DE CAILLE)
LOIN OF VEAL WITH PISTACHIOS (LONGUE DE VEAU AUX PISTACHES)
FROZEN RED FRUITS SOUFFLÉ (SOUFFLÉ GLACÉ AUX FRUITS ROUGES)

The elegantly appointed kitchen of Sheila de Rochambeau's Paris home in one wing of a handsome eighteenth-century *hôtel particulier* "is," she explains, "the heart of the house.

"For years I lived in an apartment where from my kitchen I heard my guests' laughter and conversation and I felt excluded. Nowadays, I give my dinners in the kitchen and enjoy my guests' company from beginning to end.

"Cooking is a passion. I have written for *House and Garden* and I constantly discover recipes in cookbooks, in restaurants, and in friends' homes that I try to interpret—sometimes with great trouble.

"I usually receive eight people seated or put together buffets for up to twenty, but with eight the atmosphere is ideal for conversation.

"To be relaxed is essential," notes the Comtesse de Rochambeau with her well-known charm, exu-

berance, and gaiety, "life has become so very difficult, so stressful for the majority, that dinner must
make CEOs forget their work and women forget
their worries. Very formal dinners are not my favorite thing. My kitchen is not the *Galerie des Glaces*.

"I find great inspiration in the seasons. A walk
around the market is always an opportunity for a
déclic provoked by the first artichokes, game, the first
asparagus.

"A pretty view will inspire me for a table setting.
I love the idea of a pumpkin in the fall, and on
principle I prefer to put parsley before orchids in my
'flower' arrangements."

Here at her kitchen table transformed grass-and-
all into a garden of spring flowers, Sheila de
Rochambeau offers a menu of Nests of Quail Eggs,
Loin of Veal with Pistachios, and Frozen Red Fruits
Soufflé.

Wines will include a Pouilly-Fumé followed by a
good red Bordeaux.

Marchesa Francesca Antinori

The great Italian poet Gabriele D'Annunzio described his country's table wines as "souvenirs of bottled sun."

No Italian family knows the secrets of making such popular "souvenirs" of Italy better than Florence's Antinoris, who have been making superb Italian wines ever since Giovanni di Piero Antinori was a member of the Vintners' Guild in 1385. Today the Antinoris' San Casciano wineries produce twenty-four different wines.

Here in the private dining room of the family's fifteenth-century Palazzo Antinori in Florence, the Marchesa Francesca Antinori takes time out from her rounds of charitable and cultural promotions, the pleasures of raising three daughters, and attentions to family business responsibilities to present a classic array of favorite Tuscan dishes for one of the intimate dinners for eight she prefers at her home.

The meal will begin with a great Tuscan tradition, pungent red cabbage, chicken liver, and tomato *Crostini Misti,* followed by another simple but irresistible local specialty, *Pappa al Pomodoro,* a robust tomato soup for which stale Italian white bread is a necessary ingredient. The main course will be a rich *Stracotto alla Fiorentina,* yet another mainstay of Florentine cooking, a pot roasted beef dish with a thick garlic, sage, rosemary, and basil–flavored sauce. For dessert there will be *Frutta Cotta della Cantinetta Antinori,* cooked and caramelized pears and apples, served with almond-filled *Biscotti di Prato.* The almond biscuits are to be dipped, naturally, in a slightly sweet, golden Vinsanto from the Antinori cellars.

The *crostini* and cooked fruits are served on Florentine terra-cotta plates designed by Elsa Peretti for Tiffany & Co. The sensuously formed sterling silver covered soup tureen is also an Elsa Peretti design for Tiffany's.

The splendid antique brass shell, ewer, and basin are Antinori family treasures, as is the massive brass wine cooler filled with home-grown lemons the Marchesa Antinori uses as a centerpiece.

The two massive blue and white vases holding leaves are *Faenza* majolica made by Ca'Pirota in the 1600s. The equally massive cut lead crystal candlesticks are from Tiffany's "Metropolis" collection and are made at Colle di Val d'Elsa south of Florence.

The stylish and noble setting of elegantly mixed grandeur and simplicity is backed by a painting of Michelangelo's *Campidoglio* in Rome painted by Agostino Tassi (1581–1644) hanging above a sixteenth-century Florentine sideboard, originally made for the Antinori family.

Antinori wines for the evening will include Borro della Sala, Vino Peppoli, Tignanello, Orvieto Classico Abboccato Campo Grande, and perhaps a final glass of sparkling white Marchesa Antinori Extra Brut, a family wine much favored by the great opera composer Giacomo Puccini.

Arrigo Cipriani

RICE WITH ZUCCHINI (RISOTTO AGLI ZUCCHINI)
JOHN DORY ALLA CARLINA
MERINGUE CAKE (TORTA MERINGATA AL CAFFE)

The Cipriani family's contributions to dining are legendary: Harry's Bar in Venice, the Hotel Cipriani and Harry's Dolce on the Giudecca, the Locanda Cipriani on Torcello, the Villa Cipriani in Asolo, New York's Bellini by Cipriani on Seventh Avenue, and Harry Cipriani in the Sherry-Netherland Hotel; Carpaccio, the Bellini, the Vodka Roger, the Shrimp Club Sandwich.

Here on the *fondamenta* in front of Venice's Harry's Dolce with the churches of Santa Maria della Visitazione and the Gesuiti on the *Zattere* across the Canal of the Giudecca for an operatic backdrop, international restaurateur "Doge" Arrigo Cipriani sets a table for three in classic Cipriani style: the familiar small round table conducive to friendly conversation, a pale, plain, ivory cloth flattering to the guests, simple Venetian hand-blown glasses from Murano's Nason and Moretti, a compact, unobtrusive bouquet of yellow rosebuds; and the famous Harry's Bar pitcher designed by his father Giuseppe Cipriani, who founded Harry's Bar over sixty years ago.

Having seen just about everyone and everything in his years of providing food and drink to the world's great and to those who follow in their paths, Arrigo Cipriani applauds authenticity in both food and people.

The lunch served here will include: Risotto agli Zucchini, one of the vegetable risottos pioneered long ago at Harry's Bar, in the days when Ernest Hemingway was a regular; San Pietro (or John Dory) alla Carlina, named for Arrigo Cipriani's sister; and a Torta Meringata al Caffe to complete this most Venetian meal, which is accompanied by pale yellow Livio Felluga Tocai wine in Harry's Bar's (and Tiffany's) "Bundle Pitcher."

Count and Countess Manfredi and Nally Bellati

Tagliatelli with White Truffles alla Lino (Tagliatelli alla Lino con Tartufi Bianchi d'Alba)
Pheasant with Pomegranate alla Contessa Giorgia (Fagiano al Melograno alla Contessa Giorgia)

*I*n front of the Villa Bellati built at the end of the 1600s at Campea near Treviso, the young Count and Countess Bellati take time out from their careers as photographers to offer a luncheon of house specialties: Fagiano al Melograno alla Contessa Giorgia; homemade *tagliatelli* with finely sliced white Alba truffles; and raspberries from the garden with a Croccante della Contessa Lucrezia, a brittle, nutty, giant dome-shaped "almond brittle" that accompanies ice cream with fresh fruit to perfection.

The beautiful young Countess Nally who is a much-published writer on style and the decorative arts has covered the table with rare antique Mariano Fortuny fabrics. Two massive nineteenth-century majolica vases from Faenza given to the Countess's great-grandmother by Queen Margherita of Savoy (for whom she served as lady-in-waiting) hold garden greens and flowers. A tall crystal vase made by Venetian grand-master glassmaker Archimede Seguso for Tiffany & Co. overflows with home-grown grapes. The Venetian wine goblets are also by Archimede Seguso.

The roast pheasant from the Villa Bellati's private game preserve sits invitingly in a sea of pomegranate seeds on a white Tiffany basket-weave platter from Este, while Asa Din, the family's much beloved woolly coated Jack Russell terrier, and a petit-point cushion featuring the Bellati crest worked by Countess Nally, both sit on eighteenth-century walnut chairs inlaid with the Bellati arms.

The silver luster Art Deco plates were designed by Susie Cooper for Gray's Pottery in 1929.

The silver implement next to the small plate of whole white truffles is a *taglia tartufi*. It was made for one use only—to slice truffles.

Rosita and Tai Missoni

> *FUSILLI WITH BLACK OLIVES AND CAPERS* (ALLA TAI *or* FUSILLI CON OLIVE
> NERE E CAPPERI ALLA TAI)
> *ROSITA'S SALAD* (INSALATA ALLA ROSITA)
> *PUMPKIN SOUP* ALLA ROSITA (ZUPPA DI ZUCCA ALLA ROSITA)
> *COTECHINO WITH LENTILS* (COTECHINO DI CREMONA CON LENTICCHIE)

*E*very meal at the Missonis' greenery-surrounded country house to the north of Milan presents an occasion to weave children and grandchildren, friends, collaborators, and clients into a well-choreographed and well-propped performance that is as enjoyable as it is informative.

The highly eclectic collections of art potteries, art glass, toys, textiles, and baskets that populate every surface and corner of the house, the equally eclectic mixtures of guests, and the soul-satisfying home-style Italian foods all have their stories to tell, and all participate in Tai and Rosita Missoni's view of dining as a means of communication.

The elements at Missoni dinners are, not unexpectedly, as natural and as intricately interwoven as the elements in their fashion empire's mainstay knits with their signature palette of natural dye colors: madder red, indigo blue, and yellow ocher mixed with blacks, ivories, grays, and earth tones.

Here dinner is served buffet style amongst an army of objects brought back by the Missonis from all parts of the world. There are baskets of every description which the Missonis have been avidly collecting for over thirty-five years. Their woven grasses, reeds, branches, and canes (most natural, some colored with vegetable dyes) have intentionally evident affinities to Missoni knits.

Legendary retailer Stanley Marcus once brought Tai Missoni a basket from Honduras because its colors reminded him of Missoni textiles. Contemplating the collection of baskets, Tai Missoni observes jokingly that "Missoni products have been copied throughout the world for the last two thousand years."

Here Insalata alla Rosita, an arugula, fennel, and Parmesan cheese salad, served in a "Thumb Print" terra-cotta bowl designed by fellow Italian design genius Elsa Peretti for Tiffany & Co. sits on a seventeenth-century walnut wood Florentine table surrounded by baskets. A small late-nineteenth-century *grotto* table nearby holds rice, a fundamental ingredient of Rosita Missoni's Zuppa di Zucca (pumpkin soup). The *zucca* pumpkin and leeks, the other principal ingredients of the soup, wait in an oversized basket from the basketmaker of the Tuscan village of Colle di Val d'Elsa, an artisan whose work has also been collected by Elsa Peretti.

The toy horse beside the Peretti bowl was a gift from film star Monica Vitti. The larger horse head was once a shop sign in Philadelphia.

The dinner's main dishes will be Fusilli con Olive Nere e Capperi alla Tai and Cotechino di Cremona con Lenticchie.

The dinner will be accompanied by white Tocai Rocca Rosata and red Barbaresco de Gresy wines.

Countess Marina Emo

RICE WITH PUMPKIN (RISO DI ZUCCA)
BRAISED GUINEA FOWL (FARAONA IN SALMI)
WINTER CAKE (TORTA INVERNALE)

*J*ust as the great Venetian masters such as Titian or Giovanni Bellini loved to use the lyric landscapes of the Veneto as backgrounds for their urbane saints and madonnas, the Venetian nobility since the early sixteenth century have had an ongoing love affair with the Venetian countryside, which they have dotted with superb villas of great architectural distinction. Here in anything-but-rustic *Cinquecento* splendor they continue to this day to revel in the *villeggiatura,* the sweet and sybaritic life of the villas as only the Venetians know how to live it.

One of the best-kept of the Veneto's sixteenth-century villas is the Villa Emo built in 1588 and situated between Padua and Este. A model of linear purity, its nearly cubic body stands behind a majestic columned portico. The villa, bordered by one of the world's great rose gardens, is less daunting than its more famous cousin Andrea Palladio's 1560s Villa Emo at Fanzolo di Vedelago near Castelfranco Veneto and Treviso. If guests to the villa invariably discuss the merits of the villa's attribution to Vicenzo Scamozzi, Palladio's associate and follower who presumably drew the plans, they also invariably discuss the superb traditional Italian food served by the Villa Emo's kitchens.

For centuries the noble Venetians leave the city for the country on June 13, the feast of St. Anthony, returning in the heat of the summer from mid-August to the first week in October, when they recommence the *villeggiatura* until mid-November. At the Villa Emo during the first *villeggiatura,* informal luncheons are served on long trestle tables set up between the rows of immaculately trimmed pear and apple trees that surround the villa's swimming pool. Menus are light summer fare of grilled or baked vegetables, roasted home-grown guinea hen, or fresh fish from the neighboring fishing port of Chioggia, where six centuries ago in August 1379 Pietro Emo led the Venetian defenders of the city against the Genoese forces of Pietro Doria.

On more formal occasions, and there are many, seated lunches for twenty are served by impeccably liveried and white-gloved domestics on the Villa Emo's stately portico at two round red-clothed tables. Here is one of the last places where old-fashioned Italian dishes of great complexity and refinement are still enjoyed. These surprising dishes are frequently Neapolitan more than Venetian as the Countess Marina Emo's mother was born a Princess Pignatelli and retains fine Neapolitan chefs. No one who has ever tasted it can forget the Villa Emo's *Cerino,* a giant *quenelle de veau* filled with chopped mushrooms in a rich gamy sauce and wound all about with a continuous spiral of long macaronis to resemble the spiral, cordlike candles or *cere* in Italian churches. Nor can they forget the Villa Emo's *pasticcio,* a huge sweet pasta lavishly decorated with pastry grapes and grapevines concealing inside hot pasta with a hearty and fragrantly herbed meat sauce.

Here during the autumn *villeggiatura,* the young Countess, Marina Emo, who carries on her ancestors' traditions of country living, supervises the preparation of a relatively simple summer supper in the kitchen of the Emo's *barchesse,* the elegantly proportioned dependency of the adjacent villa.

The image of plenty offered by the abundance of fall fruits and vegetables speaks eloquently of the hospitality of the Villa Emo, just as the Countess's witty use of trompe l'oeil ceramic serving dishes mimicking the ingredients of the foods she will serve speaks of the clever and lively conversations at her dinner parties, which are sometimes served in the villa's noble dining room and often take place at this kitchen table in the *barchesse.*

Her dinner, to be served on trompe l'oeil cabbage leaf plates, will begin with a colorful Riso di Zucca, a pumpkin-flavored Arborio rice dish, served in a melon-shaped covered tureen. The main course will be home-grown guinea fowl roasted and served with a variety of fall vegetables and with potatoes flavored with rosemary. There will be a white cabbage salad sweetened and accented with tiny pieces of dried figs, as well as a "red" salad of mixed *radicchio trevigiana,* and *Insalata di Chioggia.* There will then be a hot polenta with local *asiago* and *caciotta* cheeses; and for dessert, a Torta Invernale or "Winter Cake," flavored with candied chestnuts and decorated with meringue mushrooms.

The seductive mound of bright crimson *corbezzoli* or "Arbutus strawberries" will be cleaned and mixed with a little honey to accompany the cake.

The tables' spirited array of trompe l'oeil gourds, cabbages, pumpkins, melons, peppers, and red and white speckled *fagioli degli ricchi* bean pods are all made by the nearby ceramic work of Este for Tiffany & Co.

The battery of copper cooking pots hanging along the back wall of the kitchen were made for the Countess's great-great-grandmother, whose initials they still bear.

Countess Alba Giannelli-Viscardi

The ballroom of the Albrizzi Palace in Venice is thought to be the city's most splendid, and the ballroom of the family's country villa in Este is no less wonderful. Built as a free-standing garden pavilion around 1730 to accommodate the festivities of a dynastic Albrizzi-Zenobio marriage, the Villa Albrizzi's ballroom perfectly expresses the Venetian view of their countryside as a place created primarily for civilized and worldly pleasures and only incidentally as a place for agriculture.

The country ballroom has the inestimable advantage of light and air over its somber, hemmed-in city counterparts, each of its four sides having central double-glass doors flanked by tall windows

opening onto the sixteenth-century villa's vast gardens.

Here in the summer, Countess Alba Giannelli-Viscardi (née Albrizzi) vacations from her work in Milan where she runs a luxurious little jewel of a *cartoleria* in the Via Bagutta specializing in exquisitely crafted, marbleized book paper products of her own studio's production.

The ballroom pavilion with its jaunty rococo stucco decorations cheerfully painted in pastels is home during the summers alternately to Countess Alba's elite school of bookbinding and cartonnage and to her many equally elite dinner parties.

Here the central table of the ballroom's original lacquered furniture is set for a small dinner with a drawn thread work and lace tablecloth from the Venetian island of Burano. The dishes as well as the splendid white eighteenth-, nineteenth-, and twentieth-century ceramic elements that make up the magically beautiful *giardino* at the center of the table are all from the Este Ceramic just outside the villa's walls. The table will be lit by four "strolling musician" candlesticks made by Este for Tiffany & Co. The antique Venetian glasses and decanters are marked with the crown and initials "E.A." of Elsa Albrizzi, the Countess Giannelli-Viscardi's great-grandmother.

The dinner will consist of favorite family foods: to begin with Cappe Sante alla Veneziana, scallops and *langoustines* from nearby Chioggia baked in the scallop shells, to be followed by Pasticcio di Maccheroni della Contessa Giannelli-Viscardi, a pasta-filled short pastry, more Neapolitan than Venetian, flavored with meat sauce, chicken giblets, sweetbreads, and mushrooms. "Dishes must be nice to see," observes the Countess, "and the *pasticcio* looks fantastic." After the *pasticcio,* there will be a colorful salad of mixed summer greens, and for dessert *Bigné Maria Luisa,* the three Giannelli-Viscardi boys' favorite apricot jam-filled *beignets.*

The white wine for the meal comes from the vineyards of the Countess's younger brother, the Baron Ernesto Rubin de Cervin, at the Castle of Enn.

Valentino

PUMPKIN RAVIOLI WITH TOMATO AND BASIL SAUCE

Valentino's residences in Rome, Capri, and New York all speak of his profound dedication to beauty. "Had I not been a couturier," he says, "I would have been a decorator. I am obsessed by beauty in all its forms. I am a Taurus; anything I touch I embellish."

Nostalgically he recalls receptions "of unbelievable elegance," as he puts it, that he knew in Paris where he began his career at eighteen. Here at home in Rome, he brings that same remembered Parisian passion for perfection to creating the decor of an intimate dinner.

The dining room with its penchant for a romanticized orientalism was created with the help of Italian interior design giant Renzo Mongiardino to recall an eighteenth-century Sicilian veranda complete with an eighteenth-century mother-of-pearl inlaid Chinese daybed.

The table is set with flowered porcelains and

ornamented with a sterling silver Tiffany & Co. "Palm" candlestick, two eighteenth-century Meissen floral vases, and miniature crystal vases holding perfect camellias.

The inventive menus at such dinners are produced by a young English chef "who," Valentino points out, "loves to perfect dishes of unusual flavor, and add a new dimension to the charms of Italian cuisine."

A great variety of hot appetizers will be served before the dinner, which centers on Pumpkin Ravioli with Tomato and Basil Sauce accompanied by white Gavi de Gavi and red Brunello di Montalcino wines.

"My secrets?" observes Valentino, explaining the sure success of the charm and seduction of his table: "Avoid pompous menus and fussy sauces. I recommend simple foods perfectly prepared: pasta, vegetables, and sorbets."

Baron Ernesto Rubin de Cervin

Smoked Loin of Pork del Castello di Enn
(Kaiserfleisch del Castello di Enn)
Tyrolean Dumplings (Tyrolean Knödel)

*C*omposer and man of letters Baron Ernesto Rubin de Cervin divides his time between the twelfth-century story-book Castle of Enn, perched on a wooded mountainside in Italy's Alto Adige to the southeast of Bolzano, and a contemporary gem of a penthouse recently installed in the lofty attics of his family's splendidly baroque Palazzo Albrizzi in Venice.

While in residence at Enn, the Albrizzis have traditionally embraced things Tyrolean with much enthusiasm, a charming mannerism current among the Venetian nobility who summer in the mountains of the Italian South Tirol.

Here in the dining room at Enn with its early-sixteenth-century boiseries hung with Este ceramic plates decorated in the eighteenth century with the Zenobio family arms, the Baron serves a buffet dinner of local *spek* or smoked raw ham with a variety of country breads and *Bretzels* to be followed by the favorite dish of Enn's international houseguests, *Kaiserfleisch,* with *sauerkraut,* and *Tyrolean Knödel,* or smoked pork chops, fresh braised sauerkraut, and liver- or ham–flavored bread dumplings.

The buffet is ornamented with a remarkable collection of nineteenth-century Bohemian glass beakers, pitchers, and tumblers ornamented with the coats of arms of the Baron's ancestors, the Albrizzis and the Gagarins.

A dry, fruity white wine from Albrizzi family vineyards will accompany the meal.

The table's trompe l'oeil fruits and vegetables and turkeys are all contemporary ceramics from Este where Tiffany's late Design Director, Van Day Truex, initiated the making of trompe l'oeil ceramics in the late 1950s.

For dessert, guests will go out to Enn's garden to enjoy a fresh and fragrant apple strudel made from apples grown in the Adige Valley below the castle.

A wooden roe deer carved by Hammerl in nearby Innsbruck in 1884 stands proudly before the turrets of Enn. The two ceramic deer tureens are a model created at Este for Tiffany & Co.

Sybil Connolly

> PICKLED SALMON WITH CUCUMBER SAUCE
> BEETROOT AND POTATO SALAD
> HAM AND CHICKEN MOLD
> COLLARD BEEF
> SUMMER PUDDING
> MARMALADE CAKE
> CHOCOLATE CAKE

Through the fashions, textiles, interiors, and household and table furnishings she designs as well as through her writings, the "Empress" of Irish design, Sybil Connolly, is an international tastemaker whose influence touches all aspects of contemporary lifestyle.

She has dressed English royalty and American first ladies. The world's leading design magazines cover her every move. Her knowledge of gardening is legendary. The Irish press has dubbed her "The nearest thing Ireland has to royalty," and Jack Lynch, while Prime Minister of Ireland, described her as "among Ireland's national treasures."

To her friends blessed with an invitation to stay in her mews guesthouse, a little gem of Irish Georgian architecture of her own creation at the end of her garden off Dublin's Merrion Square, she is one of the world's greatest and best-organized hostesses.

No one who has enjoyed the delights of that so well and charmingly run house can forget the perfection of meals served in the small blue and white dining room or the superb collection of eighteenth-century Irish delftwares that line its walls.

Dinners almost invariably begin with a soup: carrot with homemade stock and good Irish cream or lovage with a slight celery taste. "I like simple things at home," Miss Connolly says, "poached Irish salmon, Dublin prawns with avocado mousse, rough terrines, stuffed chicken, rack of lamb, and old-fashioned homemade cakes, summer pudding, or *coeur à la crème* with strawberries. You go out for things that are exotic.

"Food is a significant part of civilization and gives us so many happy memories. My grandfather had a smokehouse, and smoked salmon and home-smoked bacon were very important when I was young, as was the smell of freshly cooked bread.

"No house would admit then to using bought bread. That would have been a terrible reflection on the house. And I'd still rather have homemade butter with that lovely golden color than caviar.

"Really," she concludes, "there's nothing nicer than good plain food very well cooked."

One of Sybil Connolly's favorite accomplishments is the design for the restoration of the "Swiss Cottage" at Caher in County Tipperary originally created in 1810 by John Nash as a romantic hideaway for the second Earl of Glengall and his mistress, and restored in 1988 through the generosity of New York's Sally Sempel Aall and the Port Royal

Foundation. Here Miss Connolly has organized a country picnic and afternoon tea including only traditional Irish recipes.

The picnic luncheon buffet set in the garden of the "Swiss Cottage" includes a layered Ham and Chicken Mold; cold spiced Collard Beef with whole-grain Irish mustard; Pickled Salmon with Cucumber Sauce; a joyously bright pink Beetroot and Potato Salad; fresh Irish soda bread, and a bright red Summer Pudding decorated with a full-blown cabbage rose from the hostess's Merrion Square garden.

The porcelains are a mixture of old Paris Angoulême with its jaunty sprigs of blue flowers and Tiffany & Co.'s "Sybil Connolly Collection" porcelains, whose black backgrounds and stylishly drawn flowers echo the late-eighteenth-century flower collages of Mrs. Delany (another Irish-born "Renaissance woman").

The coral-and-ivy-patterned tablecloth is Erin chintz designed by Sybil Connolly for Brunschwig & Fils.

Sometime after the picnic there will be a tea served in the cottage's dining room decorated with its original Dufour "Scenes from the Banks of the Bosphoros" wallpaper.

The kitchens of the Merrion Square house have provided three of Miss Connolly's guests' perennial favorites: Marmalade Cake; Uniced Chocolate Cake; and Walnut Biscuits or Dunraven Biscuits made after a recipe from Miss Connolly's great friend Nancy, Dowager Countess of Dunraven.

The Chinese lacquer red flowered porcelains are from Tiffany's "Sybil Connolly Collection." The lime-green nicotiana, the Queen Mother or Elizabeth of Clamis roses held in a blue-green 1850s English teapot are from Sybil Connolly's Dublin garden.

At the picnic, the Collard Beef, Pickled Salmon, and Beetroot and Potato Salad were rather new to Miss Connolly's kitchen's repertoire. "Usually we try out new recipes for two months after Christmas when there are fewer people to dinner," she explains. "You need the new, as no matter how good a thing is, you can't keep on with it forever."

Anoushka Hempel (Lady Weinberg)

RASPBERRY MILLE-FEUILLE
POACHED PEARS IN RED WINE FRUIT JELLY

*I*n America, the compartment marked "pudding" is somewhat sparsely populated with desserts made from printed instructions on packaging, with only an occasional homemade highlight such as English plum pudding or a more native American Indian pudding.

In England, however, "pudding" embraces everything sweet that concludes a meal. Cakes, pies, flans, *gâteaux,* tarts, mousses, ices, "fools," whips, custards, trifles, and puddings themselves, be they Christmas puddings, summer puddings, or steamed treacle puddings, are all "pudding" to the English; and no country enjoys its sweet conclusions to meals more than they.

True to the heart-warming and homey glories of English tradition which she has in the past three

decades revitalized with her well-publicized beauty, verve, and imagination, Lady Weinberg (possibly better known to the public as prominent London fashion designer Anoushka Hempel and owner of fashionable Blakes Hotel in South Kensington) has designated one room in her London home as "The Pudding Room."

Here in this intimate, dramatically black and green decorated dining room, Lady Weinberg receives her guests after the main courses of dinner are over with a glorious array of both decorative and delicious desserts.

Carrying out the Pudding Room's color scheme with an haute couture touch, the table is covered with green taffeta knotted on the corners with green ribbons. The centerpiece of miniature topiary moss trees and a crystal fishbowl bursting with cabbage leaves continues the green theme, which is accented in purple by dishes of sweet-smelling lavender heads and smart purple and green grosgrain ribbons tied in a big floppy bow about a "pudding." This pudding Anoushka Hempel Weinberg more accurately describes as a "dark froufrou chocolate *gâteau* and *ganache* torte."

The featured puddings for the evening are a Raspberry Mille-feuille, Poached Pears in Red Wine Fruit Jelly, and Fresh Peach Tart.

There is a symbolic and *faux* Christmas Pudding that has no intention of being eaten. Securely wound up in gold thread and pinned with a gold dragonfly, it sits amid the profusion of antique silver, etched and gilded crystal incense burners, votive candles, and a wealth of fruits both candied and fresh which include: figs, pomegranates, cherries, blueberries, kiwis, passion fruits, Pistachio Marzipan Apples; and grapes coated in sugar.

A collection of Georgian and Victorian etched-glass lanterns floats above the table, casting a romantic light on all the intricate details of the high-style confections. The hostess has included little silver plates of Dauphinoise cheese and oatcakes for those in a "savory" rather than a "pudding" mood.

Mrs. Galen Weston

CHOCOLATE YULE LOG
ENGLISH TRIFLE

In 1750 William Duke of Cumberland employed Henry Flitcroft to build him a "folly" on a sixty-acre plot of land covered with cedar forests some six miles from Windsor Castle. Flitcroft was then hard at work for the Duke's demanding older brother King George III on additions to Windsor. He, however, found time to build William Fort Belvedere.

The small "fort" was a romantically imposing conglomeration of oddly shaped rooms and towers complete with crenelations, "a charming frippery" as its current resident, Galen Weston, terms it.

In 1828, King George IV enlarged and rendered it somewhat less "frippish," retaining its semicircular fortification complete with thirty-one formidable cannons. These were fired once each year until 1920 by an in-house bombardier to celebrate the English sovereign's birthday.

The ever-eccentric King George IV kept a menagerie of animals and exotic birds at Fort Belvedere. The more sedate and family life–loving Queen Victoria enjoyed picnicking here. King George V's star-crossed son Edward in 1928 made the fort his home and lived in it as Prince of Wales and later during his moment as Edward VIII. That ended with his abdication in 1936.

Edward added a swimming pool, planted gardens, and with his friends, Wallis Simpson among others, brought gaiety and animation to the house.

Somewhat later Edward's nieces, Elizabeth and Margaret Rose, rode their ponies over from Windsor to play here as children.

Now, for five weeks every summer, Fort Belvedere comes back to life with dashing, polo-playing Canadian department-store king Galen Weston, Chairman and CEO of George Weston, largest private company in Canada, and his beautiful wife, Hillary.

During these summer weeks Weston plays with Prince Charles, among others, for the Maple Leaf Team at Smith's Lawn, at Windsor, and at Cowdray Park.

Here, in the dining room of Fort Belvedere, which Edward VIII had once filled with George Stubbs' horse paintings, Hillary Weston fills the table with a Christmas "hunt breakfast" of traditional English cakes and "puddings."

There is a Chocolate Yule Log and a proper sherry-spiked English Trifle complete with decorations of angelica, almonds, and a red English rose.

There is also a fine Christmas fruit cake, but for that the Westons explain, "The recipe is a secret belonging to Fortnum & Mason," the ultimate food emporium in London's Piccadilly of which Galen Weston is Vice-Chairman.

The Weston's porcelain tea and coffee service is Herend. There is Laurent-Perrier champagne for guests not in a mood for tea or coffee, as well as English cut-crystal decanters with alternate libations. Cognac is appropriately held in a ring-necked decanter from Tiffany's "English Stately Homes Collection."

The buffet at the back of the dining room holds one of Galen Weston's many polo trophies.

Mark Birley

London's preeminent restaurateur, Mark Birley, and his sister, designer and food authority Maxime de La Falaise, both inherited an artistic eye from their father, noted English painter Sir Oswald Birley.

From their mother, Rhoda Birley, they inherited the passion for cooking that had made Lady Birley one of the first to establish culinary weekends in an "English stately home." Rhoda Birley's culinary adventures at the Birley manor, Charleston, in Sussex "inspired us," Maxime de La Falaise recalls, "to try out anything in the kitchen, at any time of day or night."

No one could consider themselves really part of London's mythic "swinging sixties" unless they were a regular of Mark Birley's great supper club, Annabel's. And London night life today would lose much of its sparkle and be poor indeed without Mark Birley's three domains, Annabel's, Mark's Club, and Harry's Bar.

One of the most coveted invitations in London, however, is to be asked to lunch or dine at Thurloe Lodge, Birley's beautiful Georgian brick house near the Victoria and Albert Museum.

The vast kitchen on the ground floor of "The Lodge" is dominated by a portrait of Kate Fleet, Sir Oswald's elderly cook, known fondly to the Birley children as "Mrs. Fleet." "She was my great friend and sent me back to school with all sorts of marvelous things," Mark Birley recollects. At one end of the kitchen there is a large oval pine table and, at the other end, a professional *batterie de cuisine*. This dining room/kitchen is the scene of weekend lunch parties that often last until teatime. It is also the base for Birley's more formal Sunday lunches, when the weather encourages dining on the wide white veranda at the back of Thurloe Lodge, which overlooks one of the most splendid gardens in all the city of London.

"Eating in the kitchen is *gemütlich*, a happy way

of entertaining people you know very well. It's not for showing off, but for re-creating remembered dishes or trying new ones," Birley explains. "Caviar doesn't quite belong at a kitchen lunch party, garlic does.

"One of the best things you can eat is a perfectly cooked roast chicken, next a perfect *gigot* of lamb, crisp on the outside, pink inside.

"And the simpler the food, the better the wine . . . at Sunday lunch in the kitchen, there's no better moment to open a very good bottle of wine."

Here a typical Sunday lunch might begin with Fresh Scotch Salmon Cakes with Fried Parsley; followed by Roasted Capon served with grilled chipolata sausages, rashers of crispy bacon, Bread Sauce, and gravy," accompanied by Brussels sprouts, buttered carrots, and roast potatoes; and end with a fresh raspberry or strawberry Fruit Tart.

The early Edwardian ambiance of Mark Birley's dining table is anchored by two silver urn oil lamps with red silk shades and deep glass bead fringe. The centerpiece is a nineteenth-century Mason's Ironstone footed bowl in traditional cobalt blue, rust orange, green, and gold Imari colors which compliment the nineteenth-century English blue and white transferware dishes. The serving dishes are amply scaled antique English gadroon-edge silver, and red wine is served from a handsome English hand-cut crystal decanter which, like the crystal bowl holding eggs on the kitchen work table, is from Tiffany's "English Stately Homes Collection."

Of such comfortingly traditional English foods, Mark Birley's sister says they are "wholesome and delicious, reflecting English taste and good English ingredients."

Maxime de La Falaise

In her memorable book, *Seven Hundred Years of English Cooking,* Maxime de La Falaise pointed out that "there is no better way to enjoy our past than through the back, or kitchen door." And there is certainly no better way to gain respect for the seldom-praised glories of English cooking than to taste Maxime de La Falaise's savory re-creations of near-forgotten English dishes rediscovered in an-

tique cookbooks she collected with the encouragement of her late husband, John McKendry, who was curator of Prints at New York's Metropolitan Museum of Art.

While all the time lending her own brand of dash and stylishness to the world of high fashion in a career whose scope runs from Schiaparelli model to "style consultant" to Yves Saint Laurent, she has

found time to write cookbooks, the latest, *Food in Vogue,* a compendium of her cooking columns written for American *Vogue.*

Her downtown Fifth Avenue, New York, loft overlooking treetops and a church tower has for some ten years been the scene of her unique brand of unabashedly glamorous "family" dinners frequented by an imposing guest list of *haute bôheme* celebrities of the fashion, design, and art worlds who are also Maxime de La Falaise's closest friends.

"The walls of the loft," she observes, "are the palest possible tea-rose pink, while the ceiling is a wild pistachio that over the two-thousand-square-foot expanse loses its garishness and reflects light and shade like young trees in a forest."

Before her loft dinners, she serves "champagne kirs made with *crème de myrtilles* instead of cassis. I also make margaritas and old-fashioneds in a blender with a white of egg to make them foamy," she explains, "a trick my father learned in New York in the twenties when he was busy painting portraits of millionaires for his agent, Sir Joseph Duveen."

Here on the tile-inset work counter of her loft kitchen, Maxime de La Falaise offers her guests a dinner of favorite old English dishes: one, a Brie Tart dating back to the year 1378, and others from the fifteenth, seventeenth, and eighteenth centuries.

After the Brie Tart and Maxime's Curried Apricot and Fresh Mint Soup, there will be ground meat and slivered almond Medieval Hedgehogs; spiced Barthelmas Beef served with dilled carrots and boiled new red potatoes, Asparagus in Cream, Tomatoes Stuffed with Mushrooms, and Lady Rhoda Birley's Mushroom Bog.

Dessert will be a selection of Brown Bread Ice Cream with strawberries; a tart or Florendine of Oranges and Apples, and a Medieval Bread and Butter Pudding.

The deliciously colorful dinner will be served on a colorful assortment of flowered Imari "Halcyon," blue and yellow "Bigoudon," and blue and white "Shell and Thread" Tiffany & Co. china. The Tiffany "Shell and Thread" flat silver coordinates with the porcelain of the same name. A blue, green, and white "Merletto" Venetian glass bowl and vase made for Tiffany's by the great master glassmaker Archimede Seguso decorate the setting, which is presided over by a portrait of the hostess's mother, Lady Rhoda Birley, painted by the hostess's father, Sir Oswald Birley.

John Nicholson

Few legends endure in New York. One that does is the ever-so-stylish and charm–filled café of quintessential New Yorker "Johnny" Nicholson.

Since the first Cafe Nicholson opened its doors in the ground floor and garden of a town house on East Fifty-eighth Street aiming to be what the owners, John Nicholson, Carl Bissinger, and their collaborator/cook Edna Lewis, described as "a place where truckdrivers eat, and the food is really great," the café's classic and by now mythic menu of Roast Chicken and Chocolate Soufflé has lodged deep in the hearts of the city's more literary and talented members of café and other society, which may or may not include a few self-styled "truckdrivers."

The food at the Cafe Nicholson is, in New York terms, "really great," and what if the current café at 323 East 58th Street has neither the palm trees nor the owner's pet parrot that were an essential part of café society's props and background in the heyday of Nicholson's celebrated 1950s and 1960s premises on East Fifty-seventh Street. The landmark-quality decor is still as romantic today as even the most jaded New Yorker could demand.

Whoever truly knew the 1950s and '60s cannot help but think back with fondness of Johnny Nicholson's mirrored, tile-lined, and statue-studded café, which seemed to turn up almost daily as the background for a fashion shoot, a luxury-product ad, or for a magazine article on some highly polished facet of the "glitterati" of the day.

Regulars in those times included *The New Yorker* magazine's legendary Brendan Gill; literary giant William Faulkner, who insisted the café's food was French; cartoonist Charles Addams, who said of the relentlessly Victorian interior, "This looks like one of mine"; and architect Frederick Kiesler, who announced one evening that lamb chops were inappropriate on the menu of such a sophisticated social watering spot. With that, Edna Lewis recalled, in her 1983 *Edna Lewis Cookbook,* "Our image of truckdrivers' food began to fade, and I realized we were making a different kind of impression."

Edna Lewis left the Cafe Nicholson in 1953; but now, nearly forty years later, her legacy of the deeply satisfying, simple dishes of her native Orange County, Virginia, cuisine lingers on.

Here in today's Cafe Nicholson the house's great classic Roast Chicken is preceded by Cold Shrimps in Remoulade Sauce and followed by the Chocolate Soufflé in paper cups, which Clementine Paddleford of the *New York Herald Tribune* long ago described as "light as a dandelion seed in a high wind."

A massive Tiffany glass chandelier and Spanish Art Nouveau wall tile panels anchor the skylit room's turn-of-the-century Belle Epoque decor. The central serving table covered in grand Victorian fashion with an Oriental carpet boasts an exuberantly scaled antique brass epergne stacked with eggs; a nineteenth-century French faience black and white speckled hen and rooster, both somewhat larger than life; as well as a Tiffany & Co. French faience "Poule et Poussins" tureen all keeping attention focused on the ingredients of the meal.

Along with the chickens and eggs displayed on the table are strongly colored bouquets of blue delphinium and red and peach-colored roses in two exceptionally fine pieces of antique Tiffany & Co. silver: an 1872 "Audubon" pitcher chased with motifs of Japanese birds and flowers; and a "Japanesque" pitcher of the same period chased with lotuses and giant goldfish.

Of such generous-spirited party-table decors, Anne-Marie Schiro once noted in the *New York Times,* "There were any number of ways that Johnny Nicholson could have chosen to give a party . . . , so he decided to do everything."

Brooke Hayward

GAME PIE

$\mathcal{B}$rooke Hayward explains one of her much-admired Manhattan loft dinners: "The large, old, round library table in our living room is set with turquoise blue dinner plates and simple glasses from Tiffany's. Everything else on the table—and behind it and around it—has been picked up in years of haunting antique shops and flea fairs from California to Prague.

"The pie plate for the Game Pie central to the dinner is simple kitchen crockery. The dish for the Spinach Sautéed with Garlic and Butter is jaspé, and the cookie and bread dishes are nineteenth-century majolica. The objects and books on this table reside there all the time, as we never seem to move anything, not even for our most elaborate dinner parties; we just add more 'placements,' although we do sometimes move to the dining room which can seat ten.

"The table is skirted to the floor with robin's egg blue–glazed chintz and then overlaid with a quilted paisley cloth.

"The antique candelabra come from Italy via a dealer in London, and the alligator inkwell is English via a dealer in New York, while the sphinx candlestick and turbaned Moor tobacco jar—used here as a centerpiece—and wine ewer [with snake handles] and background urns [also with snake handles] are all majolica artifacts snatched from whatever corner of the earth yielded them up.

"A silver crab perching on the edge of the pie's crust was a pillbox in another incarnation. Its mate adorns the arrangement of fruit and vegetables that surrounds the Moor's head. Another antique pillbox, this time a brass fly (I have an endless collection of insects and reptiles), is enjoying the cheese board.

"The French Empire bronze lamp in the background is one of a pair that my long-suffering but good-natured husband [bandleader Peter Duchin] gave me as a second anniversary present. He tolerates—barely—my acquisitive nature in return for a good meal.

"The source of the Game Pie recipe is southern,

and the key ingredients are, in my case, supplied by my husband, who spends two weeks every winter hunting on a friend's plantation in Georgia.

"Peter is at least as renowned a shot as he is a musician, so there is no shortage of game with which to experiment; then too the acuity of his culinary relish is equal to that of the aforementioned accomplishments, so my only problem is how last to utilize the hampers of game that accompany him home (unplucked, of course, which is another story).

"In our lives, there are certain definite guidelines to entertaining on which we both agree, thank God:

1) *No formal dinners,* and 2) *No shortcuts.* This translates into a style, a philosophy which is very simple, if Draconian. Informal meals are *de rigueur;* picnics are ideal, particularly when guests are assigned some—*any*—function. Use only the finest ingredients, from potatoes to wine, expensive though they may be. All details other than food (table accessories, decor, combinations of people invited) should be personal, amusing, whimsical, even eccentric.

"To put it in a nutshell: hands on; take time to do it right. Otherwise don't do it at all."

Marilyn Evins

"*E*ntertaining," observes Marilyn Evins, "is certainly one of life's greatest pleasures (one I indulge too regularly and atone for by taking only the tiniest bites), and I have always found the groundwork—creating menus, preparing dishes, and presenting them with élan—to be a most gratifying process."

For many years a central figure of New York society's celebrations and one of the city's leading public relations impresarios, Marilyn Evins knows her way around the often hazardous mazes of New York fund-raising and social dinners. And if she is almost daily consulted by charity gala chairwomen on the menus that will make their events memorable, it is because of a well-earned reputation of being expert in such things through gala dinners she has had her deft hand in organizing for the New York Hospital-Cornell Medical Center, the Museum of the City of New York, the Costume Institute, and countless other institutions.

Her menus, polished and refined over time, are imaginatively, stylishly, and soundly constructed, "distinct menus," she says, "which have served me well on a number of occasions and which, I believe, are worthy of garnering attention."

Some recipes are carried on from Marilyn Evins's family traditions, such as My Mother's Lemon Pudding Cake, a delicious souvenir of early twentieth-century American party food; others, such as Bill Blass's Melba Toast and Tiny Popovers, have been garnered from friends; and many, such as Chicken Breast with Mustard Cream Sauce or Zucchini Corn Soup, are of Mrs. Evins's own able inven-

tion. All pass Marilyn Evins's criteria for foods "that look like you want to eat them."

These public-menu dishes are perfected and tried out on friends at the countless dinner parties Marilyn Evins has given in her fastidiously decorated Upper East Side apartments.

Here in the newest of her dining pavilions high up in the Tower of Fifth Avenue's Hotel Pierre surrounded by chinoiserie wall panels in the style of Pillement, specially commissioned from New York society's "court painter" Erik Filban, Mrs. Evins prepares an enticing winter supper of Salad with Three Lettuces, Deep-Fried Whitebait with Tartar Sauce, Lamb Stew, Poached Dried Fruit, and French Almond Lace Cookies.

Wines for the evening will be Château-Chalon Chardonnay, Penfold's Grange Hermitage Cabernet Sauvignon, and Château d'Yquem Sauterne.

Carrying out the room's chinoiserie theme, a variety of eighteenth- and nineteenth-century Chinese porcelains from Mrs. Evins's inclusive collection are used on the table, while an eighteenth-century Chinese ceramic Buddha rules over the buffet reflected in the dining room's Louis XV mirror.

The table is opulently decked with gold and green tapestries woven specially for the room. Large, white antique damask dinner napkins loosely folded as Marilyn Evins favors them fall chicly over the edge of the table with all their carefully studied nonchalance.

Tiffany & Co. "Metropolis" square crystal chargers lend a dramatic and stylishly contemporary grace note to the so-rich and densely textured room, and a flamboyant pair of nineteenth-century French candelabra festively light the table where guests will sit on Regency *chaises à la reine* and drink from Tiffany's "All Purpose" wineglasses.

RAVIOLONI (LARGE RAVIOLI OF RICOTTA)
RED SNAPPER LIVORNESE
RICE FRITTERS

Mrs. Sirio Maccioni

*I*t is said that "no place attracts more power and pulchritude per square inch" than Sirio Maccioni's Le Cirque on New York's East Sixty-fifth Street.

For nearly twenty years dedicated stargazers have crowded into society's favorite "canteen" to bask in the golden glow of Le Cirque's regular customers—a formidable cast of princes, billionaires, social queens, film stars, divas, tycoons, playboys, playgirls, and the occasional king, ex-American President, or rascal of the moment.

This lineup of the privileged (who by dint of hard work, birth, or adventure happen to be inordinately rich, celebrated, beautiful, or any combination thereof) flock in their turn to Le Cirque both to be in each other's reassuring company and to enjoy the always-superb cuisine (rated "four star" by the *New York Times*).

Sirio Maccioni himself takes all these social antics gracefully in his stride; and, when not juggling the seating of his status-conscious clients with the deftness and finesse of a magician, he is conferring with his chef on the nuances and refinements of his menu, whose excellence brought his glittering clientele here in the first place.

The Maccionis are Tuscan; and, from the irresistible pasta dishes that are favorite "starters" at Le Cirque to the glass of sweet Malvasia delle Lipari wine offered with coffee, the influences of great classic Italian cooking are never far away.

At home the Maccionis favor menus that are traditional in their native Tuscany, composed of dishes Mrs. Maccioni learned from her mother and grandmother. Often these will also include recipes for cakes and bread learned from her father, who owned a bakery.

Here Mrs. Maccioni prepares a Tuscan dinner of Crostini, Ravioloni of Ricotta, and Red Snapper Livornese, followed by Rice Fritters flavored with orange and lemon peel for dessert.

Her table is set with "Magnolia" and "Green Leaves" plates made for Tiffany & Co. at Este in northern Italy. Her "Montaigne Optic" stemware and Elsa Peretti "Padova" flatware are also from Tiffany's, as is her cobalt blue Elsa Peretti serving platter.

"It makes us feel good to have these Tuscan meals," Mrs. Maccioni muses, "while we are so far away from home."

Glenn Bernbaum

Whoever imagines that the privileged and celebrated devote themselves to the complexities of veal roasts stuffed with nuts and apricots or to cloyingly sweet white chocolate desserts awash in raspberry coulis is misguided; and, there to prove it is the lord of the New York "A list's" intimate lunches and dinners, Glenn Bernbaum.

For sixteen years dwellers in the stratosphere of New York society can be counted on to appear with comforting regularity in only two places, the "Suzy" column and Bernbaum's low-key, high-profile Upper East Side café, Mortimer's.

Here the great, the rich, and the hopelessly spoiled dine together on good, straightforward American fare with a regularity and devotion that borders on religion.

The short menu of Twinburgers, Crab Cakes, Designer Meat Loaf, Chicken Hash, and other unassuming dishes, all impeccably prepared and served, are targeted at Glenn Bernbaum's clientele: the remnants of conservative old monied society and the new-monied who understudy them and their highly mannered, unassuming ways.

Downstairs at Mortimer's in Bernbaum's building on the corner of Lexington Avenue and Seventy-fifth Street, society and society's dress designers, interior decorators, and "walkers" are seated in a hierarchical order whose fine tuning is a daily focus of the owner.

Upstairs in Glenn Bernbaum's private apartments, life is far more detailed in its not-at-all-understated luxuries, and far more relaxed.

Mortimer's sociably spartan decor of bentwood café chairs, bare plank floors, white tablecloths, and the occasional ficus tree and vase of flowering branches gives way upstairs to a richer blend of fine eighteenth-century French and Italian furnishings, animal sculptures, framed photos of friends and family, bibelots, leather-bound books, Chinese porcelains made into lamps, and a small collection of oil paintings that includes a *Tiger Hunt* from the studio of Peter Paul Rubens and a George Romney portrait.

The Byzantine complexity of Mortimer's seating order is unnecessary upstairs, where occasional private meals for Glenn Bernbaum's friends are served buffet-style. "Why would I do anything else when buffets are so much more pleasant," he says.

Here in the dining area of the "above-the-shop" quarters, the circular table, spread as it habitually is with a rose velvet cover, offers a typical Glenn Bernbaum buffet of Seafood Salad in Lemon Aspic, Beef Stew, and Oranges and Grapefruit Cointreau—all straightforwardly delicious.

There is also a plate of steamed mixed vegetables to accompany the stew and another dish of marzipan fruits to accompany coffee.

On the nearby coffee table, guests will find "Birdcages" hand-painted Tiffany plates, and "Faneuil" flat silver.

The buffet table is ornamented with a bouquet of fragrant fresh mimosa, silver mounted late-nineteenth-century ivory candlesticks, and an Art Nouveau crystal and silver claret jug.

In the center of all this splendor a ferocious French bronze *Lion du Senegal* splendidly sculptured by Etienne de la Brière in 1866 is effectively guarding his own buffet meal of fresh antelope.

Mrs. T. Suffern Tailer

The witty, beautiful, and always impeccably groomed Mrs. T. Suffern Tailer, has a career as ambassador-at-large for New York star couturier Adolfo which long ago won her a place in the prestigious Best Dressed List "Hall of Fame" and made her winning "square smile" (as *W* termed it) a familiar feature of the American society press.

Her equally impeccably groomed and deliciously imaginative small dinners conjured up for friends in her New York, Palm Beach, and Southampton homes have for years won her a more quietly guarded fame as a hostess who can thread her way with exemplary grace through the hauteurs of social cooking and table-setting. She has also lec-

tured from coast to coast on these talents—talents undoubtedly well-nourished by her coverage of the stylish antics of fellow haute members of American society in the pages of *Town & Country* during her long career as social editor and chronicler.

Here in the red paisley jewel-box interior of her Park Avenue apartment, whose decor has earned its own hall of fame status with an appearance on the cover of *Architectural Digest,* Jean Tailer sets a buffet of house supper specialties in front of her living room's intricately carved white marble Adam fireplace.

"My pied-à-terre is very limited for space," Mrs. Tailer points out, "so I have carefully evolved a way of entertaining to comfortably accommodate up to ten or twelve buffet style. (The dining table only seats six.)

"I set a low Chippendale table in front of the fire with an old stripped Indian paisley that harmonizes with the room's decoration.

"Then I prefer to offer the guests a good variety of flavorful dishes that are satisfying in reasonably small quantity and that don't require awkward carving or anything but a fork to eat.

"Shortly before this dinner, I went to a cook's summer school at Lorenza di Medici's at Coltibuono in Tuscany and this inspired my first course of Tuscan Bean Salad with Caviar, served in small, low Tiffany 'Swag' crystal bowls.

"The main course of supper will be an assortment of white Shrimp Cakes; pale green Zucchini Pancakes; and pale orange Sweet Potato and Sausage Cakes (or Floddies). The mix of colors pleases me as much here as the mix of tastes.

"With the platter of 'cakes' there is Cooked Cucumber Salad; Cabbage, Carrot, and Celery Slaw; and a 1950s revival Green Rice.

"Dessert will be a Rum, Chocolate, and Grand Marnier Icebox Cake decorated with candied violets, no longer a cherished secret recipe, but a cake that never fails to get 'oohs' and 'aahs' from even the most obstinately diet addicted.

"I absolutely love to cook," adds the perfect size-8 hostess, "but I love these recipes, which allow me to cook far in advance of a party."

Mrs. Tailer's buffet table is set with "Fleurs sur Fond Gris" and "Directoire—Tiffany Private Stock" porcelains. Small ivy topiary trees which Jean Tailer prefers to flowers on her already colorful table setting are held by small "Fleurs sur Fond Gris" porcelain "orange crates." The crystal salad bowls and "Hampton" candlesticks, like the "Swag" and "Nemours" decanters, are also from Tiffany's, as is the "Wyndham" flat silver.

A pair of antique Chelsea birds and some Fabergé boxes from the living room's remarkable assortment of *objets de vertu* add finishing touches to Jean Tailer's tablescape.

Gene Hovis

> CROWN ROAST OF LAMB / BRUSSELS SPROUTS WITH CHESTNUTS
> GLAZED DEVILED CARROTS
> PAN-FRIED SHREDDED POTATOES
> COFFEE PROFITEROLES WITH CHOCOLATE SAUCE AND WHIPPED CREAM

"My mother, my aunts, and even my godmother were talented and enthusiastic cooks," recalls Gene Hovis, author of *Uptown Down Home Cookbook* and Vice-President and Creative Director of New York's great department store Macy's "Marketplace" and restaurants.

"Every occasion," he continues, "from a funeral to a wedding, was observed with a food-heaped groaning board, the presence of which blunted the edge of sadness or sent the spirit of a happy time soaring.

"The cooking was straightforward and basic. No nonsense. No gimmicks. Only the best and freshest ingredients were acceptable, each brought to the peak of its flavor with appropriate cooking techniques. Fussy, pretentious food was frowned on. The desired goal was food that was disarmingly simple and honest, in which the taste of each ingredient was highlighted.

"This has been my guiding principle throughout my professional cooking career. Fashions in food are as changeable as women's hemlines and men's lapels, but simple, delicious food will never go out of style."

Here surrounded by books and polished woodwork in the beautifully appointed, good old-fashioned domestic warmth and comfort of his uptown New York apartment's library-cum-dining room, Gene Hovis offers one of his deliciously satisfying small dinner parties with all the stylishness and elegance for which he is so well known.

The buffet set on the round library table includes a rosemary-accented Crown Roast of Lamb presented on a Tiffany & Co. "Yellow Birds" French faience platter. The crown roast is filled with Brussels Sprouts with Chestnuts and surrounded with Glazed Deviled Carrots and decorated with sprigs of fresh rosemary. There are Pan-fried Shredded Potatoes and a Tomato Aspic with Vinaigrette Dressing splendidly presented on a ribbed sterling silver tray from Tiffany's. The aspic ring is filled with steamed shrimp and watercress leaves and ornamented by bright red crayfish.

Coffee, tea, and Profiteroles with Chocolate Sauce for dessert will be served in front of a colorful and whimsical nineteenth-century French hand-blocked paper screen.

The Louis XIV silver tea and coffee service from Tiffany's is elaborately chased with lambrequin motifs and sits on an octagonal "Yellow Birds" faience tray.

The profiteroles waiting with an antique American glass pitcher of warm chocolate sauce to pour over them will be served on "Platinum Grapes" plates made for Tiffany's by the Ceramiche d'Este in northeastern Italy.

Jean~Claude Nedelec

> POTATO PANCAKES WITH WILD MUSHROOM RAGOUT
> ACORN SQUASH WITH SEAFOOD RAGOUT
> WARM FRUIT COMPOTE
> CYNTHIA PEITHMAN'S LEMON CAKE

"As a child," the celebrated master chef of Glorious Food, Jean-Claude Nedelec, recalls, "I would help my mother (who, in my opinion, is still the best cook in the world) in the kitchen, and was always happiest when I could set the table. I would go through the closets and armoires and unpack the most incredible and unusual china, silver, tablecloths, and napkins—settings that were usually re-served for special occasions or that were too fragile for daily use. For me, it was the only way to do justice and pay homage to my mother's cooking."

Today Nedelec presides over a corps of forty chefs in Glorious Food's kitchen, the epicenter of American haute catering, where preparing superb dinners for five or six hundred of New York's dedicated partygoers is an almost daily challenge.

At home in his Upper East Side New York apartment, Jean-Claude Nedelec enjoys giving his own small dinners "where the setting is formal and the food sophisticated." For large groups there will be several tables with "centerpieces of fruits and vegetables and lots of candles."

"After the first course plates are removed," he explains, "guests will be directed to a side table where main-course dishes are arranged buffet style.

"What I serve for dessert," he continues, "depends on the scenario of the evening.

"Before workdays, I prefer to make it an early night, and will serve finger desserts such as miniature fruit tartlets, chocolate-covered strawberries, cookies, and so on. If it is a weekend and appropriate to stretch out the evening, I will have a dessert buffet with an abundance of sweets, some simple but others elaborate—confections such as Croquembouche, Lemon Tart, or Lemon Cake, or Oeufs à la Neige and Fruit Compote, with condiments such as kiwi and chocolate sauces, whipped cream, roasted hazelnuts, candied violets, and crystallized fruit.

"The informality of a dessert buffet is very popular. It gives guests a chance to move around and seek out people they didn't have a chance to speak to during dinner. Another reason for a dessert buffet's popularity is that people love to concoct their own desserts and postpone dieting until the next day."

Here Jean-Claude Nedelec sets his dinner table with a Tiffany "Cherry Orchard" silk scarf overlay, Elsa Peretti terra-cotta plates, "Century" flat silver, and "All Purpose" crystal, all from Tiffany's.

The dinner includes Foie Gras Grapes, Potato Pancakes with Wild Mushroom Ragout, Acorn Squash with Seafood Ragout, Wild Rice Salad with Mustard Vinaigrette, and a variety of baby vegetables.

On the dessert buffet the abundant "sweets" are presented on a variety of antique Tiffany silver serving pieces as well as in Piero Sartogo crystal bowls and an Elsa Peretti footed cake plate, all from Tiffany's collections of table furnishings.

Jane Montant

CURRIED ZUCCHINI SOUP
MARINATED SHRIMP SALAD
SCALLION BISCUITS WITH HAM
LEMON CAKE
FRESH RASPBERRIES WITH STRAWBERRY LIQUEUR

During a lifetime career at *Gourmet* magazine—as Editor-in-Chief and now as Editor-at-Large—Jane Montant evolved *Gourmet*'s characteristic style of displaying dishes on elegantly furnished tables. Under her leadership, *Gourmet* moved toward the introduction of less-elaborate menus and healthier foods in tune with today's tastes. It is no surprise that when Mrs. Montant has friends over for luncheon, she might well serve this menu of Curried Zucchini Soup, Marinated Shrimp Salad, Scallion Biscuits with Ham, Lemon Cake, and Fresh Raspberries with Strawberry Liqueur, all dishes that can be prepared ahead of time by one busy person.

Mrs. Montant sets her table with Tiffany's "Faneuil" flatware that belonged to her mother. The "Rock Cut" glass bowl and platter are also from Tiffany's. Her china is Herend picked up "piece by piece," in Vienna over a period of time as she traveled for *Gourmet*.

Mrs. Montant likes to keep flower arrangements low, like this bouquet of roses in assorted pinks—"the better to see my friends and enjoy the exchange of news and ideas."

Mimi Sheraton

CURRIED HERRING
BEET AND HERRING SALAD
GRAVLAX WITH MUSTARD SAUCE
DILLED SHRIMP AND HALIBUT SALAD

No one who loves good food should be unfamiliar with the witty, insightful, and instructive writings of New York's high priestess of food, restaurant critic Mimi Sheraton.

And, no one invited to the annual New Year's Day smorgasbord parties at her 1852 Greenwich Village town house—whatever their condition on that possibly difficult day may be—misses these delicious and so-convivial celebrations of food and friendship.

Here, the large round table in front of the front parlor's pale gray marble Victorian fireplace is covered as it always is on such occasions, with a long red damask tablecloth. The traditional holiday season colors of the table's centerpiece of holly, evergreens, and red roses is echoed by the leaves and red ribbons of "Tiffany Garland" Mason's Ironstone buffet plates. Bright orange Gravlax with Mustard Sauce on a crystal platter and silver "Wave" bowls from Tiffany's filled with yellow Curried Herring

and deep red-pink Beet and Herring Salad lend their own festive colors. The buffet also includes Dilled Shrimp and Halibut Salad in a ribbed crystal bowl, made by Reidel for Tiffany's; Swedish Meatballs; Swedish Baked Beans; Danish Liver Pâté, and a whole baked Polish ham and assorted Scandinavian breads and cookies.

The ham is carved with a Tiffany "Bamboo" carving set, and there are Tiffany pilsner glasses for guests who, like Mimi Sheraton, are partial to drinking beer with smorgasbord foods.

"My husband, Richard Falcone, and I began doing this party about ten years ago after having done small brunches for a dozen or so guests on New Year's Day for several years," Mimi Sheraton explains. "For some reason, that day seems a good one for a party, there being so many others before Christmas and so many people now go away over the holiday itself. Most are back by New Year's Day and so we enlarged our party to a late afternoon affair. We invite mainly people we like but have not seen much of during the year. A few close friends are, of course, also asked.

"My affection for Scandinavian food began in the early fifties when I wrote about interior design and home furnishings for *Good Housekeeping, Seventeen,* and *House Beautiful*'s supplement division. In those days, design innovation centered around Scandinavia and I took many trips to Denmark, Norway, Sweden, and Finland to see furniture fairs, porcelain factories, glassworks, and silversmiths. Even then, food was my passion and I sought out recipes, restaurants, and markets and felt that Scandinavian food, especially that of Denmark and Sweden, were badly represented here. I loved the simple fresh-air flavors of dill and caraway, the wonderful salmon, shellfish, game and pork dishes, and, of course, the pastries. I mastered a lot of Scandinavian cooking at home through the years, and when I decided to do this buffet, the usual smorgasbord dishes were naturals, mainly because they are easy to eat buffet style, requiring no knives. For that reason, I even slice the ham in rather small, thin, canapé-size chips. I use relatively small serving bowls that can be freshly refilled as needed because I think it uninviting to see huge bowls with contents that look picked over. It is also easier to keep foods really cold and really hot that way.

"For desserts, I serve only a few Danish cheeses and an assortment of Christmas cookies with coffee.

"We have from forty-five to fifty-five people at this party that runs from 3 to 7 P.M. I serve white and red wine, offer Danish beer, aquavit, and anything else that guests might want. There is remarkably little alcohol consumed on that day, for obvious reasons. Sparkling mineral water is the hands-down favorite."

Moira Hodgson

BEET AND WATERCRESS SALAD WITH GOAT'S CHEESE
ROAST POUSSINS WITH ROSEMARY, SHALLOTS, AND ROOT VEGETABLES
WEHANI RICE SIMMERED IN CHICKEN STOCK
SAUTÉED BABY ARTICHOKES

Here for a summer supper of Beet and Water-cress Salad with Goat's Cheese; Roast Poussins with Rosemary, Shallots, and Root Vegetables; Wehani Rice Simmered in Chicken Stock; Sautéed Baby Artichokes; and Poached Pears with Raspberry Sauce and Cream, Moira Hodgson, restaurant critic for the *New York Observer,* frequent contributor to the *New York Times,* and author of seven cookbooks, sets her buffet table with Tiffany & Co.'s "Century" flat silver and a bold mix of Tiffany ceramics which includes "Black Bamboo" dinner plates, a green trompe l'oeil cabbage tureen, and a "Portuguese Tiles" French faience tray used as a platter.

"I am addicted to unusual china and like mixing patterns and using unexpected objects like the 1920s

china maid salt and pepper server used here," Ms. Hodgson confesses.

"I like to try out new ideas in the kitchen, but am not buttressed by an army of servants nor by a limitless budget, and I often make my preparations after a full day's work, so I like to keep things fresh and uncomplicated.

"I plan menus with an eye to color and texture as well as taste. I use food in season and I pick ingredients according to what looks good in the market that day, often changing my menu at the last minute because I see something that I can't resist: baby artichokes to be sautéed in olive oil with garlic, some fresh chanterelles just in, or a particularly enticing piece of fish."

Menu

Brandhill Mussels
Cracked Stone Crab Claws
Balik Salmon on Black Bread
·
New Zealand Baby Lamb Chops
Venison Filet, Filas Artichokes
·
Rose Petal Salad, Three Greens
·
Baby Chocolate Cheesecake
·
Coffee, Kir Royale Cognac

Zack Hanle

Founder and officer of Les Dames d'Escoffier and first honoree of the James Beard Foundation, Zack Hanle has been the New York Editor of *Bon Appétit* for fifteen years. She is now the magazine's Editor-at-Large, and was once Editor-in-Chief of CBS's *Epicure* magazine. Among her "food scrivenings," as she calls them, are the pioneer *Cooking with Flowers* and the definitive *Cooking Wild Game*. An ardent picnicker, she says: "Omar Khayyám offered the best of picnic menus: the loaf, the jug, and a 'thou' of choice. If you are French, you will add some good cheese. From there, embellish at will. A picnic is the most wonderful of parties, ever piquing the mind as well as the palate.

"I have feasted far and near, with friends and family the world over, on fine and varied fare.

"Nothing was ever so refreshing and exhilarating as the foods and wines savored by waterfall and stream, on field and lawn, at seaside, in woods and gardens, on dunes and small islands reached by sundry vessels.

"I first encountered tailgate picnics at football games where simplicity was not always the rule. In recent years, menus have become more elaborate and the accoutrements of service increasingly luxurious. The best silver, crystal, china, and flower arrangements are *de rigueur*. [Here all are from Tiffany & Co.]. The upscale vehicle of the hour is the Mercedes-Benz wagon, with the only possible better perhaps, a proud vintage 'woodie' from the forties, preserved and carefully polished. Land-Rovers proliferate at the polo grounds and wagons dot outdoor concert grounds.

"Here at a pre-kickoff affair for four, plus extras for visiting guests, there is Venison-Filled Mini-Brioche, Imperial Balik Salmon, Cracked Stone Crabs, Greenshell Mussels, New Zealand Baby Lamb Chops, a Rose Petal Salad, and silken Chocolate Cheesecake in individual tarts—all with rivers of Perrier-Jouet champagne.

"It's a simple, delicious, withal elegant array of finger foods. Try all or part of the menu and, if you do, render Omar's final quatrain this way: 'And when . . . you shall pass among the guests star-scattered on the grass . . . ,' turn *up* a glass for me!"

Robert Denning & Vincent Fourcade

CURRIED FARM CORN ON THE COB
TOMATOES, SHRIMP, AND RICE
POACHED BLUEFISH WITH CURRY SAUCE

When Edith Wharton and Ogden Codman, Jr., published *The Decoration of Houses* in 1897, they set turn-of-the-century standards of American "good taste." To them these included Georgian, Louis XV, and Louis XVI Revival furnishings; luxurious silk damask curtains and upholsteries along with deep-fringed silk lampshades.

The traditions of this lavish, opulent, and aesthetic period are gloriously carried on and updated by the world-renowned New York design firm of Robert Denning and Vincent Fourcade.

Here at their Bridgehampton, Long Island, summer quarters, Robert Denning prepares a summer dinner of Curried Farm Corn on the Cob; Tomatoes, Shrimp, and Rice; Sautéed Scallops; Poached Bluefish with Curry Sauce; and fresh raspberries.

Carrying out the decorative themes of the house, the dinner will be served on "Tiffany Yellow Flowers" Mason's Ironstone plates, whose pattern is based on Aesthetic Movement Japanese Revival motifs, and coffee will be served from a superb 1870s Tiffany & Co. silver service created by Tiffany's great nineteenth-century designer, Edward C. Moore, in the firm's "Japanesque" style.

Guests will be seated on the Denning and Fourcade "Hotel Ritz Louis XVI"–style sofa, and the dinner will be lit by the Long Island summer twilight filtering through lace curtains as well as by lamps whose deep-fringed, fawn china silk shades are lined in rose, "giving pools of rose-colored light," the designers explain. "Edith Wharton atmosphere is very much the mood of the room."

Despite the assertion by Robert Denning that he has "little time and less patience with cooking, and has never entered dessertland," the house cuisine is highly regarded by those whose standards would be fully endorsed by Wharton and Codman.

Eric Boman
& Peter Schlesinger

"The guest book at Woodacres is a rather thin volume," comments celebrity photographer Eric Boman and artist/ceramist Peter Schlesinger, describing life at the rambling 150-year-old summer house they share on the South Shore of Long Island. "The idea of entertaining is not entertained—only the closest of friends are invited."

That being said, there is seldom a weekend meal served when the table is not crowded with friends. The fine early Victorian house has seen more than its share of famous visitors since the days when Franklin Delano and Eleanor Roosevelt visited Woodacres, the summer home of their friend, the legendary philanthropist Bernard Baruch.

"These days, however," Boman continues, "life here is more low-key, which doesn't mean drab.

"Tea is taken every day at five, not because of the British and their endless discussions about 'five o'clock tea' and what is and what isn't correct (that I picked up during twelve years in England), but be-

cause it coincides conveniently with the hour when Louise, the fox-terrier mistress of this house, is fed and is a good time for that relaxing ritual.

"Here, we have the fancy version, the guest tea, on the porch where it's served May to October, weather permitting."

The white painted Victorian tea table is set with Adams's Lowestoft and Tiffany's "Audubon" flat silver, designed and first produced by Tiffany & Co. in 1871 shortly after the last wing was added to Woodacres.

For tea there are house favorites, Hazelnut, Chocolate, and Sour Cherry Cake, and Nasturtium Sandwiches.

"Some variation of this cake is always at hand," says Peter Schlesinger, who frequently abandons the ceramic kilns in his studio wing of Woodacres for the Garland stove in the kitchen to throw together the delicious tea cakes.

"The basic recipe is very tolerant of substitutions," he points out. "You may omit the chocolate, exchange the hazelnuts for almonds, leave out the cherries, or add prunes. It is always rich but rather dry, with quite a bitter chocolate flavor—a grown-up cake."

"Nasturtiums," Boman adds, "are a house favorite. They encircle the porch, appear in vases, on napkins, but most importantly in the sandwiches, where they give a sharp, hot taste, not unlike that of watercress."

Many summer dinners and all winter meals at Woodacres are taken in the airy formal dining room whose tall windows on three of its sides gives it the air of a garden banqueting pavilion.

"Any dish," Eric observes, "is greatly improved by the simple effort of carrying it through the door into the dining room where there is an air of gentle formality.

"The blue of the walls has a life of its own—it changes with the light.

"The house was built on an angle, permitting its occupants to take both breakfast and dinner with the sun streaming in, on condition they dine at six, which in Bernard Baruch's time they surely did.

"My paternal grandmother's life is reflected here, in the two decanters that were the pride of her parents' humble cottage in the north of Sweden, and in the chandelier she gave her husband (but really herself) for his sixtieth birthday."

Dinner will center on the local bird, the Long Island duckling, roast with pears and Chinese spices. The Chinoiserie Duck will be accompanied by Roasted Eggplants and Wild Rice with Caramelized Onions, Mushrooms, and Jerusalem Artichokes, and all accompanied by a light red Graves wine.

The dinner will be served on antique French creamware plates and eaten with Tiffany's "Audubon" flat silver. A covered Minton tureen dated 1867 doubles as centerpiece and serving dish for the wild rice. The views in three directions to the well-kept perennial gardens provide all the flowers the setting of quiet, high sophistication requires.

"The napkins," Boman points out, "came from a dear friend's grandparents, and so have odd initials.

"This is a typical setting," he concludes. "It really changes very little, which I like."

Carolyne Roehm Kravis

HONEYDEW MELON WITH GIN AND LIME
MEDITERRANEAN LOBSTER AND FISH STEW WITH LINGUINE
TART OF FIGS WITH BLACKBERRY AND CASSIS GLAZE

New York legend has it that prominent beauty and socialite Carolyne Roehm Kravis breakfasts only on coffee and one Oreo cookie to maintain her perfect size 4/6 figure.

True or not, the tall, talented, and lovely Mrs. Henry Kravis has maintained both her perfect size 4/6 and her perfectly high-profiled social leadership position by serving as chairman of such musts of New York society as the New York City Ballet Gala, the Metropolitan Opera Gala, and the Winter Antiques Show for the Eastside Settlement House. The style she brought to such events played no small role

in the late 1980s' elevation of the gala fund-raising party to an American art form. Carolyne Roehm has also served as President of the Council of Fashion Designers of America, and all this to glowing reviews from the social press.

Her husband, financial magician Henry Kravis, has his own share of glowing reviews for his own high-profiled role in the spectacular leveraged buyouts put together by Kohlberg Kravis Roberts and Co.

In the midst of the not undaunting demands of their lifestyle in the stratosphere of success, the Kravises find time to enjoy their accomplishments in their Manhattan apartment, their Connecticut weekend house, their ski lodge in Vail, Colorado, and their summer house at Southampton, Long Island.

Here at the Southampton house Carolyne Roehm Kravis prepares a summer supper of Honeydew Melon with Gin and Lime, Mediterranean Lobster and Fish Stew with Linguine, Salade Verte, and Tart of Figs with Blackberry and Cassis Glaze. (All favorites in her well-rehearsed repertoire of party recipes.)

The supper is served on an exuberantly carved, gilt and lacquered, tile-top antique Portuguese palace table placed in front of the living room's multicolored marble fireplace. The comfortably opulent room has blue and white hand-painted tile walls in the Portuguese taste, and a collection of blue and white Chinese porcelains. The Portuguese blue and yellow color combination is enhanced by Carolyne Roehm Kravis's artful bouquets of blue hydrangeas and yellow roses.

A quizzical young Portuguese lady in a high-crowned sun hat surveys the colorful scene from a polychromed eighteenth-century Portuguese tile panel set in the wall above the fireplace. The young lady is flanked by two Chinese heads wearing parasol hats and supported by peacock feathers.

The blue and yellow "Tiffany Private Stock" porcelain "Bigoudon" plates were inspired by an eighteenth-century delft pattern, and bear an arresting resemblance to contemporary Portuguese models.

The fish stew and fig tart are served in other eighteenth-century delftware-inspired ceramics from Tiffany & Co.

Mrs. Kravis's other Tiffany table furnishings include: "Chrysanthemum" flat silver, an Elsa Peretti cobalt blue Venetian crystal dish holding gilt and silvered Jordan almonds; a "Ring Cut" ship's decanter; and cobalt blue and white "Canton" porcelains made at Vista Alegre in northern Portugal for Tiffany's.

Fruits, vegetables, herbs, lobsters, bread, and Tiffany silver beakers arranged by the hostess in the style of an eighteenth-century still-life painting add their own touch of appetizing chic and cheerfully stated opulence.

Mai Hallingby

CRAYFISH IN DILL
ANCHOVY COCKTAIL SANDWICHES
ROOSAMANNA (CREAM-OF-WHEAT FRUIT MOUSSE) / CRÈME À LA VANILLE

With close affinities to both its Baltic neighbors and Scandinavian cousins and at the same time marked by its often stormy relationship with Russia, Estonia is known for its fishing ports, its abundant wild flowers, and its "Nordic" cuisine of fish and crustaceans washed down with potato vodka and light beer accompanied by a tasty variety of fruit and berry soups and mousses. To New York society, however, its most popular export is Mai Hallingby, the tall and strikingly beautiful wife of Wall Street financial magician Paul Hallingby, Jr.

A veteran organizer of fund-raising gala events for the Boys Club, the School of American Ballet, the New York Public Library, and the Central Park Conservancy, Mai Hallingby is also a veteran hostess of the Hallingbys' more private entertainments at their homes in New York, Southampton, and the Bahamas.

Here escaping the rigorous ceremonies of "Nouvelle Society," Mrs. Hallingby prepares a poolside luncheon at her Southampton home offering her own version of nouvelle cuisine.

Although she was only two when her family fled Estonia, her mother instilled her with a profound knowledge of that country's traditions; language; and appealingly healthy, "spa-like," as she calls it, cuisine. "Above all, I like light food," she comments, "fish mousses and vegetable terrines whose different colors make them so very pretty. Then there is a favorite puree of carrots and turnips. People usually don't know what a turnip is anymore, but I like serving them cooked as I would cook little new potatoes. People are always pleasantly surprised when they taste them."

Here for a typically Estonian lunch of Crayfish in Dill; Anchovy and Herring Sandwiches; and Roosamanna, a traditional soupy red fruits mousse, all accompanied by Estonian vodka and beer, Mai Hallingby sets her poolside table covered with a silver Mylar cloth with Tiffany & Co.'s "Blue Dragon" porcelain and "Shell and Thread" flat silver.

A splendid antique silver langouste and small Tiffany silver shell dishes carry out the seashore climate of the setting, whimsically accented with some pearls from the hostess's not-so-small jewel collection.

"Crayfish are tremendously popular in Estonia," Mrs. Hallingby explains. "They have their own season, a veritable crayfish festival that lasts from Midsummer's Eve in June until September. On the first night the near-pagan outdoor celebrations around huge bonfires last throughout the luminous summer night."

The profusion of wild flowers that color the Estonian countryside in summer and that are gathered to decorate such festivities inspired Mai Hallingby's simple and simply dazzling country bouquet of intensely yellow sunflowers.

Charlotte Ford Downe

CHICKEN SALAD WITH WALNUTS
PASTA PRIMAVERA

Dubbed the "Empress of Etiquette" by the gossip columns for her popular books, magazine essays, and lecture tours on the modern dos and don'ts of social behavior, Charlotte Ford Downe knows how to make her way as gracefully as anyone along society's circuitous paths.

The same mix of good common sense, wit, and compassion she brings to her varied roles of author, civic leader, cross-country lecturer, wife, mother, and sometime teacher are brought to her additional role of hostess.

Born into the "First Family of Detroit," Charlotte Ford's education and early social training were an enviable mix of Grosse Pointe, Italy, and Paris; but throughout, her traditional American values remained with her. Here in the garden of her Southampton, Long Island, summer house, she entertains after a morning on the tennis courts with a lunch of three time-honored, fundamental American classics: Chicken Salad with Walnuts, Tomato Aspic, and a

Black Cherry Jelly Ring mold with summer fruits, all accompanied by iced tea. The only concession to "International Modern" food is a cold Pasta Primavera.

There is a large bouquet of predominantly pink mixed garden flowers which the hostess feels makes such informal and easily expandable luncheons "inviting and comfortable" with a "sunny appearance."

Summer luncheon guest lists at the Downes' are frequently expanded at the last minute, so the hostess has a fondness for food "that can be quickly prepared and will go a long way." Even then she advises, "Always have plenty of fruit and cheese handy."

Guests at this meal will eat with Tiffany's "Audubon" flat silver whose lively little birds and flowers are a perfect complement to the casual opulence of the setting.

A nineteenth-century painted tole palm tree brings its note of luxury to the table.

Mrs. Cornelius Vanderbilt Whitney

WATERCRESS SANDWICHES
BLACK WALNUT CHOCOLATE CAKE
PECAN PUFFS

The Cornelius Vanderbilt Whitney Farm in Lexington, Kentucky, has had over 450 stakes-winning horses raised on it since the time of Cornelius Vanderbilt Whitney's father, Harry Payne Whitney.

Whether at the farm or in Saratoga Springs in August, at Belmont in June, or in Florida for the winter season, the Whitneys' life centers around their racehorses and what is popularly referred to in racing circles as the "horse scene."

Every year during the July season in Saratoga Springs, New York, the Whitneys give a garden party for about five hundred local friends.

Here, as for those occasions, two Belmont Stakes trophies, both made by Tiffany & Co., are placed in the garden gazebo at Cady Hill House to serve Marylou Whitney's ever-popular New York champagne–based pink punch.

The massive sterling silver Belmont Stakes "cup" punch bowl and ladle were won by Harry Payne Whitney in 1906 with a horse named "Burgomaster." The trophy tray the cup sits on, which like the cup has horseshoe, harness, and racing bit motifs, was won in 1899 by Mr. Whitney's grandfather, William Collins Whitney, with a horse named "Jean Bereaud."

Mrs. Whitney's seven-eighths champagne to one-eighth cranberry juice punch, called a "Marylou," was "concocted," as she puts it, seven years ago when the New York State Champagne Producers asked her to suggest a new way to serve their champagne. Marylou punch is served here in Tiffany's practical "All Purpose" glasses.

The round table in the white wrought-iron gazebo is always set for the garden party with a handmade lace tea cloth that belonged to Mr. Whitney's mother, Gertrude Vanderbilt Whitney, and before her to her mother, Alice Claypoole Gwynne (Mrs. Cornelius Vanderbilt II).

Guests at the Whitneys' garden party will snack on traditional Cucumber Sandwiches and Watercress Sandwiches, frosted Black Walnut Chocolate Cake, Lemon Wafers, and Pecan Puffs.

The Lemon Wafers and Pecan Puffs are served here in Tiffany's "Wickham" crystal dishes.

The table is ornamented with one of Marylou Whitney's summer signature "garden party" hats.

Mrs. Thomas M. Bancroft

NILMA'S SORREL SOUP
LEEK AND HAM QUICHE

During Saratoga's August racing season, that "heavily booked and social month," as Mrs. Bancroft calls it, the Bancrofts' stately 1872 antebellum-style house is the setting for numerous small luncheons and dinners.

Mr. Bancroft served for seven years as Chairman of the New York Racing Association and with his brother William owns and operates the Pen-y-Bryn Farm racing stables, so conversation at the Bancroft table more often than not touches on horses and their fanciers.

Here, antique wicker chairs from the house's spectacular porches have been brought out on the lawn for an intimate lunch of the family cook, Nilma's, specialty, Sorrel Soup, and Leek and Ham Quiche, followed by Saratoga Hand Melon with strawberries, kiwis, and fresh raspberry ice cream.

The table is set with Tiffany & Co.'s "Salem" flat silver and "Laurelton Hall" china and crystal. There are pink garden roses in Baccarat vases de-

signed by Tiffany's late Design Director Van Day Truex. The silver trophy centerpiece was won by Thomas Bancroft's grandfather, William Woodward, for his horse Hypnotic's performance in 1946's Alabama, a mile-and-a-quarter grade-one race for three-year-old fillies, which takes place in Saratoga.

About thirteen miles east of the Bancrofts' house in Saratoga Springs, off Route 29, four generations of the Hand family have been growing the Hand melon (a perfect cantaloupe bearing the family's logo of a red hand on a white label). Since it was first introduced in 1925, the Hand melon has become a Saratoga racing-season tradition without which no vision of Saratoga dining could be complete.

"Many a tourist enamored of the succulent melon," Barbara Bancroft comments, "has made the mistake of bringing one or more home in the car. Sadly, they do not travel well and the odor rendered from the melons entrapped in a car is indescribable."

Bill Blass

VEGETABLE TERRINE
BILL BLASS MEAT LOAF
POTATO SKINS

ill Blass's clothes have been delighting both men and women for decades. No designer knows better than this "King of American Fashion" how to continually transform the classic into the new with flair and superbly tailored elegance, and no designer has more successfully mined the rich territories of America's affinity for English culture.

Every planned and polished detail of the late-eighteenth-century tavern building in northwestern Connecticut that Bill Blass has transformed into his country house speaks with Anglo-American authority.

The Colonial New England atmosphere of the house is reflected in the classic simplicity of the meals served in its half-paneled dining room.

"Life here," says the designer, "pretty much revolves around the dogs, so everything in the house is very casual and informal."

A typical Bill Blass country dinner prepared with traditional recipes carefully refined and perfected over the years will consist of Meat Loaf, Potato Skins, Vegetable Terrine with pepper jelly, to be followed by coffee and Lemon Meringue Pie.

The bare polished wood dining table is set with mixed English country potteries, Rattail flat silver with its pistol-handled knives, and with oversized

unornamented goblets for the red Bordeaux wine that is served at each place in individual Baccarat "Dionysus" decanters first designed for Tiffany & Co. by Bill Blass's late friend, Van Day Truex, who was Design Director of Tiffany & Co. from 1955 until 1979. The sterling silver "Capstan" salt and peppers and Corinthian-column candlesticks are also from Tiffany's.

Mr. Blass never uses flowers to decorate his tables. In this case he uses green pears in an unusual Ionic capitol-shaped container in which he often serves cheese.

The designer's fondness for meat loaf deserves special comment. Known in New York society as "designer meat loaf," it makes much applauded celebrity guest appearances on the menus of numerous

fund-raising charity balls and is a staple on the menu of Mortimer's, the favorite "watering place" of New York's elite. As Blass puts it, "Everyone seems to like it."

The food is served buffet style on a long, antique French, polished natural-oak school table guarded by a sixteenth-century German wood carving of a "gladiator" on horseback. The setting is backed by a large French Louis XV–period map of the Americas, one of four maps that quietly decorate the room.

The lemon meringue pie and coffee will also be served buffet style on another table under a massive late-Georgian silver candelabrum in front of a classic American Colonial window looking out to the yews, rhododendrons, stone walls, and assorted trees of the classic northwestern Connecticut countryside.

Mrs. John R. Drexel III

SALMON AND SOLE MOUSSE WITH RED-PEPPER MAYONNAISE
AND WATERCRESS MAYONNAISE
CROQUEMBOUCHE STONOR LODGE

Nothing in America has ever been quite so opulent as Newport in its prime; and, although the Vanderbilts' The Breakers was larger, no Newport house was ever quite so grand as coal king Edward Berwind's The Elms.

Inspired inside and out by the Château d'Asnières (designed in 1750 by Jules Hardouin-Mansart, chief architect of Versailles), The Elms (built in 1899 to 1901) was as regal as its prototype.

Here leader of Newport social "royalty," Mrs. John R. Drexel III creates a fantasy dinner in the style of her grandfather and Mr. Berwind's neighbor on Fifth Avenue, Mr. William Watts-Sherman, who used to require twelve of his private train carriages to move his family, their wardrobes, and household provisions when they left New York for the season in Newport.

Mrs. Drexel's menu of Salmon and Sole Mousse with Red Pepper Mayonnaise and Watercress Mayonnaise, Roast Loin of Veal Stuffed with Sweetbread

Mousseline and Sauce Périgueux, and Croquembouche Stonor Lodge is typical of summer dinners at the Drexels' own Bellevue Avenue home. Newport's Stonor Lodge was named for the "stately English home" where Mrs. Drexel was born the Honorable Noreen Stonor, daughter of the fifth Lord Camoys and Lady Camoys (née Miss Watts-Sherman).

The table in The Elms's stately Venetian Baroque dining room is set with "Blue Wave—Tiffany Private Stock" porcelain, "Newport" crystal, and "Olympian" flat silver, all from Tiffany & Co.

The Elms's monumental Louis XV Revival gilt bronze centerpiece and compotes are 1890 French, while all the table's lavish English silver cups, salts, and footed vegetable dish are from the Drexels' collections, as are the French Rococo Revival cherub salt stands, originally from the Paris town house of Mrs. John R. Drexel I.

The diamond tiara is a family piece worn by Noreen Drexel on state occasions.

Mrs. John G. Winslow

SEAFOOD BISQUE
ROASTED RACK OF LAMB
MADELEINES

*I*n September of 1839, wealthy Savannah, Georgia, merchant George Noble Jones wrote to America's then leading architect Richard Upjohn asking him to draw up plans in the Gothic Revival style for a "cottage containing eight chambers, besides two or three sleeping apartments for servants."

The "cottage" was the first out-of-town summer home built on the dirt road that is today Newport's glorious Bellevue Avenue; and, with its construction, Newport was on the way to becoming America's greatest summer resort.

The Civil War forced George Jones to abandon his "cottage," and he sold it on April 29, 1863, to a relative, native Newporter William Henry King. The "cottage" underwent few changes until it came into the hands of William King's nephew, China Trade millionaire David King, Jr., in 1875.

By then the grandeurs of Newport society's Gilded Age summer lifestyle had escalated beyond the capacities of Upjohn's "cottage," and David and his socially aware wife, Ella Louisa Rives King, in 1878 commissioned Stanford White of the newly formed firm of McKim, Mead & White to build a three-story addition that would house, on the ground floor, a new dining room large enough to double as a ballroom.

Stanford White was then working for Louis Comfort Tiffany on plans for a minstrels' gallery for the great hall or "Veterans' Room" of New York's Seventh Regiment Armory. When in 1880 it came time to design the ballroom/dining room of the Kings' cottage, by then renamed "Kingscote" in anticipation of its approaching splendors, White asked Tiffany to join in the decoration of the room.

Tiffany's contributions to the room's extraordinarily modern-for-1880 interior of window screens of opalescent glass bricks, wall tiles, and glass mosaics of dahlias above the room's stark Italian Siena marble fireplace are first cousins to his Tiffany glass windows, iridescent glass tile fireplace, and bird mosaic in the Seventh Regiment Armory (completed in 1880).

The addition with its Stanford White–Louis Comfort Tiffany ballroom was completed in March of 1882.

Kingscote served as the British "Summer Embassy" in 1895, and finally in 1972 the last of the King family, Gwendolin Ella Rives Armstrong, left

Kingscote to the Preservation Society of Newport County after 109 years of occupancy by her family.

Here in front of Stanford White and Louis Comfort Tiffany's luminous decor for Kingscote's dining room, Mrs. John G. Winslow, wife of the Preservation Society of Newport County's President and Chairman, sets a table for a formal summer dinner.

Mrs. Winslow's dinner will start with a Seafood Bisque of lobster, shrimp, and scallops followed by Rack of Lamb with a Dijon mustard, bread crumb, and rosemary crust, served with a mix of steamed garden vegetables: carrots, string beans, asparagus, broccoli, zucchini, and summer squash. For dessert there will be fresh Lemon Sherbet with Grand Marnier Sauce and homemade Madeleines.

"In Newport," Mrs. Winslow comments, "there is an inclination at dinners to serve too many courses. At one time, fourteen was not uncommon here, but now there is a totally different attitude about food. I find that three courses are ample, unless there is a salad after the main course. "Salad," she adds, "is not a good first course at a dinner party."

Guests at Mrs. Winslow's dinner will eat on "Tiffany Private Stock" hand-painted "Halcyon" bone china and serve themselves from passed silver platters with antique Tiffany silver serving pieces.

Both the table's exuberant bouquet of tangerine orange dahlias and Tiffany's hammered brass wall sconces which light the scene echo Louis Comfort Tiffany's Favrile glass dahlia mosaics.

Lady Mary Rothermere

SMOKED SALMON MARIE
ENGLISH SUMMER FRUIT SALAD WITH MINT

Cooling ocean breezes make the broad verandas of Lady Mary Rothermere's Newport "cottage," Four Winds, a favored summer spot for buffet luncheons.

Old-fashioned mosquito netting hangs from the veranda's arches, falling just inside the Italianate balustrade. It separates the party from the gardens as well as from the occasional New England insect, and lends an ephemeral glamor to the setting.

The menu of mixed Southern and English influences includes Smoked Salmon Marie, Roast Virginia Ham, and English Summer Fruit Salad with Mint.

Parcel-gilt English Regency armchairs provide stylish seating for guests who will eat from elaborately decorated "Breslau Castle" Royal Berlin porcelain plates from Tiffany & Co. with Tiffany's "Wyndham" flat silver.

"Wyndham" was named for the county in eastern Connecticut, not far from Newport, which was the boyhood home of Charles Lewis Tiffany who founded Tiffany & Co. in 1837.

The "Breslau Castle" pattern was first made for the Emperor Frederick the Great of Prussia by his own Royal Berlin porcelain manufactory in the late eighteenth century.

Lady Rothermere's table is enlivened by multiple examples of the charmingly unpremeditated country flower arrangements she enjoys composing with the products of her much-loved garden.

The real flowers are rivaled by the almost dauntingly lush and intricate rococo flowers of a pair of magnificent Nymphenburg porcelain tureens, also from Tiffany's.

Alyne Massey

BRIE AND CHUTNEY TARTS
TOMATO BOUILLON
ROAST QUAIL WITH APRICOT-RICE STUFFING AND SAUCE BIGARADE
LENNIE'S ROLLS
BROOK HOUSE APPLES

Hospitality and dining well are both Southern tradition and family heritage for leading Nashville and Palm Beach philanthropist, fund raiser, and socialite Alyne Massey.

Her ancestors arrived in Tennessee in the 1770s and she grew up in the state's former capital, Columbia, steeped in the Southern art of hospitality.

Among the most cherished possessions from her childhood is a cookbook compiled by her great-great-aunt while a student at Columbia Institute, an Episcopal boarding school for young women at-

tended by Mrs. Massey's mother, grandmother, and great-grandmother. True to its times, the book includes such now folkloric, regional fare as Jefferson Davis Pie and Confederate Pudding, as well as such arcane treats as Nun's Buns and Flummery.

The South's much-touted and often misunderstood traditional cooking is, Alyne Massey believes, a delicious blend of the light and flavorful (fresh vegetables and fruits, wild game, homemade breads, dressings and mayonnaises, and delicate desserts) with the unusual. "For example," she explains,

"there is only one way I would ever prepare a cured ham, and I doubt that anyone outside of Tennessee and Kentucky has ever heard of it.

"This old recipe requires two days of preparation. The ham must be about twelve pounds and must come from the left leg, because hogs habitually sleep on the right, making the left more tender. The ham is soaked overnight, then drained and scrubbed and returned to soak in fresh water containing two halved lemons, two halved onions, and a cayenne pepper. It is boiled for an hour, then ham and pot are wrapped in newspaper and a quilt and left overnight. On the second morning the rind is removed, leaving about one-fourth inch of fat. The ham is scored, pricked with cloves, covered with brown sugar, and baked at 350° for twenty minutes per pound. The result is tender, succulent, and ineffably Southern."

Alyne Massey and her late husband Jack Massey, who as founder of Kentucky Fried Chicken had a hand in the celebrity of a more popular culture of Southern cooking, always loved at once gracious and informal entertaining for both friends and charitable or business causes. However, Mrs. Massey stresses that every party should be special. "I hope the world doesn't become so informal," she states, "that hostesses fail to display their prettiest objects and use their best china and silver every now and then."

Here at Mrs. Massey's neo-Georgian Nashville home, Brook House, guests will dine in the spacious dining room at plaid taffeta–skirted tables of six on one of the hostess's typical Southern menus. With cocktails, they will have had Brie and Chutney Tarts, Caviar on Toast, and Smoked Salmon on Brown Bread. Dinner will begin with a pungent Tomato Bouillon, followed by Roast Quail with Apricot-Rice Stuffing and Sauce Bigarade served on thinly sliced Southern cured country ham; White and Wild Rice Pilaf, Haricots Verts with Toasted Almonds, and Lennie's Rolls. For dessert there will be Brook House Apples with Chocolate Ganache and Calvados Sauce.

Wines with dinner will include white Puligny-Montrachet and red Château Haut-Brion; and, with dessert, Taittinger Comtes de Champagne Blanc de Blanc.

Mrs. Massey's place settings for this dinner include "Blair House" American Pickard china created specially by Tiffany & Co. for the Presidential Guest House in Washington, D.C. (for whose Restoration Fund Mrs. Massey is a board member), Tiffany's "Hampton" flat silver, and Baccarat "Harcourt" crystal also from Tiffany & Co.

Antique English silver quail inspect the place settings.

Dessert this evening will be served in the library (where the ancestral family cookbooks are housed) on gilded and flowered antique English plates, which like the magnificent flowered urns centering Mrs. Massey's tables, were produced by Coalport.

Nancy Goldberg

NEW ORLEANS GUMBO
DOVES BRAISED IN PORT
ARTICHOKE BOTTOMS STUFFED WITH ARTICHOKES
CRÈME BRÛLÉE

Although she has with much acclaim owned and run Chicago's Maxim's, Nancy Goldberg does not come from a line of chefs.

"Gumbo was the only thing my mother cooked," explains the quintessential Chicagoan. "She learned because she couldn't get gumbo, which she loved, here in the North, so she found a good recipe from one of her friends' Southern cooks and just stuck with that, her recipe repertoire of one."

Nancy Goldberg, however, during travels in the world of art and architecture with her Bauhaus-trained, Chicago star-architect husband, Bertrand Goldberg, has picked up her own repertoire of "International Modern" recipes.

Here she prepares some house favorites that go into the Goldbergs' "half in and half out of the kitchen" dinner parties.

The dishes also find their place in boating picnics on the Chicago River where "Bud" Goldberg's land-mark Marina City skyscrapers or his more recent River City complex can be admired.

A favorite set of nineteenth-century marrow spoons inspires the preparation of Roast Marrow Bones with toast. A vast *turbotière* from France demanded a whole two-foot, fourteen-pound turbot to poach. There is naturally Mrs. Florsheim's (Mrs. Goldberg's mother's) Gumbo. A friend's son came in from the nearby farmlands with a gift of the essentials for Doves Braised in Port. Matelote of Eel, Artichoke Bottoms Stuffed with Artichokes, and a Crème Brûlée round out the menu.

A hexagonal Tiffany silver tray of fellow Chicago architect Frank Lloyd Wright is used with other Tiffany silver dishes. It reflects the dining room's Victor Vassarely tapestry, while an astonished pre-Columbian Peruvian mask and an inscrutable Chinese Sung pottery monk look on.

Betsy Bloomingdale

ERLINDA'S ROAST BONED AND STUFFED CHICKEN
FRESH PEAR ICE CREAM WITH CHOCOLATE LEAVES AND POACHED PEARS

To be a world-class charmer bringing glamor and excitement to every dinner party, including your own, takes a rare and happy mix of talent, well-nourished imagination, knowledge, and good careful planning.

Betsy Bloomingdale has never been known to arrive at the table other than bursting with informed and animated conversation on any subject; and guests arriving at her Beverly Hills home revel in how gracefully their hostess's knowing eye and taste for quality and luxury has orchestrated personalities, foods, and decor.

No hostess plans more thoroughly. "I keep loads of notes," she says, "on my own parties and also on parties I attend.

"My own parties really revolve around an honored guest, who is often from out of town, so guest lists are chosen with an eye for people to interest the guest of honor. The foods are picked to be something a little different and indigenous to California.

"And the table decor? Well, the basics are from my own wonderful garden and then I add a few other flowers if needed."

Each and every dish served at Betsy Bloomingdale's parties is photographed, and notes are taken on the recipe and presentation for future refinements.

Here the dinner revolves around a whole roast chicken, boned and filled with a truffle-laced stuffing and presented on a Tiffany & Co. "Chrysanthemum" pattern silver tray. The hostess's collection of antique English silver pheasants wander about a splendid centerpiece of red-berried pyracanthus from the garden and imported lilies flown from Holland.

"I have had guests that thought the Jordan Chardonnay and the Jordan Cabernet Sauvignon from the Alexander Valley (served in Edinburgh Thistle glasses) was a fine French Burgundy," notes the ever-supportive-of-things-Californian hostess.

Dessert will be Fresh Pear Ice Cream with Chocolate Leaves and Poached Pears served on a "Lily Pad" silver tray from Tiffany's.

"One thing I've noticed," she adds, "is how much men love an ice cream dessert, and I must say I do too."

When first married, Betsy Bloomingdale had to choose between a new mink coat and her antique Crown Derby Imari dinner service. "Young as I was, I made the right choice," she says.

Wolfgang Puck

POSTRIO LAMB AND EGGPLANT CRÉPINETTES
POSTRIO OLIVE THYME BREAD
POSTRIO DEEP-FRIED WHOLE FISH WITH CUCUMBER SALAD AND PONZU
THREE-LAYER CHOCOLATE MOUSSE

Austrian-born Wolfgang Puck may be the most influential of America's new breed of chef-restaurateurs. His accomplished and personal blend of fresh California ingredients with his classical French training have played a leading role in reviving California's culinary heritage.

Inspired by his mother, a hotel chef, Puck began his formal training at fourteen, and was shortly after apprenticed at L'Ousteau de Baumaniere in Provence. His creativity developed at a succession of three-star French restaurants, including the Hôtel de Paris in Monaco and Maxim's in Paris.

He came to the United States in 1973, beginning his American career at La Tour in Indianapolis before taking over as chef and co-owner of Los Angeles's Ma Maison.

With the publication of his last word on French cuisine *Wolfgang Puck's Modern French Cooking,* Puck broke with his French-influenced past and established that most influential and star-frequented of all Southern California's California-style restaurants, Spago on Sunset Strip, where the now-famous Puck "gourmet pizzas" were introduced.

Wolfgang Puck's only venture outside Southern California is San Francisco's Postrio, a high-ceilinged, Post-Modernist oasis of contemporary design and sophisticated menus inspired by San Francisco's Italian and Asian communities and located in the chicly renovated Prescott Hotel on Post just steps from Union Square.

Here in the Puck-trademark open kitchen in the center of Postrio's vast interior, former Spago chefs and Puck disciples Anne and David Gingrass prepare a sumptuous dinner of a "starter" plate of Puck's popular homemade charcuterie which will include David Gingrass's specialty (only served at Postrio), Postrio Lamb and Eggplant Crépinettes served with Postrio Olive Thyme Bread. There will be a fish course of Postrio Deep-fried Whole Fish with Cucumber Salad and Ponzu, and a main course of Postrio Smoked Lamb Shoulder with Garlic and Rosemary.

The fish recipe is Anne Gingrass's favorite, and in her words "a great way to eat fish."

A Postrio trio of Wolfgang Puck's own favorites: Three-Layer Chocolate Mousse, Vanilla Bean–Pistachio Cheesecake, and Chocolate-Raspberry Mousse Cake, "all intensely flavorful and not too heavy," will conclude the sumptuous and visually stimulating meal.

"With these dishes you need no table decorations," the chefs advise. "The fish decorates itself, as do the charcuterie and desserts."

The *assiette de charcuterie* is served here on a "Tiffany Garden" Limoges porcelain plate.

The deep-fried red snapper is dramatically presented on "Tiffany Private Stock—Cirque Chinois" porcelains, and the trio of Wolfgang Puck ultimate desserts, served with Cognac and coffee, are resplendent on "Tiffany Private Stock—Coeur Fleurs" porcelains hand-painted exclusively for Tiffany & Co. in Paris.

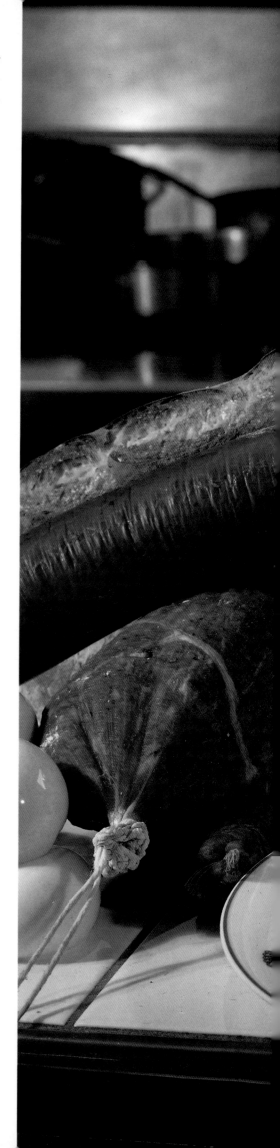

Jeremiah Tower with Mrs. Prentice Cobb Hale

LOBSTER AND ASPARAGUS RAGOUT

When San Francisco's star socialite and hostess, Denise Hale, invites guests to dinner at the Hales' French and Chinese art–filled San Francisco apartment, "I am worse," she confesses, "than the French and Chinese put together. I'm such a perfectionist, so fussy, so crazy for detail. I care very much for how things look. That's part of eating.

"I only invite friends who appreciate beautiful things, simply because I appreciate what I offer being appreciated."

Dinners at the Prentice Cobb Hales' merit appreciation. Both Hales are highly knowledgeable in things culinary.

The legendary James Beard was their close friend and gave Denise Hale private cooking lessons. ("I and Claire Boothe Luce were the only ones," Mrs. Hale proudly remembers.) And James Beard was so fond of Prentice Cobb Hale's classic California country fare that he would sit for hours eating at the Hale ranch while Mr. Hale cooked him fried fresh deer liver and quail to be washed down with cold white Haut-Brion.

Through Beard, the Hales met the chef Beard called "the next superstar in my profession," Jeremiah Tower.

"Jeremiah is almost like my brother," confides Mrs. Hale.

When asked if recipes from her southern central European childhood find their way into today's menus, Denise Hale explains why they don't.

"No one can do them as well as my grandmother. She was born Czechoslovakian, was raised in Vienna, and married a Serbian. She cooked only at Christmas and the preparations lasted a week. There was always a touch of Vienna in her cooking, but this is over. The last great meal like that came when I was five."

Prentice Cobb Hale's favorite all-American childhood meals prepared by his mother's adoring Chinese cook—tomato soup, lamb chops and baked potatoes, and apple pie and ice cream—are also things of the past.

Today with superstar chef Jeremiah Tower's help, Hale dinners like the one here will feature Lobster and Asparagus Ragout and White Chocolate–Caramel Fantasy Box for dessert.

The green floral chintz–lined dining room is decorated with a profusion of old-fashioned roses from Denise Hale's 117 rosebushes that cover a quarter acre of the Hale ranch in Sonoma County. The roses are brought to town in decorative galvanized French florist pails from Guillouard in the northwestern French city of Nantes. "This is my madness," admits Denise Hale, "but it is vitally important."

Dinner is served on a boldly patterned eighteenth-century Imari ironstone service bought while visiting Ireland's leading designer, Sybil Connolly, in Dublin, while rare K'ang Hsi *famille verte* paint boxes further ornament the table.

Dessert is served on "Tiffany Private Stock—Carrousel Chinois" porcelain plates with coffee from a "Nightcap" silver coffee service and "Flora Danica" coffee cups all from Tiffany & Co., as is the "Palm" candlestick and the "Gene Moore Circus" enameled silver acrobat performing on the Hales' dessert setting.

Anita Mardikian Pichler

> LAMB SHISH KEBAB
> BULGUR PILAF
> ROSE PETAL PRESERVES

William Saroyan, a friend and fellow country-man of the father of ever-popular San Franciscan Anita Mardikian Pichler, once wrote, "George Mardikian came to this country after having outwitted famine in his native Armenia by inventing fabulous dishes from such lowly and abundant things as grain, water, salt, imagination and poetry."

"How right Saroyan was," says Anita Mardikian Pichler. "When I was a child, I remember, my father would constantly 'tinker' in the kitchen. He would come up with incredible recipes, which I still enjoy today, and which he then served at his restaurant, Omar Khayyam's, in downtown San Francisco. For me they evoke the aromas of the casbah, the exoticism of the harem, and the high adventure of the caravan route."

Here the opulent exoticism of the Middle East flourishes at the hostess's table covered with saris and silks bought on a trip to India with her husband, Austrian artist Pepo Pichler. The inlaid Middle Eastern chairs and the lavish robes laid over them are souvenirs from time spent in Cairo and Lebanon.

On the table a wealth of Armenian *objets d'art* enliven the place setting of mixed Tiffany & Co.

"Private Stock—Directoire" and "Framboise Rose" porcelains, and "Audubon" flat silver.

As always, fruits not flowers form the center-piece of any Armenian table setting and can include grapes, pomegranates, persimmons, figs, lemons, limes, and lemon leaves, all grown in both California and Armenia.

Dinner will center around George Mardikian's recipe for Lamb Shish Kebab served with Bulgur Pilaf, a dish dating back to the ancient Hittites, and flat Lavash Armenian bread. Dessert will be beakers of fresh yogurt with homemade Rose Petal Preserves.

Amongst the table's Byzantine array of ornaments at this intimate dinner, Anita Mardikian Pichler has included a few leaves from an ancient Armenian manuscript. She explains, "These pages were presented to me and my husband on our wedding day at the Armenian monastery of San Lazzaro, located on a tiny island in the lagoon of Venice.

"My father studied there in his youth and adapted ancient recipes from such manuscripts for modern usage."

Deborah Turbeville

SQUASH, CHICKEN, AND SAUSAGE SOUP
SAUTÉED SPINACH AND RADISHES
BRAISED PORK WITH FRAGRANT PURSLANE (PORTULACA OLERACEA)

San Miguel de Allende prides itself on its populous community of artists and writers, and not least among these is that most artful of fashion photographers, Deborah Turbeville, famed for her equivocally romantic and surreal photographs of models cast off in lovely and softly lit corners of empty rooms.

Her exquisitely beautiful and elegantly simple house in San Miguel is not unlike her photographs. The unusual painted ogive arches, the scenic wall frescoes, and the reflecting pool fringed with papyrus and ferns give its courtyard an air more of the early Venetian Renaissance than of the modern central highlands of Mexico.

Here a still life of local squashes and chayotes sitting on an antique Mexican chair outside the kitchen suggests the simple vegetable dishes that Deborah Turbeville prefers for herself. Occasionally, however, friends are allowed to cook. The menu may then vary to include, as it does here on the kitchen's ample raw wood dining table, a Soup of Squash, Chicken, and Sausage served in a hollowed-out *calabaza,* Sautéed Spinach and Radishes, and Braised Pork with Purslane (*verdolaga*).

The kitchen walls are hung with *ex-votos* commemorating a variety of minor miracles, and the room, a minor miracle itself, is romantically lit by candles in Mexican peasant terra-cotta candelabra and an antique cruciform glass-and-tin lantern.

Deborah Turbeville has a fondness for pale and almost fading full-blown roses, which flower here in "Green Leaves" Este ceramic vases from Tiffany & Co., evoking the aura of Venice.

The serving plates are from the ceramic center of Dolores Hidalgo, and the dinner plates with their paintings of tropical birds in gilded cages surrounded by spirited garlands of ribbons and flowers were designed by Virginia artist Sarah Branch for Tiffany's.

Martha and Elton Hyder

MEXICAN CHICKEN, PORK, AND HOMINY STEW (POZOLE)
PAPAS CHICAS (BABY POTATOES) WITH SOLE, ARTICHOKES, AND ONIONS
BROCCOLI PIE

*E*arly in the eighteenth century, after silver was discovered around the town of Guanajuato in central Mexico's Bajío region, the new-rich Spanish colonial mining families began building palatial houses in the highland town of San Miguel de Allende and the town soon ranked among the richest and most important communities of New Spain.

San Miguel sustained its prosperity, and as is the general rule in prosperous towns, the inhabitants had an insatiable passion for building, which remains vigorous to this day.

In architecture, Spanish Colonial style predominated until the late 1800s, when an inspired Indian mason, Ceferino Gutiérrez, designed the town's dominant monument, the church of La Parroquia. This anomalous but quintessentially picturesque neo-Gothic church of local pink *cantera* sandstone sprung from Gutiérrez's fondness for postcards of European Gothic cathedrals.

Nearby, the Louis XIV Revival–style Iglesia de la Concepción built in 1891, also said to be by Ceferino Gutiérrez and ostensibly inspired by pictures of Les Invalides in Paris, boasts one of Mexico's largest domes. Together Gutiérrez's monuments give San Miguel a flamboyant and romantic skyline and lend a grand sense of event to its colonial cobblestone streets.

In 1926 the Mexican government called a halt to the delinquent styles of such high flights of fancy and declared the town a national monument, summarily protecting it from architectures unrelated to Spanish Colonial.

Just as the Palace of the Counts of Canal on the town square was San Miguel's grandest dwelling in the eighteenth century, the Quinta Quebrada back of La Concepción's great two-story pillar–supported dome is the house around which San Miguel de Allende's now eminently international and artistic social life revolves.

Elton and Martha Hyder on a visit from their native Fort Worth, Texas, bought the quinta over thirty-two years ago when it was little more than a faded souvenir of eighteenth- and nineteenth-century grandeur. Since then, Martha Hyder has succeeded with her flamboyant sense of the grand and the picturesque, as well as with the help of a small in-house army of masons, carpenters, plasterers, wood carvers, painters, stonecutters, and gardeners in converting her once-ruined Quinta Quebrada into an enchanted two-acre palace of earthly delights.

Not the least of these delights is the Mexican cooking of the Hyders' chief cook of twenty-three years, Severiana, who manages by miracles known only to her to produce glorious Mexican meals for any number of people expected or unexpected at any hour of the day or night.

Martha Hyder has over the thirty-odd years assembled an encyclopedic collection of Mexican potteries and glasswares whose rich and robust forms

and colors she orchestrates in an endless variety of handsome table settings for her nonstop schedule of entertainments.

The quinta's round poolside table sheltered by an oversized white canvas umbrella with deep crochet-lace fringe provides for small dinners of six or eight where Pozole, the region's traditional pork, chicken, and white corn stew is served with its accompanying assortments of minced vegetables and spices and refried tortillas.

The Pozole is presented in special pottery bowls made for Mrs. Hyder in Guanajuato. The round table centers on multiple vases of roses in mixed

shades of pink grouped around the umbrella pole, and is lit by two pair of ornate silver candlesticks holding vigil lights, as there would be no place for "hurricanes" to protect candles from the evening breeze.

Houseguests at the Quinta Quebrada each have suites furnished with fine Spanish Colonial antiques and decorated with a wealth of colonial paintings, wooden saints, *ex-votos*, weavings, embroideries; and, covering every available horizontal surface, *objets d'art* so numerous that the hostess warns, "Be careful. If you put something down, it's lost."

On the terraces of their suites, guests are served

early breakfasts to stave off hunger until the more formal household breakfast, which may not be served until ten or eleven.

Small impromptu meals in the local fashion can be served for members of the household at almost any time. They might be as simple as a plate of sautéed Sole, Artichokes, and Green Onions, with Papas Chicas (Mexico's much-loved baby new potatoes) served in Severiana's Dolores tile–covered kitchen on simple terra-cotta Mexican peasant plates from Guadalajara and accompanied by a glass of Spanish red wine.

Party dinners are another matter. These are served around eleven at night, or often later, after the guests have spent a couple of hours gathered around the outdoor fireplace beside the swimming pool enjoying conversation and margaritas along with the cool of the San Miguel evening and the view of the splendid dome of Ceferino Gutiérrez's Iglesia de la Concepción, which Martha Hyder will have paid the nuns to keep fully lit until her guests go into the quinta's main dining room.

Crowded into bookshelves at the end of the room, the dining room's exceptional collection of Puebla potteries lend an appropriate Spanish Colonial palace tone to the dinner setting.

A whole *cochinillo asado,* or roast suckling pig, holding an apple in its mouth and wearing a votive crown filled with flowers, by its very appearance at table transforms the dinner to a banquet.

The *cochinillo* is invariably served with one of Severiana's giant Broccoli Pies, its lattice-top crust bristling with carrot sticks as well as with white rice cooked with olive oil and chicken broth. There will be classic Chocolate Soufflés for dessert and lots of bottles of good French Burgundy standing about the table in Tiffany's "Green Leaves" ceramic wine coasters.

A plate painted with the likeness of Father Miguel Hidalgo sits with the Puebla potteries surveying the opulent scene.

It was Hidalgo, the village priest of Dolores, who on September 15, 1810, sounded the call (the famed *grito de Dolores*) to bring his parishioners together and begin Mexico's long struggle for independence from Spain. Hidalgo's ally, Ignacio José Allende, who with him led a successful attack on the Spanish garrison at Guanajuato, gave his name to the town of San Miguel de Allende, just as Hidalgo gave his to the town of Dolores.

Baron & Baroness Enrico and Sandra di Portanova

> *EGGS WITH CHORIZO*
> *SUNSET SHRIMP SURREALIST*
> *COCONUT ICE*

> *SALMON SURPRISE (BAKED MOZZARELLA WITH SMOKED SALMON)*
> *PASTA ARABESQUE*
> *PASTA JADA (JADE) OR ACAPULCO*
> *PASTA DI PORTANOVA WITH CAVIAR*

Baroness Sandra di Portanova describes Arabesque, the Acapulco home of her and her husband, Baron Enrico di Portanova, as "a cross between the Alhambra and Hadrian's Villa." Her good friend, writer Nancy Holmes, says, "Arabesque is too huge, too lovely, too impossible, too imaginative, too impractical, too fantastic to be real, to be there, to exist at all. You think what courage to even consider building it, what a wild foolishness to begin it." However, Arabesque is there, by now a landmark, on the south coast of Acapulco Bay.

Others have commented that if Marjorie Merriweather Post had married James Bond they would have gladly left both Mar-A-Lago and her seventy-room Park Avenue triplex for Arabesque.

It may be the only place on earth where the ultimate antic dream life of James Bond films is actually lived and, not surprisingly, the James Bond film *License to Kill* was set here. Within Arabesque's two-and-one-half acres, there are the master quarters, seven guest suites, three swimming pools, a living room the size of a football field with a twenty-seven-foot ceiling, a nightclub, a watchtower, a funicular to facilitate trips between the house's many levels, six kitchens, and an artificial fifty-foot waterfall.

For formal dinners, guests (and there always seem to be dozens of them at mealtimes), after watching the tropical sunset reflected in the Bay of Acapulco across the uppermost of Arabesque's swimming pools, drift up a vast curving staircase carved of spinach-green Guatemalan marble at the east end of the living room. In the dining room at the top of the stairs, tables of six or eight will have been set around the theatrical center table—a glass-topped, life-sized, kneeling wooden camel, by London's ever-ingenious master object maker Anthony Redmile.

Here, at tables decorated with gold porcelain seashells and starfish, guests will drink from seahorse glasses and enjoy Baked Mozzarella with Smoked Salmon; Pasta Arabesque with a sauce of spinach, garlic, and cream; and Tiffany Truffle, a white chocolate and raspberry dessert in the form of Tiffany & Co.'s famous blue shopping bag created at Sandra di Portanova's request to amuse Tiffany's Design Director when he visited Arabesque.

This dinner, like all large party meals at Arabesque, is cooked after the Baron di Portanova's personal recipes in the house's hotel-sized main kitchen. The Tiffany Truffle, however, was made in Houston by the Acute Catering Co., frozen, and then flown to Acapulco in time for dinner on the di Portanovas' private jet.

The unusual first course is an invention of the Baron's. Italy's little known Mozzarella al Forno (traditionally made by baking *bocconcini* wrapped in cooked ham and moistened with butter and cream) is metamorphosed by upgrading the *proscuitto cotto* to smoked salmon and adding a sauce of heavy cream, garlic, chopped Italian parsley, and pepper. The resultant Mozzarella al Salmone is, the Baron observes, "a very grand, very elegant dish that can be served as a first course as an alternative to caviar."

Days at Arabesque begin with poolside breakfasts of Eggs with Chorizo served with refried beans and guacamole, sliced mangos with lemon, and fresh orange juice.

Here, with the fringe-topped funicular car and the pool's spouting fish fountain in the background, the breakfast table is set using one of Sandra di Portanova's many Tiffany & Co. printed cotton "pareos" (this one called "Edwardian") as a tablecloth.

Somewhat later, a switch will be flipped sending thousands of gallons of water crashing toward the sea over the jumble of giant boulders beneath the house.

On a round terrace beside this not-so-miniature Niagara, Sandra di Portanova will have had luncheon tables covered with a "tropical" print and set with plates she has had painted to echo Picasso ceramics in the Mexican ceramic center of Dolores Hidalgo. Three Mexican silver vases ornamented with flat, multicolored jadeite cabochons hold local bird-of-paradise flowers and palmetto fronds.

The light lunch will center around another of the Baron's popular dishes, Pasta Acapulco, alternately called "Pasta Jada," served with slices of avocado, cherry tomatoes, and fresh salsa.

The Baron's passion for cooking was acquired as a very young man at his parents' house in Naples, "arousing," he recalls, "clearly unfounded parental concerns for my future success in the outside world.

"In Naples we weren't great meat eaters, but there was lots of chicken and fish," he remembers. "I loved some unusual things—deep-fried eels and the fried dough balls in honey called '*stroufili*' that we had at Christmas. The fried eels we called 'Neapolitan caviar.' They came alive, from Venice. You had to cut their heads off, or they tried to bite you.

"Since my parents' home in Naples, I've learned to make other things. But the exotic pastas came as early as my late teens. Of course, here or at our house in Houston I also make the best chili in the world."

The Baron has a distinctly Italian fondness for pasta, which he emphatically calls "a peasant dish." There is, however, little that any stretch of the imagination could term "peasant" in the di Portanova empire, and certainly not his celebrated Pasta di

Portanova, a nest of tagliolini with Gruyère and Parmesan filled with lots of fresh black Malassol caviar. "This," admits the Baron, "is a stride out of the territories of peasant fare."

The di Portanovas' lifelong friend, Italian artist Piero Aversa created the house's most unforgettable feature, the 1,001-nights magical rooftop terrace inhabited at first by a solitary life-sized concrete camel. "He looks lonely," Sandra di Portanova lamented. "Poor darling, make some more camels, Piero, to go with him."

More camels were added, eleven of them, some obligingly transforming themselves into furniture. Then white concrete palm trees were strewn about to create a seaside oasis of incomparable good old-fashioned romance and glamor.

The one-acre terrace, unusable by day under the fiery Acapulco sun, transfigures itself at dusk, as the lights begin to twinkle in the city of Acapulco across the bay, into a place of magic and enchantment.

Here Sandra di Portanova, Arabesque's beautiful and tireless magician, set and prop designer, choreographer, lighting director, and stage manager conjures up a private dinner set at a small round table beside her pet camels.

The table is covered with the printed lace flounces of Tiffany's "La Scala" cotton pareo. Scarlet red flowers and tapers are held in a simple and sensuous cobalt Venetian glass vase and candleholders designed by Elsa Peretti for Tiffany's.

The main course tonight is the hostess's creation of Arabesque-scaled shrimp marinated in lime juice, chili powder, onion, and Worcestershire sauce and then grilled on skewers. The Sunset Shrimp Surrealist will be followed by Coconut and Pineapple Ices.

One hundred and fifty feet above the Gulf of Acapulco, at Arabesque, the mind could easily stride over the cliffs of surrealistic conjecture.

Author's Note on the Recipes

All contributors' recipes have been scrupulously checked for both incongruities and obscurities.

Nevertheless, the author has in certain instances assumed both good common sense and a basic knowledge of cooking and of ingredients on the part of the reader.

The author feels confident to speak for the contributors and counsel, however, that the best ingredients lead to the best results when following their recipes. Tough or tasteless meats, watery or overripe fruits and vegetables, fish that is not totally fresh, underripened cheeses, bad vintages of wine, harsh vinegars, poor quality butter or olive oil, low-grade pastas, cheap chocolate, and so on and all their ilk will insure less-than-happy results.

Such things as altitude, humidity, and the ability of pots and pans to transmit heat evenly or not, as well as the idiosyncratic nature of ovens and burners, all play at times not unimportant roles in cooking where finesse is required. Times and temperatures often must be adjusted to specific circumstances.

These are all recipes of unquestioned merit that have served the contributors well through the years, and will bring enjoyment to others, if used well.

Enjoy them. Use them well.

Baked Dorades with Ripe Black Olives, Capers, and Fresh Lemon

two 3-pound dorades, scaled and thoroughly cleaned
¹/₄ cup good olive oil
salt and coarsely ground black pepper to taste
¹/₂ cup halved and pitted ripe black olives
¹/₄ cup capers
¹/₄ cup lemon pulp in small pieces, free of membranes, peels, and pips

Rub the dorades with some of the oil, then the salt and the pepper, and place them in a roasting pan. Bake them in a preheated 400°F. oven for 20 minutes, or until they are cooked. Transfer the dorades to a warm platter.

Add the remaining oil, the olives, capers, and lemon bits to the juices in the roasting pan, and simmer the mixture on the stove top for a minute or until it is hot. Pour the olive mixture over the dorades, and serve. SERVES 6.

Potato, Celery, Cucumber, and Pickle Salad

2 pounds red or waxy white potatoes, unpeeled
¹/₂ pound white celery stalks, sliced fine
1 European cucumber, peeled, seeded, and diced
2 dill pickles, seeded and diced
1 cup mayonnaise, preferably homemade
¹/₂ cup chopped Italian parsley
1 teaspoon cuminseed
salt and coarsely ground black pepper to taste

Cook the potatoes in boiling salted water until they are tender but still firm. Cut them into ¹/₂-inch pieces, and in a bowl combine them with the celery, cucumber, pickles, mayonnaise, parsley, and cumin-

seed; season with the salt and pepper. Mix well, let the salad sit for 30 minutes to 1 hour, remix, and serve. SERVES 6.

Minted Summer Fruit Salad

1¹/₂ cups peeled and sliced yellow peaches
the juice of 1 large or 2 small lemons
1¹/₂ cups Persian or Cranshaw melon balls or cubes
1 cup blackberries
1 cup red currants
¹/₂ cup whole fresh mint leaves
¹/₂ cup sugar

In a large bowl combine the peaches with the lemon juice, and mix well to prevent the peaches from browning. Add the melon balls, blackberries, currants, mint leaves, and sugar; mix gently. *Do not overmix and damage the fruit.* Serve cold but not over-chilled. SERVES 6.

Roast Tenderloin of Pork

two 1³/₄- to 2¹/₄-pound pork tenderloins
¹/₄ cup olive oil
salt and ground pepper to taste
Tarragon-Cognac Cream Sauce (recipe follows)

Coat the tenderloins with the oil, sprinkle with the salt and pepper, place them in a roasting pan, and roast them in a preheated 425°F. oven for 30 to 35 minutes. Serve the pork with the sauce.

SERVES 4 TO 6.

Tarragon-Cognac Cream Sauce

1/2 stick (1/4 cup) butter
3 tablespoons dried tarragon leaves, crumbled; or 6 tablespoons chopped fresh tarragon leaves
1/3 cup Cognac
2 cups heavy cream
salt and coarsely ground pepper to taste

In a small saucepan melt the butter over moderate heat until it is bubbly but do not blacken it, and add the tarragon. Add the Cognac, a third at a time, setting it aflame after each addition and allowing the flames to die out after each flaming. Add the heavy cream, bring the mixture to a boil, simmer it until it is reduced by half, and season with the salt and pepper. Serve the sauce with roast pork, veal or chicken. Makes about one cup.

Pan-fried Sour Apples

2 large Granny Smith or other sour apples
1 stick (1/2 cup) butter

Peel, core, and cut the apples into 6 wedges. In a skillet melt the butter over moderate heat, and in it sauté the apples until they are golden but not mushy, stirring frequently. Serve the apples with roast pork, pork chops, blood sausage, roast veal, or veal chops. SERVES 4.

Steamed Cauliflower with Beurre Noisette

1 medium cauliflower with a few leaves attached
1 to 1 1/2 sticks (1/2 to 3/4 cup) butter

Remove the stem from the cauliflower and hollow out the base, keeping the leaves attached. In a large deep saucepan steam the cauliflower in 1 inch of boiling water for 15 minutes, or until it is tender but still firm; drain it and set it on a warm serving plate. In the saucepan melt the butter, simmer until it is a rich golden brown, slowly pour it over the cauliflower, and serve at once. SERVES 6.

Baked Onions with Golden Raisins

9 or 10 medium yellow onions, or 18 flat 2-inch-wide green onions
2/3 cup olive oil
salt and pepper to taste
1 cup golden raisins

Halve the yellow onions horizontally, arrange them cut side up in a shallow baking pan, brush them well with 1/2 cup of the oil, season them with salt and pepper, and bake them in a preheated 375°F. oven for 20 minutes. (If using green onions, leave them whole.)

In the meantime, in a small bowl cover the raisins with boiling water, let them sit until plumped, drain them, and mix them with the remaining oil. Sprinkle the raisins over the onions, and bake them for 7 or 8 minutes longer. Serve the onions hot or cold with roast meats or as part of an hors d'oeuvre. SERVES 6.

Fine Green Beans with Bacon and Shallots

2 pounds fresh green beans, ends trimmed
1/2 pound lardons of fresh pork fat or sliced bacon, cut crosswise into 1/2-inch pieces
1/2 stick (1/4 cup) butter
1 cup chopped shallots
salt and pepper to taste

In a large saucepan of boiling salted water cook the green beans for 7 or 8 minutes or until tender-crisp, drain them in a colander, and refresh them under running cold water. In the saucepan in boiling water cook the lardons for 2 or 3 minutes, and drain them in a sieve. In the saucepan, cleaned, melt the butter over moderate heat, and in it sauté the lardons and the shallots for 3 or 4 minutes, until the lardons are golden but the shallots are not overcooked. Add the green beans, season with salt and pepper and cook the mixture, stirring, for 3 or 4 minutes longer. Serve at once.   SERVES 6.

Saddle of Hare in Mustard Sauce

4 saddles of hare, each halved crosswise

1 stick (1/2 cup) butter

1/2 cup white wine

a pinch of dried marjoram

a pinch of dried thyme leaves

ground black pepper to taste

2 cups heavy cream

1/4 cup Dijon mustard

Coat the saddle pieces with half of the butter; place them in a shallow roasting pan with the wine; sprinkle them with the marjoram, thyme, and pepper; and roast them in a preheated 400°F. oven for 25 to 30 minutes. Transfer the hare to a warm serving dish.

In the meantime, in a medium saucepan combine the heavy cream with the mustard, mix well, bring to a boil, and simmer until reduced by half. Pour the mixture into the roasting pan used for the hare, blend the cream mixture with the pan juices, and bring the liquid to a boil on the stove top over high heat, whisking constantly to loosen the browned bits and deglaze the pan. Pour the sauce over the hare and serve.   SERVES 4.

Boiled Pork Shoulder with Green Cabbage

one 4- to 5-pound piece salt pork shoulder with the shoulder blade (palette sale)

1 large or 2 small green or Savoy cabbages, outer leaves removed

In a kettle or large Dutch oven cover the pork shoulder with cold water, bring the water to a boil, and simmer the pork for 3 1/2 to 4 hours, or until it is very tender. Remove the pork to a large heated platter, and cut the meat into thick slices. Bring the

broth in the kettle to a rolling boil. Cut the cabbage into wedges, boil them in the broth for 7 minutes, drain them, and arrange them around the pork. Spoon some of the fatty broth from the top of the pan over the pork and the cabbage, and serve with Potatoes with Bacon and Green Onions (recipe follows).   SERVES 6.

Potatoes with Bacon and Green Onions

4 pounds small smooth-skinned red or white potatoes

1 pound lardons of fresh pork fat or sliced bacon, cut crosswise into 1/2-inch pieces

1 stick (1/2 cup) butter

1 pound green onions, trimmed, chopped coarse

1/4 cup Italian parsley leaves

salt and pepper to taste (optional)

In a large saucepan cover the potatoes with cold water, and bring the water to a boil. Simmer the potatoes for 20 minutes, or until they are cooked but still firm (very small or very fresh potatoes will take less time), and drain them. When the potatoes are cool enough to handle, cut them into 1-inch pieces, and set aside. In a saucepan of boiling water, blanch the lardons for 2 to 3 minutes to remove excess salt, drain them, and sauté them in a skillet until cooked but not crisp. Pour off most of the rendered fat, add the butter, and when it is bubbly add the potatoes, onions, and parsley. Sauté the mixture for 5 minutes, or until the potatoes just begin to color, stirring frequently. Season with salt if it is needed, and serve.

If desired, 2 tablespoons minced garlic and 1/2 cup chopped parsley can be sautéed in the butter for 1 minute before the potatoes are added (omit the parsley leaves), however, this makes the dish a better compliment to a roast than to boiled meats.   SERVES 6.

Salad of Mâche with Fried Quail, Wild Mushrooms, and Bacon

12 quail, trimmed and dressed

³/4 cup olive oil

salt and pepper to taste

2 pounds assorted mushrooms, cleaned, trimmed, and halved

¹/4 cup minced parsley

1 tablespoon minced garlic

1 pound lardons of fresh pork fat or sliced bacon, cut crosswise into ¹/2-inch pieces

THE SALAD

¹/4 cup mild red-wine vinegar

2 tablespoons Dijon mustard or Meaux whole-grain mustard

1 tablespoon salt

1 teaspoon coarsely ground black pepper

¹/2 cup olive oil

1 pound mâche frisée (curly French or Italian chicory) or escarole, rinsed, spun dry, wrapped in a clean kitchen towel, and refrigerated

In a large skillet or Dutch oven fry the quail in batches if necessary, using ¹/2 cup of the oil, for 10 minutes or until cooked, turning frequently. Season them lightly with salt and pepper and keep them warm.

In a large skillet, in the remaining ¹/4 cup of oil sauté the mushrooms, parsley, and garlic until the mushroom liquid has evaporated and the mushrooms are still damp but not wet.

In a large saucepan of boiling water blanch the lardons for 3 or 4 minutes, drain them, fry them in the pan until they are cooked but only just beginning to crisp, and remove them to paper towels to drain.

Make the salad: For the dressing, in a small bowl whisk the vinegar with the mustard, salt, and pepper until the salt is dissolved, whisk in the oil in a steady stream and whisk until the dressing is emulsified. Place the *mâche* in a large serving bowl, pour in ¹/2 cup of the dressing, and toss until the *mâche* is coated. Arrange the warm quail over the salad, scatter the mushroom mixture and the bacon on top, and dress the salad with the remaining dressing. Serve at once with a chilled red wine such as Brouilly, Vin de Cahors or even Beaujolais. SERVES 6.

Tiger Shrimp Grilled with Garlic

16 tiger shrimp (if not available use other large shrimp but the striped-shell tiger shrimp have the best flavor), shells on, butterflied

²/3 cup good olive oil

2 cloves garlic, crushed

salt to taste

In a shallow baking pan arrange the shrimp flattened out with the shell sides down. In a bowl combine the oil and the garlic, season with salt, and mix well. Coat the shrimp liberally with the oil mixture, and broil them for 3 or 4 minutes. Serve at once. SERVES 4.

Pork with Clams

one 2-pound pork loin, trimmed of fat, cut into 1-inch cubes

¹/2 cup olive oil

1 medium onion, chopped coarse

2 good small tomatoes, chopped

1 clove garlic, minced

1 teaspoon coarsely ground black pepper

¹/2 cup chicken broth or water

1 tablespoon salt

16 cherrystone clams, scrubbed

In a large deep skillet or Dutch oven brown the pork in the oil over moderate heat, add the onion, tomatoes, garlic, pepper, and the chicken broth or water. Bring the liquid to a boil and simmer the mixture, covered, for 20 to 30 minutes, or until the pork is cooked. Add the salt and the clams, and cook the mixture, covered, for 6 or 7 minutes, or until the clams are steamed. Discard any unopened clams.

Arrange the pork mixture in the center of a heated platter and surround it with the clams in their shells. For larger groups steam the clams separately, remove them from their shells, and add the meat to the pork mixture. SERVES 4.

NOTE: *For a variation, raw peeled and deveined shrimp can also be added to the pork mixture and cooked for 3 minutes.*

Potatoes with Rosemary

2 pounds small smooth-skinned potatoes, scrubbed, skins left on and cut into 1-×-1/2-inch pieces (very small new potatoes, cooked whole, are very good in this recipe)

1/2 cup olive oil

1/4 cup fresh rosemary leaves or 2 tablespoons dried rosemary

1 tablespoon salt

In a large nonstick skillet sauté the potatoes in the oil over moderate heat for 10 minutes, stirring frequently. Add the rosemary and the salt, and sauté the mixture until the potatoes are cooked and well-colored. Serve with roast meats. SERVES 4.

Kale with Garlic and Olive Oil

1 pound fresh kale, washed and large stems removed

3 cloves garlic, halved lengthwise

1/4 cup mild olive oil

salt and ground pepper to taste

In a large saucepan of boiling salted water cook the kale until just tender, and drain in a colander. In the pan simmer the garlic in the oil for 3 or 4 minutes over moderate heat, add the kale, season with salt and pepper, and cook the mixture for 2 or 3 minutes longer, stirring, or until the kale is just tender. · SERVES 4.

NOTE: *The garlic is not to be eaten, so it may be discarded before serving, however, it looks attractive mixed in the kale.*

Spinach can also be used, but it must not be boiled. Just put it in the pan with the garlic-flavored oil and cook it, covered, until it is wilted, stirring frequently. This takes only a few minutes.

Zucchini with Pepper Sauce

1/4 cup mild olive oil

2 pounds small zucchini (or use 2 pounds summer squash or 1 pound of each), trimmed, cut into 1/2- to 3/4-inch lengths

1 tablespoon Jamaican pepper sauce available in specialty food shops and some supermarkets

salt and pepper to taste

In a large saucepan heat the oil over moderate heat, add the zucchini, and mix well. Add the pepper sauce, mix well, and simmer, covered, for 10 minutes, stirring occasionally, or until the zucchini is tender-crisp. Season with salt and serve. *Do not salt the zucchini until serving or it will sweat and become mushy.* SERVES 6.

Prune Meringue Tart

THE PASTRY
2 cups all-purpose flour

1 teaspoon salt

1 1/2 sticks (3/4 cup) cold butter, cut into small pieces

4 tablespoons ice water

THE FILLING
1 pound good prunes

1 cup sugar

THE MERINGUE
3 large egg whites, at room temperature

1/2 teaspoon cream of tartar

1/3 cup sugar

1 teaspoon ground cinnamon

Make the pastry: In a bowl combine the flour and the salt, add the butter, and with a pastry blender cut it in until the mixture resembles coarse crumbs. With a fork stir in the ice water, 1 tablespoon at a time, adding only enough water to hold the pastry together, and stir the pastry until it forms a ball. Flatten the pastry into a 1/2-inch-thick disk, wrap it in plastic wrap, and refrigerate it for 20 minutes. On a lightly floured surface roll the pastry into a 10-inch round, transfer it to a 9-inch pie plate, press it lightly to line the plate, and trim and crimp the edges. Prick the bottom with a fork and bake the pastry shell in a preheated 450°F. oven for 10 to 12 minutes.

Make the filling: In a food processor puree the

prunes with the sugar, and spread the mixture into the partially baked pie shell.

Make the meringue: In a large bowl with an electric mixer combine the egg whites with the cream of tartar, beat the mixture until it is foamy, and at high speed beat the mixture until it holds soft peaks. Beat in the sugar 1 tablespoon at a time beating until the meringue holds stiff peaks.

Spread the meringue over the filling, sprinkle the top with the cinnamon, and bake the pie in a preheated 325° to 350°F. oven for 15 minutes or until the meringue is set. Serve at room temperature.

SERVES 6.

Roast Capon with Ripe Black Olives, Lemon Zest, and Sweet Italian Sausage

2 lemons

¹/2 cup olive oil

one 6- or 7-pound capon or roasting chicken, washed, patted dry, excess fat removed

2 tablespoons dried rosemary leaves, crushed

2 tablespoons salt

1 tablespoon coarsely ground black pepper

1 tablespoon dried thyme leaves, crushed

6 sweet Italian sausage links

1 cup chicken broth or water

two 6-ounce (drained weight) cans pitted medium or small ripe black olives, drained

With a vegetable peeler remove the zest from the lemons in ¹/2- to ¹/4-inch shavings. Coat them with some of the oil, and squeeze the juice from the lemons. Place the capon on a rack in a roasting pan with its wings tucked under, coat it with the lemon juice, and let it sit for 10 minutes. Brush the capon with the oil, allowing the excess to drip into the pan.

In a small bowl combine the rosemary, salt, pepper, and thyme; mix well, coat the capon with the mixture, and pat the lemon zest on top. Prick the sausages with a fork, and arrange them around the capon, rolling them in the oil that has dripped into the pan. Pour the broth or water into the pan, and bake the capon in a preheated 450°F. oven for

1 hour, basting it twice. Add the olives to the pan, reduce the temperature to 325°F., and bake for 30 to 40 minutes longer, or until the capon is cooked. Serve with Rice with Scallions, Golden Raisins and Pignoli (recipe follows).

SERVES 6.

Rice with Scallions, Golden Raisins, and Pignoli

1 cup golden raisins

2 lemon slices

¹/2 cup pignoli (pine nuts)

5 tablespoons butter

1 cup long-grain white rice

2 cups boiling water

1¹/2 teaspoons salt

2 bunches scallions, trimmed and cut into ¹/4-inch lengths (include ¹/2 of the green stem)

In a small saucepan combine the raisins, lemon slices, and enough water to cover. Bring the mixture to a boil, simmer until the raisins are soft, drain in a sieve, discard the lemon slices, and set aside. In a small skillet, sauté the pignoli in 2 tablespoons of the butter until they are golden, and set aside.

In a medium saucepan melt the remaining 3 tablespoons of butter over moderate heat, add the rice, and sauté it until it is hot and coated with the butter. Add the boiling water and the salt, mix well, and cook, covered, over low heat until three quarters of the water is absorbed. Add the scallions, mix well, and cook, covered, until all the water is absorbed. Remove the pan from the heat, and let the rice mixture sit, covered, for 10 minutes. Stir in the raisins and the pignoli, and serve.

SERVES 4 TO 6.

Fresh Leaf Spinach with Sour Cream and Nutmeg

2 tablespoons butter

1 pound fresh leaf spinach, washed, large stems discarded

1 cup sour cream

$^1/_4$ teaspoon freshly grated nutmeg

$^1/_4$ teaspoon coarsely ground black pepper

salt to taste

In a large saucepan melt the butter over moderate heat, add the spinach, cook it, covered, for 3 or 4 minutes or until it is wilted, stirring occasionally; and drain it in a colander. In the saucepan combine the sour cream, nutmeg, pepper, and salt, and heat the mixture until it is hot but not boiling, stirring. Add the spinach, mix well, and serve. SERVES 4 TO 6.

Sea Scallop, Watercress, Arugula, and Scallion Salad

1 pound sea scallops (do not use bay scallops)

$^1/_4$ cup olive oil

$^1/_4$ cup finely chopped parsley

2 bunches watercress, large stems discarded, washed and spun dry

2 bunches arugula, stems discarded, washed and spun dry, leaves broken into pieces the size of large watercress leaves

THE DRESSING

$^1/_4$ cup red-wine vinegar

1 tablespoon Dijon mustard

$^1/_2$ teaspoon coarsely ground black pepper

$^1/_2$ teaspoon salt

Pat the scallops dry with paper towels, and halve or quarter horizontally any that are very big. In a deep skillet (the scallops will cause the oil to sputter, so a deep pan is necessary) heat the oil over high heat, add the parsley, and fry it for 10 seconds. Add the scallops, fry them for 3 or 4 minutes, or just until they are cooked, stirring them gently. Drain the mixture at once, reserving the oil, and let the scallops cool to room temperature.

In a large bowl combine the watercress and the arugula, mix well and divide among 4 salad plates. In a small bowl combine the vinegar, mustard, pepper, and salt; whisk until blended, and add the cooking oil from the scallops in a stream, whisking until the dressing is emulsified. Drizzle 2 tablespoons of the dressing over each salad, and mix the remainder with the scallops until they are coated. Place a quarter of the scallops in the center of each salad, and dampen each with 1 or 2 tablespoons of the mixed juice from the scallops and the dressing. SERVES 4.

Veal Kidneys Sautéed with Juniper Berries and Gin

$^1/_2$ stick ($^1/_4$ cup) butter

2 veal kidneys, halved horizontally, cleaned of fat and white core

$^1/_2$ cup dried juniper berries softened in boiling water for 15 minutes, drained

$^1/_4$ cup gin

1 teaspoon salt

Fried Croutons (recipe follows)

In a 9-inch skillet melt the butter over moderate heat, and when it is bubbly, sauté the kidneys round side down for 5 or 6 minutes; turn them, and cook for 5 or 6 minutes longer, or just until they are cooked and still pink inside. (Do not overcook.) Transfer the kidneys to a heated dish; and, to the drippings in the pan, add the juniper berries, gin, and salt, stirring to loosen the browned bits and deglaze the pan. Carefully ignite the gin, and when the flames subside, pour the sauce over the kidneys and garnish with the croutons. SERVES 4.

Fried Croutons

6 slices good firm white bread, crusts trimmed, cut into $^1/_2$-inch squares and dried overnight

$^1/_2$ stick ($^1/_4$ cup) butter

$^1/_2$ teaspoon salt

In a large skillet melt the butter over moderate heat and when it is bubbly add the bread. Stir to coat the croutons evenly with the butter, and fry them until golden and crisp, stirring continually. Sprinkle the croutons with the salt and serve.

Roast Yellow Peppers and Radicchio with Fresh Goat Cheese

2 yellow or orange sweet peppers

two $^1/_2$-pound firm heads radicchio, any wilted leaves removed

$^2/_3$ cup olive oil

$1^1/_2$ teaspoons salt

$^1/_2$ teaspoon coarsely ground black pepper

one 4-ounce fresh goat cheese, cut into 4 pieces

Cut each pepper into 4 strips, removing the stems, ribs, and seeds, and halve each radicchio. Arrange the vegetables on a baking sheet, brush them with the oil (much of the oil will run out of the radicchio during cooking), sprinkle with the salt and pepper, and bake them in a preheated 400° to 450°F. oven for 15 minutes. Drain the vegetables, and serve them with the goat cheese.

Save the cooking oil for use in salads, fish or vegetable dishes. The peppers will have given it an appealing flavor.   SERVES 4.

Boned Rib Roast

one 4-pound beef rib roast, boned, rolled and tied

$^1/_4$ cup vegetable oil

1 teaspoon coarsely ground black pepper

1 teaspoon salt

$^1/_2$ teaspoon garlic powder

$^1/_2$ teaspoon dried rosemary leaves, crushed

$^1/_2$ teaspoon dried thyme leaves, crushed

Yorkshire pudding (recipe follows)

$^1/_2$ cup water

Rub the meat with the oil. In a small bowl combine the pepper, salt, garlic powder, rosemary and thyme; mix well. Rub the pepper mixture over the meat, place the beef on a rack in a roasting pan, and

roast it in a preheated 450°F. oven for 45 minutes, or until of the desired degree of doneness. Transfer the meat to a serving platter, remove the rack from the pan, spoon off and reserve $^1/_4$ cup of the drippings for the Yorkshire pudding, add the water to the remaining drippings in the pan, and place the pan on the stove top. Bring the drippings to a boil, scraping up the browned bits and deglazing the pan, and serve the pan juices with the roast and the Yorkshire pudding.   SERVES 4.

Yorkshire Pudding

$^3/_4$ cup all-purpose flour

1 cup milk

2 large eggs

1 teaspoon salt

$^1/_4$ cup roast-beef drippings

In a medium bowl combine the flour, milk, eggs, and salt, mix well, and let the batter sit in a cool place or refrigerate it for 1 hour.

Pour the drippings into two 8-inch square baking pans, heat each on the stove top until the drippings are sputtering, and divide the batter between the pans. Cook the mixture for a moment on the stove top and then bake the batter in a preheated 450°F. oven for 30 minutes, or until the puddings are puffed and golden with browned peaks and edges.   SERVES 4.

NOTE: *If the roast is in a very large pan the batter can simply be poured into the drippings around the roast. This will cool the pan and require cooking the roast a little longer, but the effect of the roast surrounded by the ridges and mountains of pudding can be spectacular if you have a platter large enough to serve it that way.*

Fried Green Garden Tomatoes

4 large hard green tomatoes

$^1/_2$ stick ($^1/_4$ cup) butter

1 teaspoon salt or to taste

Cut off and discard the stem and blossom ends of the tomatoes, halve the tomatoes horizontally, and fry them in a large skillet in the butter over moderate heat, turning them once, until they are tender. Season with the salt, and serve. These are excellent served with eggs in the morning in place of bacon.

SERVES 4.

China Loring's Graham-Cracker Torte

26 graham crackers, crushed

$^1/2$ cup chopped pecans

2 teaspoons baking powder

1 stick ($^1/2$ cup) butter, softened

1 cup granulated sugar

2 large eggs, separated

1 cup milk

THE BUTTER ICING

1 stick ($^1/2$ cup) butter, softened

1 pound confectioners' sugar

$^1/4$ cup heavy cream

1 teaspoon almond extract

In a bowl combine the graham-cracker crumbs, pecans and baking powder, and mix well. In a large bowl with an electric mixer beat the butter with the sugar at high speed until the mixture is light and fluffy. Add the egg yolks and the milk, mix well, and fold in the crumb mixture. In a small bowl with an electric mixer beat the egg whites at high speed until they hold stiff peaks, fold them into the batter, and spread it into two 8-inch greased pans. Bake the layers in a preheated 350°F. oven for 35 minutes, or until they are cooked but not dry. Cool the layers in the pan on a rack for 10 minutes, invert them onto the rack, and cool completely.

Make the icing: In a small bowl with an electric mixer beat the butter with the sugar until the mixture is light and fluffy. Add the cream and the almond extract, mix well, and use to sandwich the torte layers together. If desired, sweetened whipped cream can be used instead of the icing, but the icing is recommended.

MAKES ONE 8-INCH TORTE, SERVING 6 TO 8.

China Loring's Date Bars

1 cup all-purpose flour

1 teaspoon baking powder

$^1/4$ teaspoon salt

1 stick ($^1/2$ cup) butter, softened

1 cup granulated sugar

3 large eggs, separated

1 cup chopped dates

1 cup chopped pecans

confectioners' sugar for dusting

In a bowl combine the flour, baking powder, and salt, and mix well. In a large bowl with an electric mixer beat the butter with the sugar at high speed until the mixture is light and fluffy. Add the egg yolks, one at a time, beating well after each, and fold in the flour mixture, the dates, and the pecans. In a small bowl with an electric mixer beat the egg whites at high speed until they hold stiff peaks, fold them into the batter; spread it into a greased 13-x-9-inch baking pan, and bake in a preheated 375°F. oven for 12 minutes. While the mixture is hot, cut it into bars in the pan, and sprinkle them with the confectioners' sugar.

MAKES ABOUT TWO DOZEN.

China Loring's Holland Butter Cookies

2 cups all-purpose flour

$1^1/2$ teaspoons ground cinnamon

$^1/2$ teaspoon salt

2 sticks (1 cup) butter, softened

1 cup sugar

1 large egg, separated

1 cup chopped or shaved almonds

In a bowl combine the flour, cinnamon and salt, and mix well. In a large bowl with an electric mixer beat the butter with the sugar at high speed until the mixture is light and fluffy. Add the egg yolk, and mix well. In a 13-x-9-inch baking pan pat the dough into a thin layer, brush it with the egg white, beaten until blended but not frothy, and sprinkle it with the almonds. Pat the nuts into the dough, and bake in a preheated 375°F. oven for 10 to 12 minutes, or until golden. *Check the cookies frequently the last few minutes of cooking time so they do not burn.* While the mixture is hot, cut it into bars in the pan. MAKES ABOUT TWO DOZEN.

Grandma Webster's Molasses Cake

2 cups all-purpose flour

2 tablespoons baking powder

$^1/_2$ teaspoon ground allspice

$^1/_2$ teaspoon ground cinnamon

$^1/_2$ teaspoon ground cloves

$^1/_2$ teaspoon ground ginger

$^1/_2$ teaspoon baking soda

1 stick ($^1/_2$ cup) butter, softened, or $^1/_2$ cup other fat (bacon drippings were originally used in this recipe)

$^1/_2$ cup brown sugar

$^1/_2$ cup dark molasses

2 large eggs, separated

$^1/_2$ cup milk

granulated sugar for glazing

Into a large bowl sift the flour combined with the baking powder, spices, and baking soda. In a large bowl with an electric mixer beat the butter with the sugar at high speed until the mixture is light and fluffy, add the molasses, egg yolks, and the milk, and mix well. Add the flour mixture, and mix well. In a small bowl with an electric mixer beat the egg whites at high speed until they hold stiff peaks, and fold them into the batter. Pour the mixture into a shallow 13-x-9-inch greased baking pan, and liberally sprinkle the top with the granulated sugar. Bake the cake in a preheated 375°F. oven for 30 minutes, or until the cake tests done.   SERVES 8 TO 10.

Chilled Fresh Pea Soup

2 pounds fresh or frozen peas

1 small onion, quartered

6 fresh mint leaves, or $^1/_2$ teaspoon dried mint

1 teaspoon salt

3 cups chicken broth

1 cup sour cream

3 scallions, trimmed, chopped fine

salt and pepper to taste

In a large saucepan combine the peas, onion, mint, salt, and chicken broth. Bring the liquid to a boil, and simmer for 7 or 8 minutes. In a blender puree the mixture in batches until it is thick and smooth, and serve hot or chilled. In a small bowl combine the sour cream with the scallions, mix well, season with salt and pepper, and add a dollop of the mixture to the soup.   SERVES 6.

Smoked Salmon Mousse

3 envelopes unflavored gelatine

1 quart chicken broth

6 scallions, trimmed, chopped

1 tablespoon dried dillweed

2 pounds smoked salmon, sliced

1 tablespoon dried dillseed

1 tablespoon coarsely ground black pepper

vegetable oil for greasing the mold

Cucumber and Sour Cream Sauce (recipe follows)

In a small bowl sprinkle the gelatine over 1 cup of the broth, and let the mixture sit for 5 minutes, until the gelatine is softened. In a large saucepan bring the remaining broth to a boil, add the scallions and the dillweed, and simmer for 3 or 4 minutes. Remove the pan from the heat, add the gelatine, stir until it is dissolved, and add the salmon. Let the mixture sit for 2 or 3 minutes. In a blender puree the mixture in batches, transfer it to a bowl, add the dillseed and pepper, mix well, and pour the mixture into an oiled 2-quart ring mold. Chill the mold for 6 to 24 hours.

When ready to serve, loosen the edges of the mousse with a knife, dip the mold into a large bowl or basin of warm water, dry off the mold, and invert it onto a large platter. Or, instead of dipping the mold in the warm water, wrap it in a warm, damp kitchen towel for 15 seconds and turn out the mousse. Serve the mousse with the sauce. SERVES 8.

Cucumber and Sour Cream Sauce

1 large European cucumber, peeled, seeded, and chopped into
   very small chunks

2 tablespoons salt

1 pint sour cream

6 scallions, trimmed and minced

1 teaspoon coarsely ground black pepper

2 dashes hot red-pepper sauce

In a large bowl combine the cucumber and salt, and mix well. Let the mixture sit for 15 minutes, until the cucumbers have sweated, and pat them dry with paper towels. To the cucumbers add the sour cream, scallions, pepper, and hot-pepper sauce; mix well.

Beet, Walnut, Onion, and Sausage Omelette

10 large eggs

1 tablespoon salt

1 teaspoon baking powder

1 teaspoon coarsely ground black pepper

1 stick ($^1/_2$ cup) butter

1 cup diced cooked beets

1 cup chopped onion

1 cup crumbled cooked sausage meat

$^1/_2$ cup chopped parsley

$^1/_2$ cup crumbled walnuts

In a large bowl combine the eggs, salt, baking powder and pepper, and mix well. In a large skillet over moderate heat melt half of the butter, and in it sauté the beets, onion, sausage, parsley, and walnuts for 4 minutes, or until the onions are golden but not soft. In another large skillet over moderate heat melt the remaining butter, and when it is bubbly add the eggs. As they cook around the edges, lift the cooked part up, allowing the liquid egg to run under the edges, and cook and lift until there is only a very little semi-liquid egg left on top. Immediately turn off the heat, spread the beet mixture across the center, fold the omelette over itself, and slide it onto a warm platter. SERVES 6.

Conchita's Cheese Soufflé
(SOUFFLÉ AU FROMAGE CONCHITA)

1 stick (¹/2 cup) butter

1 tablespoon vegetable oil

2 tablespoons all-purpose flour

6 cups milk, scalded

grated nutmeg to taste

salt and pepper to taste

8 large eggs, separated, the whites at room temperature

1³/4 cups (7 ounces) grated Emmental or other firm, flavorful imported Swiss cheese (see Note)

In a large saucepan melt the butter in the oil over low heat, stir in the flour, and cook the roux, stirring, for 3 minutes. Remove the pan from the heat, add the scalded milk, in a steady stream, whisking vigorously until the sauce is thick and smooth, and bring it to a boil, stirring. Remove the pan from the heat, let the mixture cool slightly, season with the nutmeg and salt and pepper, and beat in the egg yolks one at a time until they are blended. Let the mixture cool until it is lukewarm, and stir in the cheese.

In a large bowl with an electric mixer beat the egg whites at low speed until they are foamy, and at high speed beat them until they hold soft peaks. Carefully fold the egg whites into the cheese mixture just until no white streaks remain, pour the mixture into a buttered deep 2-quart soufflé dish or deep oven-safe bowl, and place the soufflé in a cold oven. Turn the temperature to 400°F. and bake the soufflé for 30 minutes, or until it has risen and is golden on top and hot but still quite runny on the inside. (If your oven preheats by the broiler unit in the top of the oven, preheat the oven to 300°F. and gradually increase the temperature so that the broiler unit will not cook the top of the soufflé before it has had a chance to rise.)

After guests have had a first serving, return the soufflé to a 250°F. oven so that the rest of the soufflé will stay hot, as guests usually demand seconds. SERVES 6.

NOTE: *For best results, use only a flavorful imported Swiss cheese.*

Conchita's Seafood Quiche
(QUICHE AUX FRUITS DE MER CONCHITA)

8 large eggs

2 heaping tablespoons all-purpose flour

1 cup crème fraîche

2 cups milk

1³/4 cups (7 ounces) grated imported Swiss cheese

¹/2 pound unshelled mussels, cooked

¹/2 pound scallops, cooked

salt and pepper to taste

In a large bowl whisk the eggs until blended, add the flour and the crème fraîche, and mix well. Beat in the milk, cheese, mussels, and scallops; season with salt and pepper, and pour the mixture into a buttered baking dish. Bake the quiche for 1 hour, or until the custard is set. SERVES 6.

NOTE: *If desired, place the quiche in a roasting pan on the middle rack in a preheated 375°F. oven. Add enough boiling water to the roasting pan to come three quarters of the way up the sides of the baking dish, and bake the quiche until the custard is set.*

Fillets of Sole with Artichoke Hearts

6 large or 12 small sole fillets

flour for dredging

salt and pepper to taste

2 sticks (1 cup) butter

12 artichoke hearts

3 tablespoons finely chopped Italian parsley (optional)

lemon halves for garnish

Dredge the fillets in the flour seasoned with salt and pepper, shaking off the excess flour mixture. In a large skillet in batches or using several skillets, fry the fillets in two thirds of the butter for 2 to 3 minutes on each side. While the fillets cook, in another skillet fry the artichoke hearts in the remaining butter until they are golden brown. Serve the fillets and artichokes sprinkled with parsley and accompanied by the lemon halves. SERVES 6.

Stuffed Vegetables

3 to 5 pounds assorted vegetables: tomatoes, onions, peppers, Japanese eggplants, zucchini

THE STUFFING
1 pound cooked ham, ground
1 pound sausage meat, cooked
1 tablespoon finely chopped fresh basil leaves
1 tablespoon snipped chives
1 tablespoon finely chopped parsley
1 tablespoon finely chopped fresh tarragon leaves
4 large eggs

Cut off and discard a thin slice from the blossom end of each tomato, the top of the onions and peppers, and one side of the eggplants and zucchini, and scoop out the insides, leaving a ¼- to ½-inch-thick shell. Invert the tomatoes onto paper towels to drain. Blanch the remaining vegetables in boiling salted water for 2 minutes. Remove the eggplants and zucchini, cook the onions and peppers for 3 minutes longer, remove them, and invert all the vegetables onto paper towels to drain well.

Make the stuffing: In a bowl combine the ham, sausage, basil, chives, parsley, tarragon, and eggs; mix well. Spoon the stuffing into the vegetables, and arrange the vegetables in a large roasting pan. Add ¼ inch boiling water to the pan, and cover the pan with aluminum foil. Bake the vegetables in a preheated 350°F. oven for 30 minutes, or until the filling is hot and the vegetables are tender. SERVES 6 TO 10.

Spanish Meatballs
(ALBONDIGAS)

THE MEATBALLS
2 pounds ground beef round
4 large eggs
¼ cup chopped parsley
2 cloves garlic, crushed
2 to 3 dashes cayenne
salt and black pepper to taste
flour for rolling the meatballs
vegetable oil for frying

THE SAUCE
4 or 5 onions, chopped fine
¼ cup vegetable oil
1 pound fresh tomatoes, pureed, or more if more sauce is desired
salt and pepper to taste

Make the meatballs: In a large bowl combine the beef, eggs, parsley, garlic, and cayenne. Season with salt and pepper, and mix well. Form the mixture into 1-inch balls, roll them in flour, and in batches, fry them in very hot oil until they are browned on all sides. Drain them in a large strainer.

Make the sauce: In a large saucepan fry the onions in the oil over moderately low heat, stirring occasionally, until they are golden. Add the tomato puree, and bring the liquid to a boil. Simmer the sauce for 20 minutes, season with salt and pepper, add the meatballs, and simmer them in the sauce for 15 minutes. SERVES 8 TO 10.

Braised Veal Shank
(JARRET DE VEAU)

2 tablespoons butter
2 tablespoons oil
1 veal shank
2 cups small white onions, peeled
1 cup pitted niçoise olives
½ teaspoon dried thyme leaves, crushed
1 bay leaf
½ cup dry white wine
salt and pepper to taste

In a large skillet melt the butter in the oil over moderately high heat, and brown the veal pieces on all sides. Remove the veal from the pan, add the onions, and brown them on all sides in the drippings. Add the veal, olives, thyme, bay leaf, and wine, and season with salt and pepper. Bring the liquid to a boil, and simmer the mixture, covered, over low heat for 3 hours, or until the veal is tender, turning the veal and stirring the mixture occasionally. SERVES 4.

Stuffed Chicken

2 large (3 1/2 to 4 pounds each) grain-fed chickens

THE STUFFING
1/2 stick (1/4 cup) butter

1 onion, diced fine

1 clove garlic, crushed

2 tablespoons Cognac

2 cups fresh white bread crumbs (no crusts)

3 slices ham, minced

2 or 3 large eggs

2 tablespoons minced fresh tarragon leaves

salt and pepper to taste

4 carrots, peeled, sliced

4 leeks, trimmed, washed, sliced

4 turnips, peeled, diced

1 celery stalk, diced

2 cabbages, cut into wedges

4 onions, minced

10 tablespoons butter

1 cup white wine

Remove the gizzards and the livers from the chickens, rinse the innards and the chickens well under cold water, and pat them dry with paper towels. In a small saucepan cover the gizzards with water, bring the water to a boil, and simmer for 45 minutes, or until the gizzards are tender.

Meanwhile, prepare the stuffing: In a large skillet melt the butter and sauté the onion until it is golden. Add the garlic, and sauté until tender. Remove the mixture to a large bowl. In the hot drippings sauté the chicken livers over moderately high heat until they are browned on the outside but pink in the center. Add the Cognac, set it aflame, and stir the livers until the flames subside. Mince the gizzards and livers, add them to the bowl with the onion mixture, and stir in the bread crumbs, ham, eggs, and tarragon. Season with salt and pepper, and mix until combined.

Lightly pack the stuffing into each chicken, and sew them up with kitchen string. Place them in a kettle with enough salted water to cover, add the carrots, leeks, turnips, and celery, and bring the liquid to a boil. Simmer the chicken and the vegetables, covered, for 1 1/2 hours or until the chickens are done and the vegetables are tender.

When the chickens and vegetables have cooked for 1 hour, in a large saucepan of boiling salted water cook the cabbage wedges for 3 minutes, drain them, return them to the pan, and set them aside.

In a skillet sauté the onions in the butter until they are golden, and add the onion mixture to the cabbage with the wine. Bring the wine to a boil and simmer the mixture, covered, for 30 minutes, or until the cabbage is tender.

Transfer the chickens and the vegetables to a serving platter. Serve the cabbage mixture with the chickens and vegetables. SERVES 10 TO 12.

Stacked Vegetable Omelettes

(OMELETTES EN PILE)

12 large eggs, beaten

6 tablespoons butter

FILLINGS
(ONE OR TWO PER OMELETTE)
1/2 cup sautéed chopped tomatoes

1/2 cup sautéed diced eggplant

1/2 cup sautéed chopped onion

1/2 cup sautéed sliced zucchini

1/2 cup sautéed chopped sweet green pepper

1/4 cup mixed chopped fresh basil, chives, parsley, and tarragon

In an omelette pan make an omelette with 2 to 4 of the eggs and 2 tablespoons butter per omelette, adding one of the fillings to each omelette. Arrange the omelettes in a stack as you would pancakes. (*We have a habit of using 1 or 2 omelettes made only of herbs.*) SERVES 6.

Conchita's Rice Pudding
(GÂTEAU DE RIZ CONCHITA)

1 quart milk

1 cup raw long-grain white rice

THE CRÈME ANGLAISE
1 quart milk

³/4 cup sugar or to taste

12 large egg yolks

8 ounces crème fraîche or sour cream

12 sugar cubes

1 cup water

In a large saucepan bring the milk to a boil, add the rice, and mix well. Over moderately low heat simmer the rice for 20 minutes, or until it is tender.

In the meantime make the crème anglaise: In the top of a double boiler over simmering, not boiling water, combine the milk, sugar, and egg yolks. Heat the mixture, stirring constantly, until it is thick enough to coat the back of a spoon. When the rice is cooked, add the crème anglaise and the crème fraîche to the rice, mix well, and set aside.

In a small saucepan combine the sugar cubes with the water, and stir the mixture until the sugar is dissolved. Over moderate heat cook the mixture, swirling the pan frequently, until the sugar is caramel-colored, and pour it into a heat-safe mold. Add the rice mixture, mix well, and refrigerate the mold for several hours, or until it is set. Just before serving, unmold the rice mixture onto a serving dish.

SERVES 12.

Conchita's Chocolate Cake
(GÂTEAU AU CHOCOLAT CONCHITA)

THE CAKE
1 stick (¹/2 cup) unsalted butter, softened

¹/2 cup sugar

4 large eggs, separated

4 ounces bittersweet chocolate, melted and cooled

¹/4 cup all-purpose flour

1 cup ground blanched almonds

THE FROSTING
1 stick (¹/2 cup) unsalted butter, softened

8 ounces semisweet chocolate

Make the cake: In a large bowl with an electric mixer beat the butter with the sugar until the mixture is fluffy, and beat in the egg yolks one at a time until they are blended. Fold in the chocolate, and then the flour and the almonds. In another bowl with an electric mixer beat the egg whites at high speed until they hold soft peaks, and fold them into the batter mixture until no white streaks remain. Pour the batter into a buttered 10-inch tube pan, and bake the cake in a preheated 375°F. oven for 40 minutes, or until a cake tester inserted in the center of the cake comes out clean. Let the cake cool in the pan for 10 minutes, and invert it onto a rack to cool completely.

Make the frosting: In the top of a double boiler over hot, not boiling, water, melt the butter with the chocolate, stir until smooth, and stir in enough water to make the frosting of spreading consistency. Chill the frosting slightly, and use it to cover the cake.

SERVES 10 TO 12.

Conserved Goose
(CONFIT D'OIE)

1 goose, quartered

salt to taste

2 pounds fresh chestnuts, shelled

1 bay leaf

1 sprig fresh rosemary

1 sprig fresh thyme

¹/₂ pound fresh cèpes, stemmed

2 pounds potatoes, peeled, sliced (optional)

2 tablespoons chopped parsley (optional)

2 cloves garlic, minced

Heavily sprinkle the goose pieces with salt, place them in a large bowl, covered with plastic wrap, and refrigerate them for 24 hours. Pat them dry with paper towels, removing most of the salt, and arrange the goose pieces in a single layer with the skin sides up in a deep roasting pan. Cook them in a preheated 325°F. oven for 2 to 2¹/₂ hours or until they have rendered most of their fat. Remove the pan from the oven, drain the goose pieces, and set them on a platter. Let the fat stand until it is cool, sieve about 1 cup of the fat into a large bowl, add the goose pieces, pour the remaining fat through a sieve over them to cover them completely, and refrigerate the goose, covered with waxed paper, for 1 to 3 days.

Before serving, in a saucepan cover the chestnuts with water. Tie the bay leaf, rosemary, and thyme together with kitchen string, add the bouquet garni to the water, and bring the liquid to a boil, covered. Simmer the chestnuts for 40 minutes, or until they are tender when tested with a skewer, and drain them. In a skillet, brown the chestnuts in some of the goose fat, and place them in a roasting pan. In the drippings in the skillet brown the cèpes, and place them with the chestnuts. In the drippings in the skillet brown the potatoes, cooking them over moderately low heat until they are tender, adding more goose fat if necessary. Place them in the roasting pan. Add the goose pieces to the roasting pan with the fat, and heat them in a preheated 350°F. oven until they are hot. Remove the goose pieces, cut them into serving portions, and arrange them on a warm platter surrounded by the chestnuts, the cèpes, and the potatoes. Sprinkle the potatoes with the parsley and the garlic.   MAKES 10 TO 12 SERVINGS.

Salad of Asparagus Tips

2 cups asparagus tips

1 tablespoon Meaux wine vinegar

1 teaspoon Dijon mustard

2 tablespoons olive oil

2 tablespoons peanut oil

truffle slivers

In a saucepan of boiling salted water cook the asparagus for 4 minutes, or until they are tender-crisp, drain them, and slice them. In a serving bowl whisk the vinegar with the mustard until blended, and whisk in the olive and peanut oils until the mixture is thickened. Add the asparagus, toss the salad until it is coated with the dressing, and sprinkle it with the truffle slivers.   SERVES 4.

Brioche with Candied Fruits
(BRIOCHE DU SUD-OUEST)

THE BRIOCHE
1 cake of yeast

¹/₂ cup milk

4 cups all-purpose flour

6 large eggs

a pinch of salt

1 tablespoon sugar

10 tablespoons butter, softened

¹/₂ pound candied fruits, chopped

THE SAUCE
one 12-ounce jar orange and mandarin marmalade

¹/₄ cup water

Make the brioche: In a bowl dissolve the yeast in ¹/₄ cup of the milk, warmed, and stir in 1 cup of the flour until the mixture is blended. Let the mixture stand at room temperature covered with plastic wrap for 2 hours.

In a large bowl whisk 5 of the eggs with the remaining 3 cups of flour until the mixture is blended. Add the remaining ¼ cups of milk, and mix well. Add the salt, sugar, and gradually beat in the butter until it is blended. Add the yeast mixture, mix well, and let the dough stand, covered with a damp kitchen towel, at room temperature for 5 or 6 hours. Reserving ¼ cup of the candied fruit for garnish, stir the remainder into the dough, and pour the dough into a large buttered brioche mold to fill it two thirds full. Let the dough stand covered with a clean damp kitchen towel at room temperature for 1 hour, or until the dough has risen to the top of the mold. In a small bowl beat the remaining egg until it is blended and gently brush the top of the dough with enough of the egg to glaze it. Bake the brioche in a preheated 350°F. oven for 25 to 35 minutes, or until a cake tester comes out clean. Cool the brioche in the pan on a rack.

Make the sauce: In a small saucepan combine the marmalade with the cup water, stir the mixture until it is blended, and bring the sauce to a boil. Boil it for 5 minutes. Serve the sauce with the brioche, sliced, and garnish with the reserved chopped candied fruit.

SERVES 8 TO 10.

L A   B A R O N N E   G U Y   D E   R O T H S C H I L D

Monkfish with Creamed Leeks
(LOTTE À LA CRÈME DE POIREAUX)

3½ pounds trimmed monkfish fillets, cut into rounds

1½ cups dry white wine

12 medium leeks (about 4½ pounds), trimmed, split, washed well, and sliced fine

3 shallots

salt to taste

In a baking dish arrange the fillets in a single layer, and pour the wine over the fish. Bake the fillets, covered, in a preheated 350°F. oven for 20 minutes or until the fish is cooked.

In the meantime, in a large saucepan combine the leeks and the shallots, add enough water to cover them, and season with salt. Bring the liquid to a boil, and cook the vegetables, covered, for 10 minutes, or until they are tender. Drain them, purée them through a food mill, and keep the sauce warm.

Transfer the fillets to a serving platter, and serve them covered with the leek sauce, accompanied by the Puree de Pommes de Terre *Parfumée au Safran* (recipe follows). SERVES 6.

Pureed Potatoes with Saffron
(PURÉE DE POMMES DE TERRE PARFUMÉE AU SAFRAN)

1 cup milk

2 cloves garlic, crushed

½ teaspoon crumbled saffron threads

2½ to 3 pounds boiling potatoes, peeled, cooked, and mashed

½ stick (¼ cup) butter (optional)

saffron threads for garnish

In a small saucepan bring the milk to a boil, add the garlic and the crumbled saffron, and steep the mixture, covered, for 5 minutes. In a large bowl combine the potatoes and the butter, and stir in enough of the hot milk mixture to reach the desired consistency. Garnish the potatoes with the saffron threads.

SERVES 6.

Lamb Curry
(CURRY DE PRÉ SALÉ)

1 onion, chopped

¹/4 cup good olive oil

3 pounds trimmed lamb shoulder (from pré salé *lamb, if possible), cut into 1-inch cubes*

2 tablespoons all-purpose flour

2 tablespoons curry powder

1 quart chicken broth

¹/4 pound celery root, peeled and diced

4 tomatoes, peeled, seeded, and cut into small pieces

¹/2 pint crème fraîche or heavy cream

2 Golden Delicious apples, peeled, cored, and diced

salt and pepper to taste

cooked white rice

In a 3-quart Dutch oven sauté the onion in the oil for 2 or 3 minutes, until it is tender, then add the lamb, and sauté it until very slightly browned on all sides. Stir in the flour, and cook the mixture, stirring frequently, for about 8 minutes. Mix in the curry and enough of the chicken broth to cover the meat. Add three quarters each of the celery root and tomatoes, bring the liquid to a boil, and simmer the mixture, covered, for 1¹/2 hours.

Transfer the meat to a bowl, and to the sauce in the pan add the crème fraîche or cream. Simmer the mixture for 2 or 3 minutes, add the meat, the remaining celery root and tomatoes, and the apples. When the mixture is heated through, season it with salt and pepper and serve it with the rice.   SERVES 4.

St. Marcel Cake
(GÂTEAU ST. MARCEL)

3¹/2 ounces bittersweet chocolate

1 stick (¹/2 cup) unsalted butter

³/4 cup sugar

2 large eggs, well beaten

1 tablespoon all-purpose flour

Crème Anglaise (recipe follows)

In the top of a double boiler over hot, not boiling, water combine the chocolate, butter, and sugar, and heat the mixture, stirring, until it is smooth and the sugar is dissolved. Remove the pan from over the water, and mix in the eggs and the flour. Pour the mixture into a *moule à manquer* or a slope-sided round mold, and steam the *gâteau*, covered, over simmering water for 1 hour, adding boiling water as necessary, or until a cake tester comes out clean. Invert the *gâteau* onto a warm serving dish, and serve it with warm Crème Anglaise on the side.   SERVES 4.

Vanilla Custard Sauce
(CRÈME ANGLAISE)

¹/3 cup sugar

1 tablespoon cornstarch

4 large egg yolks

1³/4 cups milk

1 teaspoon vanilla extract

In a small bowl mix the sugar with the cornstarch, and beat in the egg yolks until blended. In a small saucepan bring the milk to a boil, add a little of it to the egg-yolk mixture, and whisk until blended. Pour the egg-yolk mixture into the hot milk in the saucepan, and cook the mixture over moderate heat, stirring constantly, for 5 minutes, or until the sauce coats the back of a spoon. Remove the sauce from the heat, stir in the vanilla until blended, and keep the sauce warm until serving. Or pour it into a small bowl, cover with plastic wrap placed directly on the surface of the sauce to prevent a skin from forming, and refrigerate the sauce until it is cold.
MAKES 1¹/2 CUPS.

Quail Egg Nests
(NIDS D'OEUF DE CAILLE)

THE PUREE
1¹/₂ cups broccoli flowerets, or 2 cups packed watercress leaves
2 teaspoons butter, softened
1 to 2 tablespoons heavy cream (if using the watercress)
salt and pepper to taste

THE HOLLANDAISE
3 large egg yolks
1 stick (¹/₂ cup) butter, cut into ¹/₂-inch wide pieces
the juice of ¹/₂ lemon
freshly grated nutmeg to taste
ground white pepper to taste
salt to taste

four 4-inch baked puff-pastry tart shells
16 hot, poached quail eggs

If a watercress puree is desired, make it after the hollandaise as it will become bitter if made ahead. The broccoli puree can be kept warm while making the hollandaise. To make the puree: In a small saucepan of ¹/₂ inch of boiling salted water cook the broccoli or the watercress just until tender. Drain it, place it in a bowl, and mash the broccoli with the butter until smooth, and season with salt and pepper to taste. Or finely chop the cooked watercress, mix it with the butter and the heavy cream, and season with salt and pepper.

Make the hollandaise: In the top of a double boiler over hot, not boiling, water, whisk the egg yolks with the butter until the butter is melted and the mixture is thickened and smooth. Remove the top from over the water and continue to whisk the mixture for 2 minutes. Whisk in the lemon juice until it is blended, and season with the nutmeg, white pepper, and salt. Return the mixture to heat over hot water, whisking constantly until the sauce thickens.

Spread the broccoli or watercress puree over the bottom of each tart shell, top each with 4 of the poached quail eggs, and cover the eggs and the puree with the sauce. SERVES 4.

Loin of Veal with Pistachios
(LONGUE DE VEAU AUX PISTACHES)

one 5-pound loin of veal, boned, trimmed, and rolled
1 cup salt-pork lardons, or ¹/₂-inch pieces of sliced bacon
1 cup pistachio nuts
salt and pepper to taste
steamed small green vegetables (optional)

With the tip of a paring knife make small slits over the outside of the veal roll, and alternately insert the lardons and pistachios into the slits. Place the veal in a roasting pan, season the meat with salt and pepper, and roast it in a preheated 425°F. oven for 1 hour, or until it is cooked, basting it frequently with its juices. Serve the veal with the vegetables. SERVES 8.

Frozen Red Fruits Soufflé
(SOUFFLÉ GLACÉ AUX FRUITS ROUGES)

2 cups well-beaten white farmer cheese
2 cups heavy cream, softly whipped
3 cups raspberry pureed and sieved (2 cups raspberry coulis)

THE SAUCE
¹/₂ cup blackberries
¹/₂ cup black currants
¹/₂ cup red currants
¹/₂ cup raspberries

In a bowl combine the farmer cheese, whipped cream, and raspberry coulis, and mix gently until combined. Lightly pack the mixture into an aluminum foil-lined 8-cup soufflé dish, and freeze it for 2 hours, or until it is firm.

Make the sauce: In a saucepan combine the blackberries, black and red currants, and the raspberries, heat the mixture to a boil, and cook it just until it is juicy, stirring the fruits gently but making sure they remain firm. Cool the mixture, and refrigerate it until it is cold.

To serve: Wrap a hot, clean kitchen towel around the soufflé dish for 15 seconds, or until the soufflé melts slightly, or dip the dish into a bowl of warm water and dry it off. Unmold the soufflé onto a serving dish and gently remove the foil. Pour the sauce over the soufflé.   SERVES 6 TO 8.

MARCHESA FRÀNCESCA ANTINORI

Mixed Tuscan Crostini
(CROSTINI MISTI)

RED CABBAGE
4 slices Tuscan bread, toasted
garlic cloves, crushed
red cabbage, sliced, boiled, and drained well
good Tuscan olive oil
salt to taste

Rub the toasts lightly with garlic, cut each slice crosswise into thirds, top each piece with some of the cabbage, sprinkle with the oil, and season with salt.

CHICKEN LIVER
the heart of an onion, chopped fine
olive oil
6 chicken livers, sieved
about 1/4 cup mixture of anchovies, chopped fine; capers; and gherkins, chopped fine
dry white wine
chicken broth
4 slices Tuscan bread, toasted

In a large heavy skillet fry the onion in the oil over moderately low heat. Add the chicken livers, and cook the mixture, stirring, for 5 to 6 minutes. Stir in the anchovy mixture. Cook the liver mixture, stirring, for 10 minutes. Add enough of the wine to wet the mixture, and cook it, stirring, until the wine evaporates. Add a little of the broth, and cook the mixture, stirring, until it is of spreading consistency. Cut each toast slice crosswise into thirds, and cover each piece with some of the liver mixture.

TOMATO
garlic, minced, to taste
fresh gingerroot peeled and minced, to taste
olive oil
Italian plum tomatoes, sieved
salt to taste
4 slices Tuscan bread, toasted

In a large heavy skillet fry an abundant quantity of the garlic and ginger in the oil over moderately low heat. Stir in the tomatoes, and season with salt. Bring the mixture to a boil and boil it for 10 minutes, stirring, until it is of spreading consistency. Cut each toast slice crosswise into thirds, and top each piece with some of the tomato mixture.   SERVES 8.

Tuscan Tomato Soup
(PAPPA AL POMODORO)

1 leek, washed well, chopped fine
4 cloves garlic, minced
1 chile pepper, seeded, chopped fine
1 pint olive oil
1 heaping tablespoon tomato paste
2 cups chicken broth
salt and pepper to taste
2 1/2 pounds Italian plum tomatoes, peeled, seeded, and chopped
chopped, fresh basil, to taste
1 pound stale white bread, broken into small pieces

In a large heavy saucepan fry the leek, garlic, and chile in the oil over moderately low heat, stirring. Add the tomato paste and tomatoes, bring the mixture to a boil, and simmer it for 10 minutes. Add the broth, season with salt and pepper, and return the mixture to boiling; and boil for 5 minutes. Stir in an abundant amount of the basil and all the bread. Let the mixture stand for 20 minutes, and then whisk it until the bread is broken down and the mixture is smooth. If the mixture is too thick, whisk in more of the broth, and serve the mixture hot, drizzled with a little additional olive oil.

Serve with Vino Peppoli. SERVES 8.

Florentine Braised Beef
(STRACOTTO ALLA FIORENTINA)

one 3-pound boneless beef pot roast

8 carrots, peeled

1 celery heart

¹/₄ pound bacon, cut into small pieces

4 onions

1 cup good olive oil

1 bunch fresh rosemary

1 bunch fresh sage

fresh basil leaves

6 cloves garlic, chopped fine

salt and pepper to taste

1 750 ml. bottle red wine (Antinori)

4 heaping tablespoons tomato paste

4 pounds Italian plum tomatoes, quartered

beef broth (optional)

Make two lengthwise cuts in each side of the beef, and into each cut put 1 carrot, 1 celery heart and a quarter of the bacon pieces. Tie the meat with kitchen string to seal the meat around the stuffing. Chop coarse the remaining carrots and celery and the onions.

In a large flameproof casserole heat the oil over moderately high heat until it is hot but not smoking, and in it brown the beef, add the chopped carrots, celery, and onions, add the herbs and garlic, season with salt and pepper, and add the wine. Bring the liquid to a boil, and simmer the mixture, stirring frequently, until the wine has nearly evaporated. Stir in the tomato paste, and simmer the mixture for 3 to 4 minutes. Add the tomatoes, and if they do not cover the meat add enough of the broth until they do. Bring the liquid to a boil, and simmer the mixture for 2 hours, or until the meat is tender, turning it frequently to keep it from sticking to the bottom of the casserole.

Transfer the meat to a cutting board and remove the strings. Sieve the sauce, slice the meat, and serve it with the sauce under and on top of the slices.

Serve with Tignanello Antinori. SERVES 8.

Rice with Zucchini
(RISOTTO AGLI ZUCCHINI)

2 quarts rich chicken broth

14 ounces small zucchini, cut crosswise into $^{1}/_{2}$-inch-thick rounds

1 onion, chopped fine

a pinch of salt

2 tablespoons vegetable oil

10 tablespoons unsalted butter

1 pound Arborio rice (Italian short-grain rice, available at specialty food stores)

2 tomatoes, diced

fresh basil, chopped

fresh parsley, chopped

3 $^{1}/_{4}$ ounces Parmesan cheese, grated, or to taste

In a saucepan bring the broth to a simmer and keep it at a bare simmer. In a large heavy saucepan cook the zucchini and onion with a pinch of salt in the oil and 4 tablespoons of the butter over moderately high heat, stirring, until the vegetables are tender. Transfer the vegetables to a bowl, leaving the fat in the pan.

Add 4 tablespoons of the butter to the fat in the pan, increase the heat to high, and when the butter begins to bubble, add the rice, stirring for 1 minute to toast the rice, thus preserving all its starch, and to coat it well with the fat. Add a scant $^{1}/_{2}$ cup of the hot broth and cook the mixture, stirring, until the broth is absorbed. Continue adding the broth, about $^{1}/_{2}$ cup at a time, stirring constantly so that the rice does not stick to the bottom of the pan; adjust the heat only so that the mixture does not burn but is not low enough to slow down the cooking, and let each portion of broth be absorbed before adding more, until the rice is tender but *al dente*. The total cooking time should be about 20 minutes.

When all the liquid has been absorbed, stir in the zucchini mixture, tomatoes, chopped basil and parsley to taste, the remaining 2 tablespoons of butter, and the Parmesan. SERVES 6.

John Dory
alla Carlina

a handful of parsley sprigs, minced

capers

about 5 gherkins, chopped

4 to 5 tomatoes, seeded and diced

olive oil for frying

24 skinless sole fillets (2 $^{1}/_{4}$ to 3 pounds)

about $^{1}/_{2}$ cup all-purpose flour

salt and pepper to taste

1 stick ($^{1}/_{2}$ cup) butter

4 to 5 drops Worcestershire sauce

the juice from 1 lemon

In a bowl combine the parsley, capers, and gherkins. In a large skillet sauté the tomatoes in a little olive oil until they are hot, and transfer them to a bowl.

Dredge the fillets in the flour, seasoned with salt and pepper, shaking off the excess. In the skillet, cleaned, heat a thin layer of the oil over moderately high heat until it is very hot, and in it brown the fillets on both sides in batches, transferring them when they are done to a large shallow baking dish. Sprinkle the parsley mixture and then the tomatoes over the browned fillets.

In the oil used to fry the fish, melt the butter over moderately high heat and add the Worcestershire and lemon juice, scraping up the brown bits in the pan. Pour the mixture over the tomatoes in the baking dish, and bake the fillets in a preheated 450°F. oven for 5 minutes, or until the fillets are cooked through. Serve with rice pilaf or steamed potatoes. SERVES 6.

Meringue Cake (A Variation on Trifle)
(TORTA MERINGATA AL CAFFE)

THE CAKE
3 large eggs, at room temperature
$^1/_2$ cup granulated sugar
$^1/_4$ teaspoon vanilla extract
1 scant cup all-purpose flour

THE COFFEE CREAM
1 large egg yolk
1 tablespoon granulated sugar
1 teaspoon all-purpose flour
2 espresso cups of good, very hot coffee
$1^1/_2$ cups heavy cream, whipped

THE MERINGUE
5 large egg whites, at room temperature
1 cup granulated sugar
the juice of $^1/_2$ lemon
$^1/_4$ teaspoon vanilla extract
castor or superfine sugar to color the meringue

Make the cake: In a large bowl with an electric mixer beat the eggs with the sugar until the mixture is thick and pale and forms a ribbon when the beaters are lifted, and beat in the vanilla. Fold in the flour just until it is combined, pour the batter into a greased and floured 8-inch round cake pan, and bake in a preheated 300°F. oven for 20 minutes, or until the cake is golden and a cake tester comes out clean. Cool the cake in the pan on a rack. When the cake is thoroughly cooled, remove it from the pan, and slice it horizontally into 4 layers.

Make the coffee cream: In a small saucepan whisk the egg yolk and the sugar until thick and light, whisk in the flour and then the coffee, and bring just to a boil over moderately low heat, whisking constantly. Remove the pan from the heat, let the mixture cool, whisking frequently, and fold in the whipped cream. Fill the cake layers with the coffee cream and place the cake on a heat-safe dish.

Make the meringue: In a large bowl with an electric mixer beat the whites until they hold soft peaks, add the sugar, 1 tablespoon at a time, beating, and whip the whites until they hold glossy and stiff but not dry peaks. Beat in the lemon juice and vanilla just until blended, and cover the cake with the meringue.

Sprinkle the meringue with castor sugar and heat for 1 to 2 minutes, or just until golden, in a preheated 500°F. oven. SERVES 6 TO 8.

Tagliatelli with White Truffles alla Lino

(TAGLIATELLE ALLA LINO CON TARTUFI BIANCHI D'ALBA)

1/2 pound (about 2 cups) all-purpose flour

2 large eggs

1 teaspoon salt

1/4 cup Italian olive oil

butter

fresh sage leaves, chopped, to taste

sliced white truffles for garnish

Sift the flour into a mound on the work surface. With your fist, make a well in the center and add the eggs, salt, and oil. Using your fingertips, mix the eggs with the salt and oil, gradually incorporating the flour from the insides of the well into the egg mixture until the liquid is blended with enough of the flour to form a soft dough, and then incorporate the rest of the flour. Using both hands, knead the dough for about 10 minutes, or until it is smooth and not sticky. Wrap the dough in plastic wrap and leave it to rest for 30 minutes before shaping the tagliatelli.

Place the dough on a floured board and roll it out to 1/16-inch thickness. Roll up the sheet of pasta and with a sharp knife, cut the roll crosswise at 1/4-inch intervals. Unroll the tagliatelli to their full length and place them on a lightly floured surface to dry for a minimum of 10 minutes.

In a large saucepan of salted boiling water boil the pasta for a few minutes, until it is *al dente*. Drain the pasta and place it in a serving dish. In a small saucepan, melt the butter, stir in the sage, pour the mixture over the pasta, and toss to coat. Garnish with the sliced truffles.   SERVES 2.

Pheasant with Pomegranate alla Contessa Giorgia

(FAGIANO AL MELOGRANO ALLA CONTESSA GIORGIA)

one 3-pound pheasant

one lemon, halved

2 sticks (1 cup) butter

sprigs fresh rosemary

bacon slices

1 cup heavy cream

1/2 cup fresh pomegranate juice

pomegranate seeds for garnish

In a large bowl of water soak the pheasant with the lemon halves for 30 minutes. Drain the pheasant, pat it dry, and stuff it with 1 stick of the butter and the rosemary sprigs. Cover the pheasant with the bacon slices and place it breast side up on a rack in a roasting pan with the remaining stick of butter in the pan. Roast the pheasant in a preheated 350°F. oven, basting frequently with the pan juices, for 1 to 1 1/2 hours, or until it is tender. (Do not let the bacon burn. If the bacon starts to get too brown, remove it from the bird and reserve.)

When the pheasant is cooked, remove it to a platter, remove the rack from the pan, and add the heavy cream and pomegranate juice to the pan juices. On top of the stove, boil the liquid, whisking frequently, until it is reduced by half. Serve the sauce with the pheasant and garnish it with the bacon and the pomegranate seeds.   SERVES 3 TO 4.

Fusilli with Black Olives and Capers alla Tai
(FUSILLI CON OLIVE NERE E CAPPERI ALLA TAI)

4 to 5 cloves garlic

1/4 cup olive oil

2 pounds canned Italian plum tomatoes, well-drained

salt to taste

1/4 cup chopped capers

30 oil-cured black olives, pitted and chopped

paprika to taste

1 pound fusilli

In a skillet sauté the garlic in the oil over moderate heat until they are tender; add the tomatoes, season lightly with salt, and cook the mixture, stirring occasionally, for 15 minutes. Stir in the capers, olives, and paprika, and cook the mixture for 15 minutes longer. In a kettle in 1 gallon of boiling salted water cook the pasta until it is *al dente*. Drain it in a colander, transfer it to a serving dish, toss it with the tomato mixture, and serve it at once.   SERVES 4.

Rosita's Salad
(INSALATA ALLA ROSITA)

1 bunch of arugula, stems discarded, washed well, and spun dry

1 fennel bulb, cut into thin strips

Parmesan cheese to taste, shaved into curls with a vegetable peeler

extra-virgin olive oil to taste

1 tablespoon red wine vinegar

salt and pepper to taste

In a large bowl combine the arugula, fennel, and Parmesan. In a small bowl, whisk the oil with the vinegar and salt and pepper; drizzle the dressing over the arugula mixture, and toss lightly to coat.
SERVES 4.

Pumpkin Soup alla Rosita
(ZUPPA DI ZUCCA ALLA ROSITA)

1 leek, split, washed, chopped fine

olive oil

one 4 1/2-pound pumpkin, seeded, peeled and diced

3 chicken-flavor bouillon cubes

7 cups water

3 cups cooked rice

chopped parsley

grated Parmesan cheese

In a large saucepan sauté the leek in the oil until it is tender, add the pumpkin, and sauté for 3 minutes. Add the bouillon, dissolved in 1 cup of boiling water, and the rest of the water, bring the liquid to a boil, and simmer the mixture, covered, for 20 to 30 minutes, or until the pumpkin is tender. In a blender or food processor puree the mixture in batches, return it to the saucepan, cleaned, and stir additional bouillon dissolved in boiling water if the soup is too thick. Add the rice and parsley. Serve the soup with the Parmesan.   SERVES 8 TO 10.

Cotechino with Lentils
(COTECHINO DI CREMONA CON LENTICCHIE)

1 pound dry lentils

1 cotechino sausage (a flavorful sausage most often in the skin of a pig's foot—can be found at Italian butchers—it is traditionally eaten at New Year's)

3 quarts cold water

1 onion, chopped fine

1/4 cup olive oil

1 tablespoon chopped tomato

salt and pepper to taste

Tie up the lentils in a square of cheesecloth, and soak them in a large bowl of water for 2 1/2 hours. After the lentils have soaked for 30 minutes, in a kettle combine the cotechino with the cold water, bring to a boil over low heat, and simmer gently, covered, for 2½ hours (do not prod the sausage with a fork at any time during its cooking). Let the cotechino rest in its cooking liquid until serving.

In a large heavy saucepan sauté the onion in the oil for 3 minutes, or until it is tender, add the lentils, drained, enough water to cover them, and the to-mato. Season with salt and pepper, and bring to a boil. Simmer the mixture, covered, for 1½ hours or until the water is absorbed and the lentils are tender, adding more water if necessary during cooking. Serve the lentils surrounded by thick slices of cotechino. SERVES 6 TO 8.

Rice with Pumpkin
(RISO DI ZUCCA)

5 cups chicken broth

1 onion, chopped fine

1 clove garlic, minced

½ stick (¼ cup) butter

¼ cup Italian olive oil

2 pounds pumpkin, seeded, peeled, diced

2 cups Arborio rice (Italian short-grain rice, available at specialty food stores)

salt and pepper to taste

In a saucepan bring the broth to a simmer and keep it at a bare simmer. In a large heavy saucepan cook the onion and garlic with the butter and oil over moderately low heat, stirring, until they are softened. Add the pumpkin, and cook the mixture, stirring, for 8 minutes. Add the rice, and over moderately high heat, cook it, stirring for 2 to 3 minutes, until the rice is coated well with the fat. Add a scant ½ cup of the hot broth and cook the mixture, stirring, until the broth is absorbed. Continue adding the broth, about ½ cup at a time, stirring constantly so that the rice does not stick to the bottom of the pan, adjusting the heat only so that the mixture does not burn but is not low enough to slow down the cooking, and letting each portion of broth be absorbed before adding more, until the rice is tender but *al dente*. The total cooking time should be about 20 minutes. When the rice is creamy, season with salt and pepper. SERVES 6 TO 8.

Braised Guinea Fowl
(FARAONA IN SALMI)

1 guinea fowl

about 5 tablespoons butter

salt and pepper to taste

2 cups chicken broth

carrot and onion slices for flavoring the broth

1 bay leaf

½ pound carrots, sliced

3 celery stalks, chopped fine

1 medium onion, chopped coarse

3 tablespoons all-purpose flour

¼ cup port

Place the guinea fowl on a rack in the roasting pan, rub the breast with a small knob of butter, season well with salt and pepper, and add the broth to the pan. Roast the fowl in a preheated 400°F. oven for 40 minutes, basting frequently. Transfer the fowl to a large chopping board, and pour the pan juices into a medium saucepan. Remove the whole leg and wing joints and the breast meat, place on a plate, and cover loosely with aluminum foil. Add the bones, carrot and onion slices for flavoring the broth, and the bay leaf, and season with salt and pepper. Add enough water to the pan with the cooking juices to cover the bones and bring the liquid to a boil over moderately low heat. Simmer, uncovered, for about 30 minutes, strain the broth, and set it aside.

In a heavy flameproof casserole cook the sliced carrots, celery and chopped onion in the remaining butter over moderate heat, covered, until they are softened. Add the flour and cook the roux, stirring, for 1 minute. Remove the casserole from the heat, then whisk in the broth and port, a little at a time, and bring the sauce to a boil, whisking until it is thickened. Season with salt and pepper to taste, add the meat and joint pieces, and cook the mixture, covered, in a preheated 325°F. oven for about 30 minutes. SERVES 4.

Winter Cake, or "Torta Invernale"

THE SPONGE CAKE
1 cup all-purpose flour

1 tablespoon baking powder

¹/2 teaspoon salt

1 stick (¹/2 cup) butter, softened

1 cup granulated sugar

3 large eggs, separated, the whites at room temperature

THE FILLING
1 pound marrons glacés (candied chestnuts, available at specialty food shops)

¹/2 cup heavy cream, or more, if needed

6 tablespoons coffee-flavored liqueur

THE ICING
1¹/2 sticks (³/4 cup) butter, softened

one 1 pound box confectioners' sugar

2 tablespoons milk

1 teaspoon vanilla extract

8 meringue mushrooms (optional)

Make the cake layers: In a bowl sift the flour and combine it well with the baking powder and salt. In a bowl with an electric mixer cream the butter with the sugar until the mixture is light and fluffy, then add the egg yolks, one at a time, beating well after each addition. Fold in the flour mixture, and combine well. In another bowl with an electric mixer and clean beaters beat the egg whites until they hold stiff peaks but are not dry, and fold half of them at a time into the cake batter. Divide the batter among 3 buttered and floured 8-inch round cake pans, and bake the cake layers in the middle of a preheated 350°F. oven for 20 minutes, or until a tester comes out clean. Cool the cake layers in the pans for 10 minutes, turn them out onto racks, and let them cool completely.

Make the filling: Reserve 4 marrons glacés, press the remainder through a potato ricer into a bowl, and whisk in enough of the heavy cream to make the mixture of jam consistency.

Make the icing: In a small bowl with an electric mixer beat the butter with half of the sugar at low speed until the mixture is blended. Gradually add the milk, vanilla and remaining sugar. Beat the icing at medium speed until it is smooth and fluffy.

Sprinkle the cake layers with the liqueur, and sandwich them together with the filling. Cover the cake with the icing, decorate the top with the reserved marrons glacés, halved, and arrange the meringue mushrooms, if desired, around the edge. SERVES 12.

Venetian-Style Scallops
(CAPPE SANTE ALLA VENEZIANA)

16 sea scallops

16 langoustines (langoustes)

1 cup white wine

1 shallot, minced

½ stick (¼ cup) butter plus additional for baking

¼ cup all-purpose flour

8 crayfish, cooked, shelled

Cook the scallops and the *langoustines* separately in water, drain. Reserving 1 cup cooking liquid from the *langoustines*, shell them and set aside. In a small saucepan bring the wine and shallot to a boil, and boil the liquid until it is reduced by half. In another saucepan melt 4 tablespoons of the butter, add the flour, and cook the roux over moderately low heat, stirring, for 3 minutes. Add the reserved cooking liquid from the *langoustines* and the reduced wine mixture in a stream, whisking, and simmer the mixture, whisking occasionally, for 10 minutes.

Arrange 8 scallop shells on a jelly-roll pan, place 2 scallops, 2 *langoustines,* and a crayfish in each shell, spoon 2 tablespoons sauce over the fish in each shell, dot the mixtures with the remaining tablespoons of butter, and bake in a preheated 400°F. oven for 3 to 4 minutes, or until hot.   SERVES 8.

Macaroni Pie della Contessa Giannelli-Viscardi
(PASTICCIO DI MACCHERONI DELLA CONTESSA GIANNELLI-VISCARDI)

THE SHORT PASTRY

4 cups all-purpose flour

2 tablespoons sugar

1 teaspoon salt

2 sticks (1 cup) cold butter, cut into bits

3 large egg yolks

1 large egg white

3 to 4 tablespoons ice water

THE FILLING

1 pound leftover beef or veal pot roast, minced, with its cooking juices

2 cups sliced mushrooms, sautéed in butter

1 cup finely chopped cooked chicken giblets

1 cup coarsely chopped cooked sweetbreads

salt and pepper to taste

butter

1 pound maccheroni (macaroni—any of the shorter tubular-type pastas), cooked and drained

1 cup grated Parmesan cheese

1 large egg white, lightly beaten

In a large bowl combine the flour, sugar, and salt. Cut in the butter with a pastry blender until the mixture is crumbly. In a small bowl, mix the egg yolks, egg white, and 1 tablespoon of ice water until blended, pour into the flour mixture, and mix with a fork until it forms a dough, adding up to 1 more tablespoon of ice water if necessary. Gather the dough into a ball and flatten slightly to form a disk, cover the dough with plastic wrap, and refrigerate it for 30 minutes.

In a large saucepan cook the minced beef or veal and its cooking juices, the mushrooms, giblets, and sweetbreads, until the mixture is a thick sauce. Season with butter and salt and pepper to taste, and stir in the *maccheroni* and Parmesan until the mixture is combined well.

Divide the pastry in half. Roll out one piece of the pastry ¼-inch thick on a lightly floured surface, fit it into a buttered 10-inch springform pan, leaving a 1-inch overhang and reserving the pastry scraps, and fill the pastry shell with the meat mixture. Roll out the remaining piece of the pastry ⅛-inch thick, arrange it over the filling, reserving the pastry scraps, and crimp the edges together decoratively. Lightly combine and reroll the pastry scraps, cut out decorative leaves and flowers, brush the top of the *pasticcio* with the egg white, and arrange and attach the pastry leaves and flowers. Cut a few vent holes in the pastry with the tip of a knife, and bake the *pasticcio* in a preheated 375°F. oven for 40 minutes, or until the pastry is cooked.   SERVES 8.

Maria Luisa's Fritters
(BIGNÉ MARIA LUISA)

¼ cup lukewarm water

about 8 cups all-purpose flour

2 ounces yeast

¼ cup sugar

2 large eggs, lightly beaten

1 stick (½ cup) butter, melted

a pinch of salt

2 cups milk

about ½ cup apricot jam

vegetable oil for deep-frying

confectioners' sugar

In a large bowl stir together the yeast and lukewarm water until the yeast is dissolved, and let the mixture stand for 5 minutes, or until the mixture is slightly foamy. In a large bowl make a well in the flour, and in it pour the yeast mixture, sugar, eggs, butter, salt, and milk, and stir to combine. Turn out the dough onto a lightly floured surface and knead it for 10 minutes, or until it is soft and manageable, adding only as much additional flour as necessary to keep the dough from being sticky. Put the dough in an oiled bowl, turning to coat it with the oil, and let it rise, covered with plastic wrap, in a warm place for 1½ hours or until it is double in bulk. On the floured surface, roll the dough out ¼-inch thick and cut out rounds with a floured 2½-inch round cutter. Put 1 teaspoon of the jam in the center of half of the dough rounds, cover each with another dough round, and pinch the edges together to seal. Let the *bigne* rise, covered, in a warm place for 1 hour, or until they are puffy looking.

In a kettle heat 2 inches of the oil until it registers 375°F. on a deep-fat thermometer. Into it drop 3 or 4 *bigne* at a time, turning them as they rise to the surface, and fry them, turning them 3 or 4 more times, for a total cooking time of 2 to 3 minutes, or until they are golden. Transfer the *bigne* with a slotted spoon to paper towels to drain, and sprinkle them with the confectioners' sugar before serving.   MAKES ABOUT 20.

Pumpkin Ravioli with Tomato and Basil Sauce

THE PASTA DOUGH
2¹/₂ to 3 cups all-purpose flour

1 tablespoon salt

3 large eggs, beaten lightly

THE FILLING
¹/₂ uncooked boneless chicken breast

2 tablespoons ground hazelnuts

1 cup well-drained, pureed cooked pumpkin flesh from a
    medium pumpkin (reserve the pumpkin for serving)

1 large egg yolk

THE SAUCE
4 carrots, peeled and diced

2 celery stalks, diced

1 onion, diced

1 teaspoon salt

1 tablespoon olive oil

one 28 ounce can peeled Italian tomatoes

2 cups chicken broth

2 tablespoons chopped fresh basil leaves

2 to 4 tablespoons olive oil or heavy cream

*M*ake the pasta dough: In a food processor blend 2¹/₂ cups of the flour, salt, and eggs until the mixture just begins to form a ball, adding more flour to make a firm, not sticky, dough. Turn out the dough onto a lightly floured surface, and knead it a few times. Let the dough stand, covered with an inverted bowl, at room temperature for 1 hour.

Make the filling: In a food processor puree the chicken with the hazelnuts, and in a bowl combine the chicken mixture with the pumpkin and egg yolk.

Mix until blended, place the mixture in a pastry bag fitted with a ¹/₄-inch plain tip, and refrigerate the bag while making the sauce and pasta sheets for the ravioli.

Make the sauce: In a large saucepan sauté the carrots, celery, and onion with the salt in the oil for 10 minutes, or until they are tender. Add the tomatoes and chicken broth, bring the liquid to a boil, and simmer it for 45 minutes. Sieve the sauce into another saucepan, and keep it warm until serving. Just before serving, add the basil.

Make the ravioli: Divide the pasta dough into 8 pieces, flatten each piece into a rectangle with two sides the width of the pasta machine rollers, and work with one rectangle at a time, keeping the remainder under an inverted bowl. For each piece of pasta dough, dust the pasta rectangle lightly with flour, and feed it through the rollers several times to knead the dough, folding the dough and dusting it lightly with flour each time. Adjust the rollers to the next setting, roll out the pasta sheet without folding it, and continue to roll it through increasingly lower settings to make a thinner dough with each rolling, until it is rolled through the machine set on the next to the lowest setting. Repeat with another sheet of pasta. Pipe button-sized portions of the filling over one rolled pasta sheet, spacing the mixture 1¹/₂ inches apart, and cover the filled sheet with a plain pasta sheet, pressing lightly around the filling to press out air bubbles and to attach the 2 pasta sheets, using a little water to glue the sheets together. Cut out the ravioli with a pizza cutter. Repeat with the remaining pasta rectangles and the filling.

In a large kettle of boiling salted water cook the ravioli for 2 to 3 minutes, or until they are *al dente,* drain them in a colander, transfer them to a large bowl, and toss them with the oil or cream. Serve them in the empty warmed pumpkin shell with the sauce.   SERVES 4.

Smoked Loin of Pork del Castello di Enn

(KAISERFLEISCH DEL CASTELLO DI ENN)

one smoked loin of pork
fresh sauerkraut braised in champagne with juniper berries
mashed potatoes
a sauce of blueberries stewed with a little sugar

In a Dutch oven cover the pork with water, bring the water to a boil, and simmer the pork for 30 minutes. Remove the pork from the liquid, drain it, slice it into "chops," and serve it with the sauerkraut, potatoes, and sauce.

Tyrolean Dumplings or Tyrolean Knödel

$1/2$ onion, chopped fine
$1/2$ cup chopped parsley
$1/4$ pound minced speck or Westphalian ham
1 stick ($1/2$ cup) butter
1 pound dry white bread, broken up into $1/4$-inch crumbs
$1/2$ cup sifted all-purpose flour
$1/2$ cup milk
2 large eggs, beaten
2 quarts beef stock

In a skillet fry the onion, the parsley, and speck in the butter over moderately low heat, stirring, until the onion is tender. Add the bread crumbs and fry the mixture, stirring, until the crumbs are golden, and let the mixture cool. In a large bowl combine the flour, milk and eggs. Beat just until combined well. Add the crumb mixture, and stir until a thick dough forms, adding some water if the dough is too dry. With the palms of your hands, shape the mixture into big balls, cook the *knödel,* covered, in a kettle of boiling salted water until they are puffy and a cake tester comes out clean, and drain them.

Meanwhile, in a large saucepan bring the stock to a boil. Add the cooked *knödel,* heat them for a few minutes, and serve.   MAKES 8 TO 10 DUMPLINGS.

NOTE: *For liver* knödel, *substitute finely chopped liver for the speck.*

Pickled Salmon with Cucumber Sauce

THE PICKLING LIQUID
4 cups water
2 large carrots, sliced thin
2 medium white onions, sliced
6 sprigs fresh parsley
1 tablespoon salt
1 cup white-wine vinegar
1 teaspoon cracked black pepper
1 teaspoon fresh tarragon leaves
1 teaspoon lemon-thyme leaves, or 1 sprig fresh thyme

3 to 4 pounds fresh skinless salmon fillets

THE SAUCE
1 cucumber, peeled, seeded, and grated
1 cup heavy cream
1 tablespoon finely chopped fresh tarragon leaves
1 teaspoon salt
1/2 teaspoon coarsely ground black pepper
1 or 2 dashes cayenne
1 teaspoon lemon juice

*I*n a fish poachér large enough to hold the salmon fillets but not so large as to require an excessive amount of pickling liquid, over moderately high heat, bring the water, carrots, onions, parsley, salt, vinegar, pepper, tarragon, and lemon-thyme to a boil. Add the salmon fillets and, if necessary, enough boiling water to just cover the fillets, reduce the heat to allow the water to barely simmer, and poach the fillets for 15 minutes. Transfer the fillets to a shallow porcelain baking dish, arrange the carrots and on-ions on top of the fillets, pour in enough of the pickling liquid to cover, and refrigerate for 24 hours or more.

Make the sauce: In a bowl combine the cucum-ber, cream, tarragon, salt, black pepper, cayenne, and lemon juice, and stir until blended. Transfer the mixture to a sauceboat or serving bowl.

To serve, drain the salmon and serve it with the sauce. SERVES 6 TO 8.

Beetroot and Potato Salad

1 1/2 pounds beets, trimmed, leaving 2 inches of the stem ends
1 1/2 pounds red or white potatoes (do not use large baking potatoes)
2 fennel bulbs, chopped coarse
1 cup sour cream
1/2 cup mayonnaise
1 tablespoon salt
1 teaspoon coarsely ground black pepper

*I*n a large saucepan cover the beets with cold wa-ter, bring the water to a boil, and simmer the beets, covered, for 20 to 25 minutes, or until the beets are tender but still firm. Drain the beets under running cold water, remove the skins and stems, and when the beets are cool enough to handle, dice coarse. While the beets cook, in another large saucepan cover the potatoes with cold water, bring the water to a boil, and simmer the potatoes, covered, for 40 to 50 minutes, or until the potatoes are tender but still firm. Drain the potatoes under running cold water, and when the potatoes are cool, peel and dice coarse.

In a large bowl, combine the diced beets, diced potatoes, chopped fennel, sour cream, mayonnaise, salt, and pepper, and stir gently until blended. The salad will have a very bright pink color and is most attractive served on a bed of California red leaf lettuce. SERVES 12.

Ham and Chicken Mold

one 3- to 3 1/2-pound stewing hen
2 tablespoons salt
2 pounds cooked ham, chopped coarse
1/2 cup finely chopped parsley
2 large eggs, hard-boiled, sliced, the all-white pieces discarded

*I*n a kettle cover the hen with cold water, add the salt, and bring the water to a boil. Simmer the hen for 45 minutes, or until it is completely tender. Transfer the hen to a colander, and when cool enough to handle, remove the meat from the skin and bones, and chop coarse. Return the skin and bones to the kettle with the cooking liquid from the hen, and simmer the mixture for 15 minutes. Strain the stock into a bowl, and skim off the fat. In a bowl combine the ham and parsley.

Line the bottom of a 2-quart bowl with 6 or 7 of the egg slices, moisten them with 2 tablespoons of the stock, and cover with alternate layers of the chicken and the ham mixture (2 layers of each). Press down firmly on the layers but not so hard as to disturb the egg-slice pattern on the bottom. Pour in enough stock to barely cover the top layer, but not so much as to end with a liquid cover. Cover the bowl with plastic wrap, and refrigerate for 24 hours before serving.

To unmold, run a knife around the top inch of the mold to loosen it, then either dip the bowl in a larger bowl or sink of hot water or wrap the bowl in a hot, wet kitchen towel for 15 seconds, and turn out the mold onto a serving plate.   SERVES 8.

Collard Beef

one 3-pound beef brisket
1 tablespoon salt
1 teaspoon ground allspice
1 teaspoon ground cloves
1 teaspoon ground ginger
1 teaspoon grated nutmeg
1 teaspoon cracked black pepper
1 teaspoon dried sage, crushed
1 teaspoon dried thyme, crushed
8 slices lean bacon
4 bay leaves
whole-grain Irish mustard

Have the butcher cut the brisket with the grain into 3 "slabs." In a bowl mix the salt, allspice, cloves, ginger, nutmeg, pepper, sage, and the thyme, and rub the mixture over the slabs of brisket on all sides. Place 4 slices of bacon between each layer, and tie the brisket securely with kitchen string 3 times in each direction to make a "package" that will keep its shape in cooking. Place the brisket in a deep baking dish with the bay leaves and enough water to cover it, and braise it, covered, in a preheated 425°F. oven for 3 to 3½ hours, or until the meat is tender, adding water when necessary to keep the brisket covered.

Drain, cool, and refrigerate the brisket, covered with plastic wrap, for 24 hours. Remove the strings and serve the brisket neatly sliced with the mustard.
SERVES 6.

Summer Pudding

slices white bread, preferably 1 day old, crusts removed
2 pounds raspberries
¼ pound red currants (if available, if not, they are not necessary)
sugar to taste

Line the bottom and sides of a 1-quart pudding basin with the bread slices overlapping, and cut the bread so it is level with the top of the bowl.

In a saucepan combine the raspberries, currants, and sugar, and bring the mixture to a simmer over moderate heat, gently stirring just until the sugar melts, the raspberries are crushed, and the liquid boils. Pour the hot fruit mixture into the prepared bowl, cover the top with bread, and trim the bread so it is even with the edge of the bowl. Cover the bread with plastic wrap, put a weighted plate or saucer (whichever fits best) on top, place the basin on a large plate, and leave overnight. To serve the pudding, remove the plate and the plastic wrap, and invert the pudding onto a serving dish.   SERVES 6.

Marmalade Cake

1 stick (½ cup) butter or margarine
1 cup superfine sugar
2 large eggs
1 cup plus 2 tablespoons sifted self-rising flour
2 rounded tablespoons marmalade with the peel

Grease a 2-pound loaf pan, and line it with parchment or waxed paper. In a bowl with an electric mixer cream the butter or margarine with the sugar until the mixture is light and fluffy; add the eggs, 1 at a time, beating, and fold in the flour a third at a time. Add the marmalade and blend the mixture until it is combined well. Pour the batter into the prepared pan, smooth the top, and bake in the middle of a preheated 350°F. oven for 1 hour, or until a tester comes out clean, checking the cake after 30 minutes and covering the top with a piece of parchment paper or aluminum foil if the cake browns too quickly. Cool the cake in the pan for 20 minutes, invert it onto a rack, and let it cool completely.   SERVES 6 TO 8.

Chocolate Cake

6 ounces dark chocolate

2 sticks (1 cup) unsalted butter

2 cups superfine sugar

1¹/₄ cups self-rising flour

a pinch of salt

3 large eggs, lightly beaten

¹/₃ cup ground almonds

¹/₃ cup ground rice

3 tablespoons milk, heated

In the top of a double boiler over hot, not boiling, water, melt the chocolate, stirring occasionally; re-move it from the heat, and let it cool. In a large bowl with an electric mixer cream the butter with the sugar at high speed until the mixture is light and fluffy. At low speed add the flour mixed with the salt alternately with the eggs, beginning and ending with the flour mixture and beating the batter after each addition until it is just combined. Add the almonds, rice, and chocolate, beating just until combined, and beat in the hot milk. Pour the batter into a buttered 9- to 10-inch tube pan, and bake in a preheated 350°F. oven for 1 hour, or until a cake tester comes out clean. Cool the cake in the pan for 20 minutes, invert it onto a rack, and let it cool completely.

SERVES 10.

ANOUSHKA HEMPEL
(LADY WEINBERG)

Raspberry Mille-Feuille

¹/₂ pound puff pastry

Crème Pâtissière (recipe follows)

four ¹/₂-pint boxes fresh raspberries

confectioners' sugar

Roll out the pastry onto a lightly floured surface to a ¹/₈-inch-thick rectangle, and with a fork prick it all over to prevent the pastry from rising. Transfer the pastry to a large baking sheet and refrigerate it for 10 minutes. Bake the pastry in a preheated 425°F. oven for 10 to 15 minutes, or until it is lightly browned and cooked through, and cool it on the baking sheet on a rack. Cut the pastry into 3 equal narrow rectangles, cover one side of each of 2 rectangles with half of the crème patissière and then half of the raspberries, carefully lift one filled pastry rectangle onto the other filled pastry rectangle, and top it with the remaining pastry rectangle. Sprinkle the top with the confectioners' sugar.   SERVES 8.

Crème Pâtissière

6 large egg yolks

¹/₂ cup castor or superfine sugar

6 tablespoons all-purpose flour

2 cups milk

1 vanilla bean

confectioners' sugar

In a bowl combine the egg yolks, sugar, flour, and a little of the milk, and mix well. In a medium sauce-pan combine the remaining milk and the vanilla bean, heat to a boil, and pour the milk mixture in a stream into the egg-yolk mixture, whisking con-stantly. Pour the mixture into the saucepan, cleaned, and cook it over moderately low heat, stirring until it comes to a boil, and boil for 2 minutes. Pour the mixture into a metal bowl to cool, and sprinkle it with the confectioners' sugar to prevent a skin from forming.

Poached Pears in Red Wine Fruit Jelly

1 lemon

8 small William pears

zest of 1 orange, removed with a vegetable peeler

1 bottle good red wine

1/2 cup sugar

1/4 cinnamon stick

1 whole clove

4 envelopes unflavored gelatine

1/2 cup water

Remove the lemon zest using a vegetable peeler, halve the lemon, and squeeze the juice into a bowl. Peel and core the pears, and rub them with the lemon juice to prevent them from browning. In a large saucepan combine the lemon zest, orange zest, wine, sugar, cinnamon and clove, and stir the mixture until the sugar dissolves. Arrange the pears close together but not touching in the saucepan, cover them with waxed paper and then the lid, bring the wine mixture to a boil, and simmer the pears for 15 to 20 minutes, or until they are tender. Cool the pears in the wine mixture.

When the pears are cool, remove them from the pan, and set aside. In a small bowl, sprinkle the gelatine over the 1/2 cup of water, and let the mixture stand for 5 minutes, or until the gelatine is softened. Heat the wine mixture until it is very warm, add the softened gelatine, and stir until it is dissolved. Pour half of the gelatine mixture into a serving bowl, and refrigerate it until set. Arrange the pears on top, add the remaining gelatine mixture, and refrigerate it until it is set. Once the jelly has set, the pears should give the impression of floating on top.   SERVES 4.

Chocolate Yule Log

THE CAKE

6 large eggs, separated

1 cup castor or superfine sugar

4 to 6 ounces unsweetened chocolate, melted and cooled

1 1/2 cups all-purpose flour

1 tablespoon confectioners' sugar

THE ICING

1 cup heavy cream

6 ounces bittersweet chocolate, melted and cooled

1 teaspoon vanilla extract

THE FILLING

1 cup heavy cream

2 tablespoons confectioners' sugar

Make the cake: In a large bowl with an electric mixer beat the egg yolks with the sugar at high speed until the sugar dissolves. Beat in the chocolate until it is blended; and fold in the flour just until it is combined. In a large bowl with an electric mixer beat the egg whites at high speed until they hold stiff peaks, and fold them into the cake batter until no white streaks remain. Pour the mixture into an oiled jelly-roll pan lined with oiled waxed paper, and bake the cake in a preheated 350°F. oven for 15 minutes, or until the cake shrinks back from the edges of the pan and springs back when lightly pressed with a fingertip. Sprinkle the cake with the confectioners' sugar, cover it with a damp, clean kitchen towel and a baking sheet, and invert the cake onto the towel. Remove the jelly-roll pan, and gently peel the waxed paper from the cake. Starting at one short end, roll up the cake and the towel jelly-roll fashion (it will crack slightly), and let it cool completely on a rack.

Make the icing: In a small saucepan combine the heavy cream and chocolate, and heat the mixture over low heat, stirring frequently, until the chocolate melts and the icing is smooth. Chill the mixture for 30 minutes, or until it is thick enough to spread.

When the cake is completely cool and the icing is thick, make the filling: In a small bowl with an electric mixer beat the heavy cream with the sugar until the mixture holds stiff peaks.

Carefully unroll the cake, spread it with the filling, and reroll it without the towel. Place the cake seam side down on a serving plate, and cover it with the icing.   SERVES 10.

English Trifle

THE SPONGE CAKE
3 large eggs, separated

1 cup granulated sugar

1 teaspoon grated lemon zest

$^1/_4$ cup boiling water

1 tablespoon lemon juice

1 cup sifted cake flour

$1^1/_2$ teaspoons baking powder

$^1/_2$ teaspoon salt

2 cups light cream

$^1/_4$ cup granulated sugar

4 large egg yolks

1 tablespoon vanilla extract

one 12-ounce jar seedless raspberry jam

$^1/_2$ cup sherry

3 cups heavy cream

$^1/_2$ cup confectioners' sugar

2 cups raspberries, sweetened to taste

sliced bananas (optional)

sliced pears (optional)

candied angelica (optional)

toasted slivered almonds (optional)

Two days before serving, make the cake: In a large bowl with an electric mixer beat the egg yolks at high speed until they are light yellow. Add the sugar and lemon zest, and beat at high speed for 5 minutes, or until the sugar is dissolved. Add the boiling water and the lemon juice, and beat at high speed for 5 minutes, or until the mixture is cool. In a sieve combine the flour, baking powder, and salt, sift the mixture over the egg-yolk mixture, and fold in just until the dry ingredients are moistened. In a small bowl beat the egg whites with an electric mixer at high speed until they hold stiff peaks. Pour the batter into two 9-inch round cake pans lined with parchment paper, and bake the layers in a preheated 350°F. oven for 20 minutes, or until the tops spring back when gently pressed. Cool the cakes in the pans for 10 minutes, invert them onto a rack, remove the papers, and let them stand overnight or until they are slightly stale.

The day before serving: In a medium saucepan heat the light cream with the sugar, stirring until the sugar is dissolved and the cream is hot. In a bowl beat the egg yolks until blended and whisk in the hot cream mixture in a steady stream until the mixture is blended. Pour the mixture into the saucepan, cleaned, and cook it over low heat, stirring constantly, until it coats the back of a spoon. Pour the mixture into a bowl, and refrigerate it covered with plastic wrap placed directly on the surface to prevent a skin from forming.

Cut the cake layers into finger-length pieces, spread one side of each piece with the jam, and sprinkle the cake pieces with the sherry. In a large bowl with an electric mixer beat the heavy cream with the confectioners' sugar until it holds stiff peaks. Arrange half of the cake pieces, jam side up, in a glass bowl, cover them with half each of the raspberries, bananas and pears, cover the fruit with half of the custard and then one quarter of the sweetened whipped cream. Repeat the layers of the cake, fruit, custard, and whipped cream. With the remaining whipped cream in a pastry bag fitted with a rosette tip, decorate the top of the trifle, and garnish it with the angelica and almonds. Red roses also look very pretty on top. Refrigerate the trifle for at least 12 hours before serving.   SERVES 10 TO 12.

Fresh Scotch Salmon Cakes

1 stick (¹/₂ cup) butter
1¹/₄ cups all-purpose flour, plus additional for dredging
1¹/₂ cups milk, scalded
1 pound cooked salmon, flaked
¹/₂ cup chopped parsley
freshly grated nutmeg
salt and pepper to taste
1 large egg, beaten lightly
fine fresh white bread crumbs
vegetable oil for frying
lemon wedges
Parsley Sauce (recipe follows)
Deep-fried Parsley (recipe follows)

In a small saucepan melt the butter over low heat, stir in the 1¹/₄ cups flour, and cook the roux, stirring, for 3 minutes. Remove the pan from the heat and add the scalded milk in a stream, whisking vigorously until the mixture is thick and smooth, and bring the sauce to a boil, stirring. Simmer the sauce for 5 minutes, and stir in the salmon, parsley, and nutmeg, and salt and pepper. Spread the mixture in an even layer in a jelly-roll pan, cover with plastic wrap, and refrigerate for a few hours, until well chilled.

For each fish cake, lightly pat one eighth of the salmon mixture into a ball, flatten into a ¹/₂-inch-thick cake, dredge in flour, coat with the egg, letting the excess drip off, and coat with the bread crumbs. In a large heavy skillet heat the oil over moderately high heat and sauté the fish cakes, turning them with a spatula, until golden brown. Serve with the lemon wedges and the parsley sauce, and garnish with the deep-fried parsley. SERVES 4.

Parsley Sauce

¹/₂ stick (¹/₄ cup) butter
2 tablespoons all-purpose flour
1¹/₂ cups milk
2 tablespoons heavy cream
2 tablespoons chopped parsley
1 large egg, hard-boiled, chopped coarse
salt and pepper to taste

In a small saucepan melt the butter over low heat, stir in the flour, and cook the roux, stirring, for 3 minutes. Remove the pan from the heat, add the milk in a stream, whisking vigorously until the sauce is thick and smooth, and bring it to a boil, stirring. Stir in the heavy cream and strain the sauce through a fine sieve into another small saucepan. Gently stir the parsley and egg into the sauce, and season with salt and pepper.

Deep-Fried Parsley

vegetable oil for deep-frying
sprigs fresh parsley, washed well and dried very well

In a large heavy saucepan heat 1¹/₂ inches of oil until very hot. With the parsley in a frying basket or sieve, plunge the parsley into the oil and cook it until the hissing stops. Lift out the basket and drain the parsley well on paper towels.

Roasted Capon

one 5-pound capon
root vegetables, chopped coarse
vegetable oil
chicken broth
crisp rolls of bacon
grilled chipolata sausages
Bread Sauce (recipe follows)

Place the capon on a rack in a roasting pan with the root vegetables, brush the capon and vegetables with the oil, and roast them in a preheated 325°F. oven for 1¹/₂ hours, basting the capon and vegetables every 10 minutes with the pan drippings and the oil, and turning the vegetables as they brown.

Remove the capon and vegetables to a serving platter and remove the rack from the pan. Skim the fat from the pan, place the pan with the pan juices on the stove top over moderately high heat, add the chicken broth, scraping up the brown bits in the pan, and reduce the liquid until it is thick enough to coat the back of a spoon. Strain the gravy through a fine sieve into a sauceboat, and pass it and the bread sauce with the capon, bacon, and sausages.

SERVES 6.

Bread Sauce

1¹/₂ cups milk

1 small onion

2 cups fine fresh brown bread crumbs

freshly grated nutmeg

salt and pepper to taste

2 tablespoons butter

*I*n a small saucepan heat the milk with the onion over moderately low heat until the milk boils, and stir in the bread crumbs. Let the sauce stand over very low heat, or place the pan in another pan of simmering water for 20 minutes. Remove the onion, season the sauce with the nutmeg and salt and pepper, and whisk in the butter until blended.

MAXIME DE LA FALAISE

Brie Tart

"Take a crust inch deep in a trap; take yolks of eggs raw and cheese ruayn and meddle it and the yolks together and do thereto powder, ginger, sugar, safron, and salt, do it in a trap, bake it well and serve it forth."
—*The Forme of Cury, 1378*

THE PASTRY

3 cups all-purpose flour

¹/₄ teaspoon salt

1 stick (¹/₂ cup) butter

6 to 8 tablespoons ice water

¹/₂ cup cold vegetable shortening

THE FILLING

2¹/₂ cups heavy cream

¹/₄ pound Brie, rind discarded

1 teaspoon saffron threads, crushed

1 teaspoon sugar

¹/₂ teaspoon ground ginger

salt and pepper to taste

3 large eggs

2 large egg yolks

*M*ake the pastry: In a bowl combine the flour and the salt. Add half of the butter, and with a pastry blender, cut it into the flour mixture until it resembles coarse crumbs. Add the ice water, 1 tablespoon at a time, mixing with a fork until the pastry holds

together. On a lightly floured surface with a lightly floured rolling pin, roll out the pastry into a 5-inch-wide strip. Dot two thirds of the length of the surface of the pastry with half of the shortening, and fold the dough crosswise into thirds like you would fold a letter, with the plain end of the pastry folded first over the shortening on the middle of the pastry strip. Sprinkle the pastry with flour, wrap it in plastic wrap, and refrigerate it for 20 minutes. When chilled, roll out the pastry into a 5-inch-wide strip, dot two thirds of the length of the surface with the remaining butter, fold up the dough as for the first rolling, and roll it out again into a 5-inch-wide strip. Dot two thirds of the length of the surface with the remaining shortening, fold it into thirds, sprinkle it with flour, and chill it, covered, for 20 minutes. Roll out the pastry, fold it into thirds again, and chill it, covered, until ready to make the tart.

Make the filling: In a small baking dish combine the heavy cream, the Brie, and the saffron, and bake the mixture, covered, in a preheated 200°F. oven for 20 to 30 minutes, or until the cheese has just melted and the saffron has dissolved and colored the cream. While the cheese mixture bakes, roll out the pastry on a lightly floured surface, fit it into a 10-inch quiche dish, prick it lightly with a fork, and when the cheese mixture is out of the oven, bake the pastry shell in a preheated 425°F. oven for 10 minutes.

Transfer the cheese mixture to a blender or food processor and blend it until it is smooth. Add the sugar and the ginger, and blend well, seasoning carefully with salt and pepper. In a bowl beat the eggs and egg yolks until blended, add the cheese mixture, and beat until the mixture is blended. Pour e cheese mixture into the partially baked pastry shell, and bake it in a preheated 350°F. oven for 30 minutes, or until the filling is set and puffy.

SERVES 5 TO 6.

Maxime's Curried Apricot and Fresh Mint Soup

1 pound (2 cups) chicken cooked

8 dried apricots, poached in 1 cup water and drained (reserve the poaching liquid)

2 tablespoons butter

1 tablespoon curry powder

a pinch of cayenne

salt and black pepper to taste

2 tablespoons all-purpose flour

3 cups homemade chicken broth

1 cup heavy cream

4 tablespoons finely chopped fresh mint leaves

6 sprigs fresh mint for garnish

In a blender, combine the chicken, 4 of the apricots, and the poaching liquid from the apricots, and puree the mixture. In a nonstick saucepan melt the butter over moderately low heat, add the curry powder and cayenne, season with salt and pepper, and stir in the flour. Cook the roux, stirring, for 1 minute, and pour in the chicken broth in a steady stream. Bring to a boil over moderately high heat, stirring, and add the chicken mixture, the 4 remaining apricots, minced, and the heavy cream. Simmer the mixture, stirring occasionally, for 15 minutes, until it is reduced slightly, and stir in the chopped mint. Let the mixture infuse over low heat, covered, for 5 minutes, and adjust the seasoning before serving. Serve each portion garnished with a mint sprig. The soup can also be chilled and served cold. SERVES 6.

Medieval Hedgehogs
(YRCHOUNS)

"Take Piggis mawys, & skalde hem wel; take groundyn Porke, & knede it with Spicerye, with pouder Gyngere, & Salt & Sugre; do it on the mawe, but fille it nowt to fulle; then sewe hem with a fayre threde, & putte hem in a Spete as men don piggys; take blaunchid Almaundys, & kerf jem long, smal, & scharpe, & frye jem in grece & sugre; take a litel prycke, & prykke the yrchouns, An putte in the holes the Almaundys, every hole jalf, & eche fro other; ley hem then to the fyre; when they ben rostid, dore hem sum whyth Whete Flowre, & mylke of Almaundys, sum grene, sum blake with Blode, & lat hem nowt brone to moche, & serve forth."

—Two fifteenth-century cookery books

This must have been a nursery dish to amuse children in the mid-fifteenth century!

2 pounds (4 cups) ground pork, veal, or chicken, or a mixture of these

2 tablespoons coarse bread crumbs

2 large egg yolks, beaten

1 tablespoon butter, softened

2 teaspoons salt

1/2 teaspoon ground ginger

1/2 teaspoon ground mace

1/4 teaspoon ground black pepper

2 pitted black olives, cut into eighths

1/3 cup slivered almonds

4 tablespoons vegetable broth

lettuce leaves

In a bowl combine the ground meat, bread crumbs, egg yolks, half of the butter, the salt, ginger, mace, and pepper, and mix gently. Form the mixture into balls with a little snout. Place a sliver of olive into the snout and make eyes with the remaining olive slivers. Stick the almonds into the remaining ball to make quills. Place the hedgehogs in a deep baking pan with the vegetable broth and bake, covered, in a preheated 375°F. oven for 1 hour, basting occasionally with the remaining butter, melted into the vegetable broth in the pan. Serve on the lettuce leaves, a hedgehog's favorite meal. SERVES 8.

Barthelmas Beef

"To make barthelmas beef:

Take a fat brisket of beef and bone it and put it into so much water as will cover it, shifting it three times a day for three days together, then put it into as much white wine and vinegar as will cover it; and when it hath lyen twenty-four hours, take it out and drye it in a clothe, then take nutmeg, ginger, cinnamon, cloves and mace of each a like quantity, beaten small and mingled with a good handfull of salt. Strew both sides of the beef with this, and roul it up as you do Brawn; tye it as close as you can, then put it into an earthen pot, and cover it with some paste, set it into the oven when household bread and when it is col, eat it with mustard and sugar."

—Hannah Wolley, 1664

ground cinnamon

ground cloves

ground ginger

ground mace

ground nutmeg

salt

a beef brisket

cooked root vegetables if serving the brisket hot, or a blend of mustard and brown sugar to taste if serving the brisket cold

In a small bowl mix equal amounts of the cinnamon, cloves, ginger, mace, and nutmeg. In a flour shaker combine an equal amount of the spice mixture and salt, and sprinkle the mixture over the brisket. Place the brisket in a deep baking dish with enough water to cover it, cover the dish tightly with aluminum foil, and then cover the foil with the lid to the dish. Bake the brisket in a 350°F. oven for 30 minutes to the pound of meat, or until the brisket is tender when tested with a thin skewer. Drain the brisket, and serve it hot with the root vegetables or cold as a salad with the mustard mixture.

Asparagus in Cream

"Take your large asparagus, and cut them in pieces, half an inch long, as far as they are green; then stove them in clear strong broth till crisp and tender; season them with pepper, salt, and nutmeg and a little onion; then toss them up thick with the yolks of eggs beat up in a little white wine and cream, and some thick butter, and so serve them, and garnish with lemon."

—John Farley, 1783

2 large egg yolks

1 cup heavy cream

a pinch of nutmeg

1 pound asparagus, trimmed, lightly cooked

salt and pepper to taste

4 crispy French rolls

3 tablespoons butter

In the top of a double boiler combine the egg yolks and heavy cream, and cook, stirring, over simmering, not boiling water, until the mixture is hot and thickened, and coats the back of a spoon. Transfer the mixture to a blender or food processor. Reserve 4 or 8 perfect asparagus spears. Cut the remaining asparagus into 1-inch pieces, place them in the blender with the egg-yolk mixture, puree, and season with salt and pepper.

Split open the rolls, discard some of the bread from inside them, and in a skillet sauté the rolls in the butter over moderate heat; or, brush the rolls with the butter, melted, and brown them in a hot oven. Fill each roll with some of the pureed asparagus mixture, and arrange 1 or 2 of the reserved asparagus spears on top so that the tips are visible. Cover with the top of the rolls. SERVES 4.

Brown Bread Ice Cream

A traditional English country house dessert since time immemorial.

> 1 pint vanilla ice cream, softened
>
> 1 1/2 cups coarse brown- or black-bread crumbs, dried in the oven
>
> 2 tablespoons Cognac
>
> 1 pint strawberries steeped in liqueur of choice to taste

In a bowl combine the ice cream, bread crumbs, and Cognac, and stir the mixture until blended. Refreeze the ice-cream mixture until it is firm, but not hard, and serve it with the steeped berries. SERVES 4.

Medieval Bread and Butter Pudding

"Soupes dorye:
Take gode almaunde mulke y-draw wyth wyn, an let
hem boyle togederis, an caste ther-to Safroun & Salt; an
than take Paynemayn, an kytte it an toste it, an wete it
in wyne, an ley it on a dysshe, an caste the syryp ther-
on. An than make a dragge of powder Gyngere, Sugre,
canel, Clowes, Maces, an caste ther-on. When it is
y-dressid, an serye thanne forth for a pottage gode."
—Two fifteenth-century cookery books

> 10 slices of brioche bread
>
> 1 stick (1/2 cup) butter, softened
>
> 1 cup white wine
>
> 2 1/2 cups half-and-half
>
> a pinch of saffron
>
> a pinch of salt
>
> 4 large eggs
>
> 3 tablespoons sugar
>
> almond extract to taste
>
> 1/4 teaspoon ground cinnamon
>
> 1/4 teaspoon ground cloves
>
> 1/4 teaspoon ground ginger
>
> 1/4 teaspoon ground mace
>
> additional ground cinnamon, cloves, ginger, and mace for garnish

Spread the bread slices with the butter, arrange them in layers with the crusts up in an earthenware baking dish, and sprinkle the bread with a little of the wine. In a small saucepan combine the half-and-half, saffron, and salt, and heat the mixture over moderately low heat, stirring, until it is almost to a boil. In a bowl, whisk the eggs with the sugar until blended, and add the hot milk mixture in a stream, whisking, and beat in the remaining wine, almond extract, cinnamon, cloves, ginger, and mace until the mixture is combined well, and pour it over the buttered bread. Place the baking dish in a roasting pan on the middle rack of a preheated 350°F. oven, pour enough boiling water into the roasting pan to come halfway up the sides of the baking dish, and bake the pudding for 25 minutes, or until the custard is set. Sprinkle with a dusting of additional spices and serve the pudding warm. SERVES 6 TO 8.

NOTE: *The quantity of custard and spices may be doubled if a richer, creamier dessert is desired; the bread absorbs a lot of the liquid. When reheated, this dish will swell up again in the pan like a soufflé!*

Roast Chicken with Herbs

1 teaspoon Provence herbs (optional)
1 teaspoon salt
$^1/_2$ teaspoon freshly ground pepper
$^1/_2$ teaspoon dried thyme leaves, crumbled
one 3-pound chicken or 3 poussins
3 tablespoons butter, softened
3 tablespoons water

In a small bowl combine the Provence herbs, the salt, pepper and thyme, and mix well. Wash the chicken inside and out under cold water and pat it dry with paper towels. Using a spatula, spread 1 tablespoon of the butter over the inside of the chicken, and sprinkle the inside with 1 teaspoon of the herb mixture. Truss the chicken, rub the remaining 2 tablespoons of butter over the outside, sprinkle the chicken with the remaining herb mixture, and refrigerate it for 1 hour.

Place the chicken on a wire rack in a roasting pan, and bake it in a preheated 450°F. oven (425°F. if using poussins) for 45 minutes, or until it is cooked. Remove the chicken to a warm platter, remove the rack from the pan, skim off and discard any fat from the pan juices, and with the pan on the stove top over moderately high heat, bring the pan juices and the 3 tablespoons water to a boil, scraping the pan to remove any browned bits. Serve the pan juices with the chicken. Have the rest of the meal ready when the bird is cooked so the chicken does not stand for more than a few minutes after it is taken from the oven.

SERVES 6.

Chocolate Soufflé with Whipped Cream and Chocolate Sauce

2 tablespoons butter
2 tablespoons all-purpose flour
1 cup milk
$^1/_2$ vanilla bean
4 ounces bittersweet chocolate, finely grated
$^1/_3$ cup boiling water
3 large egg yolks
3 tablespoons granulated sugar
$^1/_4$ teaspoon salt
5 large egg whites
confectioners' sugar for garnish
Hot Chocolate Sauce (recipe follows)
whipped cream

In a large heavy saucepan melt the butter over moderate heat, stir in the flour, and cook the roux, stirring, for 3 minutes; remove the pan from the heat. In a small saucepan combine the milk and vanilla bean, bring the milk to a boil, pour it through a sieve into the roux in a stream, whisking vigorously until the mixture is thick and smooth, and bring it to a boil, stirring. Remove the pan from the heat, and add the chocolate and boiling water, stirring until the chocolate melts. Add the egg yolks, one at a time, beating well after each, the sugar and the salt. Stir the mixture vigorously for 4 or 5 minutes, or until it is smooth and shiny. (The mixture can be kept warm for 30 minutes with waxed paper placed directly on the surface to keep a skin from forming.)

In a large bowl with an electric mixer beat the egg whites at high speed until they hold soft peaks, and with a rubber spatula or large flat spoon fold them into the soufflé mixture. Spoon the mixture into a heated 2-quart soufflé dish or into 4 to 6 individual heated soufflé dishes to fill them three quarters full. Place the soufflé in a preheated 450°F.

oven, increase the temperature to 475°F. for 5 minutes to make up the heat loss when the oven was opened, and return the temperature to 450°F. Bake the soufflé for 20 to 25 minutes and the individual soufflés for 12 to 13 minutes. Remove the soufflé from the oven, dust it with the confectioners' sugar, and serve it with the chocolate sauce and whipped cream. SERVES 4 TO 6.

Hot Chocolate Sauce

1¹/₂ ounces bittersweet chocolate, grated

2 tablespoons sugar

a small piece of vanilla bean

1 cup water

In a small saucepan combine the chocolate, sugar, vanilla bean and water; bring the mixture to a boil over moderate heat, stirring, and simmer it for 15 to 20 minutes, stirring frequently. The sauce may be made ahead of serving and reheated.

Game Pie

2 ounces dried morels

1 cup warm water

¹/₂ pound double-smoked bacon, diced fine

2¹/₂ sticks (1¹/₄ cups) butter

24 pearl onions

1 pound shallots, peeled

1 bunch carrots, peeled, cut diagonally into ¹/₂-inch pieces

5 cups well-flavored chicken broth

1¹/₂ pounds button mushrooms, cleaned, trimmed

¹/₄ cup vegetable oil

12 doves (optional)

8 venison sausages

8 quail

2 pheasants, quartered

8 cloves garlic, crushed

one 10-ounce package frozen baby peas

1 cup dry white wine

1 cup Armagnac

1 cup crème fraîche

1 cup all-purpose flour

¹/₂ cup chopped parsley

1 tablespoon dried thyme leaves, crushed

2 tablespoons Worcestershire sauce

5 or 6 dashes hot red-pepper sauce

salt and freshly ground black pepper to taste

one 17¹/₂-ounce package frozen puff pastry, thawed

1 large egg, beaten

In a small bowl soak the morels in the warm water for 15 minutes. In the meantime, in a large Dutch oven sauté the bacon in 4 tablespoons of the butter until crisp. Add the onions, shallots, and carrots, sauté the mixture for 5 minutes, and add 1 cup of the broth. Bring the liquid to a boil, simmer it for 5 minutes, and set it aside.

In a large skillet sauté the mushrooms in the oil over moderately high heat until they are browned, and add them to the vegetable mixture. Smear the doves (if using), sausages, quail, and pheasants with the garlic, sauté them in the skillet in 4 tablespoons of the butter, in batches, until they are browned on all sides, and set them aside.

Strain the morels through a double thickness of cheesecloth, squeezing the morels to extract their liquid, and reserve the liquid. Rinse the morels under cold water to clean them well, and add them and the peas to the vegetable mixture in the Dutch oven.

In a bowl combine the remaining 4 cups of broth with the morel liquid, wine, Armagnac, and crème fraîche. In a large saucepan melt 1¹/₂ sticks of the butter over moderate heat, stir in the flour, and cook the roux for 3 minutes, stirring. Add the broth mixture, 1 cup at a time, whisking vigorously until the mixture is thickened and smooth. Bring the mixture to a boil, whisking, and simmer it for 3 minutes. Add it to the vegetable mixture with the parsley, thyme, Worcestershire, hot-pepper sauce, and salt and pepper.

Arrange the sausage mixture in a large pie dish and add the vegetable mixture. Shake the dish to settle the ingredients, and let them cool completely. Note: *The pie can be made up to this point and refrigerated overnight.*

Insert an upside down spice jar in the center of the mixture to raise the pastry. Roll out the pastry as the package label directs, joining the seams if necessary, and cover the pie dish with the pastry. Trim the edges of the pastry and use the scraps to decorate the top. Make a few slits in the pastry for vent holes, brush the pastry with the beaten egg, and sprinkle it with salt. Bake the pie on the middle rack of a preheated 450°F. oven for 25 minutes. Remove the pie from the oven, lower the rack one notch, and bake the pie at 400°F. for 20 minutes, placing a sheet of aluminum foil over the pie to prevent overbrowning. Let the pie sit for 10 minutes before serving.

SERVES 12 TO 16.

MARILYN EVINS

Fried Whitebait

2 pounds fresh whitebait

clarified butter and vegetable oil for deep-frying

all-purpose flour seasoned with salt and pepper for dredging

several lemons, the zest removed with a vegetable peeler and carved into twists, and the lemons sliced

small bunches fresh basil

Tartar Sauce (recipe follows)

Thoroughly rinse the whitebait in cold water, and pat them dry with paper towels. In a large deep skillet heat $1/8$ inch of the clarified butter with $3/4$ inch of vegetable oil until it is very hot. Roll the whitebait, a few at a time, in the flour, and place them in a frying basket. Fry them in the hot fat just until they curl up slightly—but do not let them brown—and turn them out onto paper towels to drain. Pat them with paper towels to absorb any excess fat. Repeat until all the whitebait are fried, place them on a platter with the lemon zest, sliced lemons, and basil. Serve the fried whitebait with the tartar sauce.

SERVES 4.

Tartar Sauce

THE MAYONNAISE

2 large egg yolks

1 tablespoon Dijon mustard

$1^{1}/4$ cups light olive oil or peanut oil

1 teaspoon salt

$1/8$ teaspoon white pepper

2 tablespoons lemon juice

1 tablespoon finely chopped chervil (optional)

1 tablespoon finely chopped chives

1 tablespoon finely chopped parsley

1 tablespoon finely chopped tarragon leaves

1 tablespoon capers

1 small sour pickle, chopped fine

Make the mayonnaise: In a small bowl beat the egg yolks and mustard together, and slowly add the oil, beating continually. Add the salt, pepper, and lemon juice, and beat for a few seconds longer. Put the mayonnaise in a cool place until using.

In a small bowl combine the mayonnaise, chervil (if desired), chives, parsley, tarragon, capers, and the pickle, and mix until blended.

Compote of Dried Fruit with Devonshire Cream

1/2 pound dried Australian apricots

1/2 pound large dried Australian peaches

1/2 pound dried Australian pears

1/2 pound extra-large prunes with pits

1/4 pound dried apples

1/4 pound dried mangoes

1/2 pound dried Michigan Bing cherries

1/2 pound dried Michigan sour cherries

2 large (1.5 litre) bottles mineral water

2 750 ml. bottles very fine white drinking wine

the zest of 3 lemons, removed with a vegetable peeler

1 vanilla bean, split lengthwise

curled ribbons of candied peel from 6 lemons

very cold Devonshire cream

milk (optional)

Rinse all the dried fruit. In a kettle, combine the mineral water, wine, lemon zest, and vanilla bean; bring the liquid to a boil, and reduce it by half. Add the apricots, peaches, pears, prunes, apples, and mangoes. (The juice should just cover the top of the fruit.) Bring the liquid to a boil, add the Bing cherries and the sour cherries, and simmer the fruit just until it is *al dente*—just chewy, not tender. Remove the kettle from the heat, and cool the fruit until it is warm, not hot.

Serve the compote with masses of the candied peel and the Devonshire cream, placed on the side. (The cream should be the consistency of sour cream—it should not form stiff peaks. If it is too thick, add a bit of milk.)   SERVES 10 TO 12.

French Almond Lace Cookies

2/3 cup blanched almonds, ground fine in a blender

1/2 cup sugar

1/2 cup margarine

1 tablespoon all-purpose flour

2 tablespoons milk

In a heavy saucepan combine the almonds, sugar, margarine, flour, and milk. Cook the mixture, stirring, over moderate heat until the margarine melts. Drop teaspoonfuls of the mixture at least 2 inches apart onto greased baking sheets, and bake the cookies in batches in the middle of a preheated 350°F. oven for 8 minutes, watching the cookies carefully, until they are golden. Let the cookies cool briefly, and with a metal spatula, working with one cookie at a time, loosen the cookies from the sheet, drape them with the rough side out over a rolling pin (or an exceptionally clean broom handle!), and let them stand until they are completely cool.   MAKES ABOUT TWO DOZEN COOKIES.

Ravioloni
(LARGE RAVIOLI OF RICOTTA)

THE PASTA DOUGH
2¹/₂ to 3 cups all-purpose flour
a pinch of salt
3 large eggs, beaten lightly

THE FILLING
²/₃ cup ricotta cheese
¹/₂ cup grated Parmesan cheese
¹/₃ cup cooked chopped, fresh spinach
1 tablespoon finely chopped parsley
1 medium egg, beaten lightly
freshly grated nutmeg to taste
salt to taste

butter to taste, softened
additional grated Parmesan to taste
fresh sage leaves, minced, to taste

Make the pasta dough: In a food processor blend 2¹/₂ cups of the flour, the salt, and eggs until the mixture just begins to form a ball, adding more flour if necessary to make a firm, not sticky, dough. Turn out the dough onto a lightly floured surface, and knead it a few times. Let the dough stand, covered with an inverted bowl, at room temperature for 1 hour.

Make the filling: In a bowl, mix the ricotta with the Parmesan, spinach, parsley, egg, and nutmeg, and salt until blended.

Make the ravioloni: Divide the pasta dough into 8 pieces, flatten each piece into a rectangle with two sides the width of the pasta machine rollers, and work with one rectangle at a time, keeping the remainder under an inverted bowl. Dust the pasta rectangle lightly with flour, and feed it through the rollers on the widest setting of the pasta machine. Fold the rolled pasta in half, and feed it through the rollers several times to knead the dough, folding the dough and dusting it lightly with flour each time. Adjust the rollers to the next setting, roll out the pasta sheet without folding it, and continue to roll it through increasingly lower settings to make a thinner dough with each rolling, until it is rolled through the machine set on the next to the lowest setting.

Repeat with another sheet of pasta. Spoon teaspoonfuls of the filling mixture over one rolled pasta sheet, spacing the mounds 3 inches apart, and cover the filled sheet with a plain pasta sheet, pressing lightly around the mounds to press out air bubbles and to attach the 2 pasta sheets, using a little water to glue the sheets together. Cut out the ravioloni using a round, square, or other shape cutter. Repeat with the remaining pasta rectangles and the filling.

In a large kettle of boiling salted water cook the ravioloni for 2 to 3 minutes, or until they are *al dente,* drain them in a colander, transfer them to a large bowl, and toss them with the butter, Parmesan, and sage. SERVES 4.

Red Snapper Livornese

4 red snapper fillets
flour for dredging
¹/₂ cup olive oil
¹/₂ cup finely chopped parsley
2 cloves garlic, chopped fine
1 cup crushed peeled Italian plum tomatoes
¹/₄ cup white wine
salt and pepper to taste

Lightly dredge the fillets in the flour, shaking off the excess. In a large skillet fry the fillets in the oil over moderate heat, transfer them to a plate, and in the fat in the skillet sauté the parsley and garlic for about 30 seconds; add the tomatoes and wine, and simmer the mixture, stirring occasionally, for 15 minutes. Add the fillets to the tomato mixture, season with salt and pepper, and simmer the mixture, covered, for 5 minutes. SERVES 4.

Rice Fritters

3 cups milk

1 cup Arborio rice (Italian short-grain rice, available at specialty food shops)

3 tablespoons granulated sugar

lemon zest, removed with a vegetable peeler, to taste

orange zest, removed with a vegetable peeler, to taste

2 large eggs, beaten lightly

1/2 cup all-purpose flour

vanilla extract to taste

vegetable oil for deep-frying

confectioners' sugar

In a medium nonstick saucepan bring the milk to a boil, stir in the rice, granulated sugar, lemon zest, and orange zest, and simmer the mixture, stirring frequently with a wooden spoon, until the rice is cooked. Remove the pan from the heat, and let the mixture stand until it is cool. Remove the lemon and orange zest, chop them fine, and stir them into the rice mixture. Add the eggs, flour, and vanilla, and stir until the mixture is blended. In a large deep skillet fry spoonfuls of the mixture in 2 inches of the oil, turning the fritters as they brown. Transfer them with a slotted spoon to paper towels to drain, and sprinkle them with the confectioners' sugar.

SERVES 4.

GLENN BERNBAUM

Seafood Salad in Lemon Aspic

THE ASPIC

3 envelopes unflavored gelatine

5 cups warm chicken broth

3/4 cup fresh lemon juice

the zest of 2 lemons, removed with a vegetable peeler, slivered

salt and ground white pepper to taste

olive oil for greasing the mold

10 avocado slices (from 1 1/2 avocados)

THE SALAD

20 large shrimp, peeled, deveined, cooked, chilled, and halved lengthwise

1 1/2 pounds lump crabmeat, free of shells

1 1/2 pounds cooked lobster meat, cut into 1/2-inch pieces, including 1 intact claw for garnish

THE DRESSING

1 1/2 cups mayonnaise

1/2 cup lemon juice

6 tablespoons snipped chives

salt and pepper to taste

watercress sprigs for garnish

Make the aspic: In a large bowl sprinkle the gelatine over 1 cup of the chicken broth, and let it stand for 5 minutes, or until the gelatine is softened. Pour in the remaining 4 cups of warm broth, and stir the mixture until the gelatine dissolves. Add the lemon juice, lemon zest, and season with the salt and white pepper. Place the bowl in a larger bowl of ice and water, and let the mixture stand, stirring frequently, until it is the consistency of raw egg whites. Remove the bowl from the ice water, ladle enough of the thickened aspic into an oiled 10-inch ring mold to fill it 1/2 inch, and gently push the avocado slices into the aspic using a paring knife to cut the slices to fit the curve of the mold. Refrigerate the mold until the aspic is set. Stir and gently warm the remaining aspic in a bowl of tepid water to keep it from setting while the avocado mixture sets. Fill the mold with the remaining aspic, thickened to the point that the lemon zest is suspended in it. Refrigerate the mold for 2 hours, or until it is set.

Make the salad: In a large bowl combine the shrimp, crabmeat, and lobster, and mix gently to keep the lumps of crabmeat intact. Refrigerate the mixture while preparing the dressing.

In a small bowl combine the mayonnaise and lemon juice, and whisk the mixture until it is smooth. Add the chives and season with salt and pepper. Using a rubber spatula gently fold half of the dressing into the seafood mixture, adding more dressing until the mixture is of the desired consistency, and adjust the seasoning to taste.

To serve, unmold the aspic by dipping the mold in a basin of warm water for a few seconds, releasing the aspic from the mold by running your index finger around the mold to allow air between the aspic and the mold, and invert the mold onto a chilled 16-inch platter. Carefully lift the mold from the aspic, using your fingers to release the mold or place a warm, damp kitchen towel over the mold. Spoon the salad into the center of the ring, arrange the watercress around the mold, and garnish the top of the salad with the lobster claw.   SERVES 10.

Beef Stew

5 pounds stewing beef, cut into 1-inch cubes

1 750 ml. bottle dry red wine

1/2 cup olive oil

1/2 cup all-purpose flour

2 tablespoons butter

fresh or canned beef stock

1 1/2 cups coarsely chopped carrots

1 1/2 cups coarsely chopped celery

1 1/2 cups coarsely chopped onions

1 cup red-wine vinegar

salt and pepper to taste

BOUQUET GARNI

2 bay leaves

2 cinnamon sticks

2 sprigs fresh thyme, or 1 teaspoon dried thyme

1 teaspoon fennel seeds

1 teaspoon dried oregano leaves, crushed

6 white peppercorns

4 whole cloves

1/4 cup anisette

1/4 cup muscatel wine

1 cup cooked carrots

24 pearl onions, cooked

12 medium mushroom caps, sautéed

3 tablespoons chopped parsley

The day before serving: In a large bowl combine the beef and the wine, mix well, cover with plastic wrap, and marinate the mixture in the refrigerator overnight.

The next day, drain the beef, pat it dry with paper towels, place it between sheets of waxed paper, and pound the meat gently with a meat mallet. In a large Dutch oven brown the meat in the oil in batches over moderate heat, and remove it to a large bowl. In the drippings in the pan brown the flour,

stirring it constantly, then add the butter, and stir it until it melts and blends with the flour mixture. Return the meat to the pan and stir it to mix it with the flour mixture. Add enough of the beef stock to cover the meat; add the carrots, celery, chopped onion, vinegar, and bouquet garni tied in a square of cheesecloth. Season with salt and pepper, and stir the mixture until it is combined. Bake the stew, covered, in a preheated 350°F. oven for 2 to 2 1/2 hours, or until the meat is tender when pressed with a fork, stirring the stew occasionally.

Transfer the meat and vegetables to a large bowl with a slotted spoon, discard the bouquet garni, bring the liquid to a boil over moderate heat, and simmer it for 15 to 20 minutes, or until it is reduced to coating consistency. Stir in the anisette and muscatel, return the meat mixture to the pan, and set it aside until ready to serve. Just before serving, reheat the stew over moderate heat stirring it constantly, and add in the cooked carrots, pearl onions, and mushrooms; sprinkle the parsley on top.

SERVES 10.

Oranges and Grapefruit Cointreau

2 cups plus 2 tablespoons sugar

2 cups plus 2 tablespoons water

1/4 cup Cointreau or other orange-flavored liqueur

8 navel oranges

6 small firm pink grapefruits

mint sprigs for garnish

In a small saucepan combine 2 cups of the sugar with the 2 cups of water, stir the mixture until the sugar dissolves, bring the syrup to a boil over moderate heat, simmer it for 10 minutes, and pour it into a large bowl to cool. Stir the Cointreau into the cooled syrup, and set it aside.

Remove the zest from 2 of the oranges and 2 of the grapefruits, and cut it into julienne strips. In a clean small saucepan combine the remaining 2 tablespoons of sugar with the 2 tablespoons of water, stir the mixture until the sugar dissolves, and add the strips of zest. Bring the mixture to a boil over moderately high heat, and boil it, stirring constantly, until the sugar is caramelized and the zest is well coated with the caramel.

Peel and remove the pith from the oranges, cut

them crosswise into ³/₈-inch-thick rounds, and place them in the bowl with the syrup. Peel and remove the pith from the grapefruits, section them, add the sections to the syrup mixture, and toss the mixture until the fruit is coated with the syrup. Sprinkle the fruit mixture with the caramelized zest, garnish it with the mint sprigs, and chill it until ready to serve. SERVES 10 TO 12.

Tuscan Bean Salad with Caviar

three 15-ounce cans white kidney beans (cannellini)
1 cup finely chopped sweet white onion
¹/₂ cup chopped Italian parsley
1 tablespoon coarsely ground black pepper
1 teaspoon salt
¹/₂ cup Italian olive oil
about 12 ounces black caviar

In a large bowl combine the beans, onion, parsley, pepper, salt, and oil, and toss to mix well. Spoon the mixture into 6 small bowls, and top the mixture in each with a generous tablespoonful (about 2 ounces) of the caviar. SERVES 6.

Shrimp Cakes

1¹/₂ pounds shrimp, shelled, deveined, and chopped
one 8-ounce can water chestnuts, chopped fine
6 scallions, chopped fine
1 tablespoon finely grated peeled gingerroot
1 tablespoon finely crushed Szechuan peppercorns
1 large egg yolk
about 1 cup fine dry bread crumbs
about ¹/₂ stick (¹/₄ cup) butter

In a large bowl combine the shrimp, water chestnuts, scallions, gingerroot, peppercorns, and egg yolk, mixing well, and let the mixture stand for 1 hour. Shape the mixture into 6 cakes, coat them with the bread crumbs, and fry them in butter for 4 minutes on each side. SERVES 6.

Small Zucchini Pancakes

2 cups shredded zucchini (use only small zucchini)
¹/₂ cup specialty flour for gravies and sauces
2 large eggs, beaten
1 teaspoon salt

¹/₂ teaspoon pepper
about ¹/₂ stick (¹/₄ cup) butter

In a bowl combine the zucchini and flour; mix well. Add the eggs, salt, and pepper, and mix thoroughly. In a skillet fry tablespoonfuls of the zucchini mixture in butter for 3 minutes on each side to make 14 to 16 pancakes. SERVES 6.

Sweet Potato and Sausage Cakes
(FLODDIES)

1 cup chopped sweet white onion
about ¹/₂ stick (¹/₄ cup) butter
1 pound sweet Italian sausage, cooked and crumbled
2 cups mashed cooked sweet potatoes
1 teaspoon salt
¹/₂ teaspoon pepper
2 tablespoons mayonnaise

In a skillet sauté the onion in 2 tablespoons of the butter for 5 minutes. Transfer the onion and butter to a bowl, add the sausage, sweet potatoes, salt, pepper, and mayonnaise, stir the mixture until it is combined, and form it into 6 "cakes." In the skillet, cleaned, fry the cakes for 4 to 5 minutes on each side over low heat in the remaining butter. SERVES 6.

Cooked Cucumber Salad

3 European cucumbers, pared, halved lengthwise, seeds
  removed, and the halves cut crosswise into $^1/_4$-inch-thick
  "crescents"

1 750 ml. bottle Chardonnay blanc or other dry white wine

1 tablespoon salt

THE DRESSING

$^1/_4$ cup Italian olive oil

$^1/_4$ cup white wine vinegar

$^1/_2$ teaspoon ground pepper

In a medium saucepan combine the cucumbers, wine, and salt, bring the wine to a boil, and simmer the mixture for 30 minutes. Drain the cucumbers thoroughly, cool them, and refrigerate them until cold.

Make the dressing: In a small bowl, whisk the oil, vinegar, and pepper until combined. In a salad bowl, toss the cucumbers with the dressing until they are coated.   SERVES 6.

Cabbage, Carrot, and Celery Slaw

$^1/_2$ green cabbage, grated

3 large carrots, grated

1 head of celery, grated

6 scallions, chopped fine (optional)

THE DRESSING

$^1/_2$ cup mayonnaise

$^1/_2$ cup sour cream

the juice of $^1/_2$ lemon

1 tablespoon salt

1 teaspoon black pepper

a dash of cayenne

In a large bowl combine the cabbage, carrots, celery, and scallions. In a small bowl combine the mayonnaise, sour cream, lemon juice, salt, and peppers; whisk the dressing until it is combined. Pour the dressing over the cabbage mixture, and toss it until it is coated.   SERVES 6.

Green Rice

1 cup long-grain rice

1 stick ($^1/_2$ cup) butter

1 teaspoon salt

scant 2 cups hot water

$1^1/_2$ cups coarsely chopped sweet white onion

two $10^1/_2$-ounce cans minced clams, drained

3 cups chopped parsley

1 cup (4 ounces) shredded yellow Cheddar cheese

In a skillet sauté the rice in 2 tablespoons of the butter, add the salt and hot water, and cook the rice until it is tender. Pour the rice onto a jelly-roll pan, and let it dry until the rice grains separate easily.

In a large deep skillet sauté the onion in the remaining butter until it is tender, adding the clams and parsley for the last 2 minutes. Add the rice and cheese, and heat, stirring, until the mixture is hot.
                                    SERVES 6.

Rum, Chocolate, and Grand Marnier Icebox Cake

2 envelopes unflavored gelatine

$^3/_4$ cup water

4 ounces unsweetened cooking chocolate

1 cup sugar

2 large egg yolks

3 tablespoons dark rum

1 quart heavy cream

2 tablespoons Grand Marnier

ladyfingers (optional)

In a small saucepan sprinkle the gelatine over water, let it stand for 5 minutes to soften, and heat the gelatine over low heat until it is dissolved. In the top of a double boiler over hot, not boiling, water, melt the chocolate, stirring, until it is smooth. Stir in $^2/_3$ cup of the sugar, and stir until the sugar is dissolved; add the egg yolks, rum, and 3 tablespoons of the dissolved gelatine, and mix until combined. Pour the mixture into a bowl, and refrigerate it, stirring occasionally, until it is cool and thickened to the consistency of egg whites.

Meanwhile, in a bowl with an electric mixer beat half of the heavy cream until it holds stiff peaks. Beat in the remaining ⅓ cup of sugar, the Grand Marnier, and the remaining dissolved gelatine, and beat until the mixture is blended. Refrigerate the mixture until the chocolate mixture is thick.

Whip the remaining heavy cream until it holds stiff peaks, and fold it into the chocolate mixture. In a waxed paper-lined 2-quart soufflé dish or in a ladyfinger-lined 2-quart springform pan layer the chocolate and Grand Marnier mixtures in 4 alternate layers beginning with the Grand Marnier mixture. Refrigerate the cake for several hours, and invert it onto a cake plate.   SERVES 6.

GENE HOVIS

Crown Roast of Lamb

3 racks of lamb, about 18 chops in all, trimmed and tied into a crown by the butcher
¼ cup olive oil
½ stick (¼ cup) butter, softened
2 tablespoons minced garlic
2 tablespoons finely chopped fresh rosemary
salt and freshly ground black pepper to taste
Brussels Sprouts with Chestnuts (recipe follows)

Bring the meat to room temperature, and rub it with the oil, butter, garlic, and rosemary; season it with the salt and pepper, and place it in a medium roasting pan. Cover the top bones with aluminum foil, and roast the meat in a preheated 400°F. oven for 20 to 35 minutes, or until it is pink. Let the roast rest for 15 minutes, loosely covered with aluminum foil, before carving. Remove all the foil, and fill the center of the roast with the Brussels sprouts and chestnuts.   SERVES 6.

Brussels Sprouts with Chestnuts

2 pounds Brussels sprouts
½ cup fine dry bread crumbs
1 stick (½ cup) butter
1 cup finely chopped shallots
2 cups whole chestnuts (cooked fresh or canned, not in syrup)
1 teaspoon lemon juice
salt and freshly ground black pepper to taste
1 tablespoon fresh dill, chopped

Wash the sprouts, cut off the stems, remove any loose or discolored leaves, and with the tip of a paring knife, cut a cross in each stem. Soak the sprouts in a bowl of ice water for a few hours to slightly loosen the leaves. Drain the sprouts, steam them in a pan of boiling salted water for 8 minutes, and drain them.

In a skillet brown the bread crumbs in 2 tablespoons of the butter, and set them aside. In the skillet, cleaned, sauté the shallots in the remaining butter until they are limp but not browned. Add the sprouts and the chestnuts, and cook them, covered, for 5 minutes, shaking the pan frequently, until the sprouts are tender-crisp. Add the lemon juice, season with the salt and pepper, and stir in the dill. Spoon the mixture into the crown roast and sprinkle it with the bread crumbs.

Glazed Deviled Carrots

8 or 9 large carrots (about 1½ pounds)
1 stick (½ cup) butter
¼ cup light-brown sugar
½ teaspoon dry mustard
salt and ground white pepper to taste
½ to 1 teaspoon hot red-pepper sauce
¼ cup dry vermouth
fresh parsley or dill, chopped

Scrape the carrots, cut them into 3- to 4-inch-long shoestrings, and place them in a bowl of cold water. In a 12-inch skillet melt the butter over moderate heat but do not brown or burn it. Add the brown sugar, mustard, salt and white pepper, the hot-pepper sauce, and vermouth; mix well and heat through. Drain the carrots quickly, leaving whatever moisture adheres to them, and toss them in the butter mixture until they are coated. Simmer the carrot mixture, covered, for 12 to 15 minutes, or until the carrots are tender-crisp, removing the lid for the last 5 minutes of cooking time to reduce the sauce and to glaze the carrots. Sprinkle the mixture with the parsley or dill.   SERVES 6.

Pan-fried Shredded Potatoes

2 to 2¹/₂ pounds Idaho baking potatoes, peeled

1 onion, grated

2 tablespoons butter

about 2 tablespoons vegetable oil

salt and freshly ground pepper to taste

fresh parsley, chopped

In a large saucepan, cover the potatoes with boiling salted water, boil them for 9 to 10 minutes, and drain and cool them. (*Note:* This may be done a day in advance of serving and the potatoes refrigerated.) Shred the cooled potatoes into a bowl using the coarse side of a grater such as one used for cabbage. Refrigerate the potatoes until ready to use as they are less likely to stick to the skillet if chilled. Add the onion to the potatoes, and toss the mixture lightly to combine.

In a 10- to 12-inch cast-iron skillet melt the butter in the oil over moderate heat, add the potato mixture, season it with salt and pepper, and gently press the mixture around the sides of the pan. Cook the potato mixture for 12 to 15 minutes, or until it is crusty and browned on the bottom, checking it frequently to make sure it isn't sticking to the pan, and adding more oil if necessary.

Place a large plate over the pan, invert the pan over the plate, and turn out the potato mixture onto the plate. Slide the potato mixture back into the pan to cook on the other side, adding more oil if it is needed. Season the potato mixture with salt and pepper, cook it for 12 to 15 minutes longer, gently slide it onto a round heated serving dish, sprinkle it with the parsley, and cut it into pie-shaped wedges.

SERVES 4 TO 6.

NOTE: *If doubling the recipe, use two skillets.*

Coffee Profiteroles with Chocolate Sauce and Whipped Cream

THE PÂTE À CHOU
1 stick (¹/₂ cup) butter

1 teaspoon granulated sugar

¹/₂ teaspoon salt

1 cup water

1 cup all-purpose flour

4 large eggs

THE CHOCOLATE SAUCE
8 ounces semisweet-chocolate morsels

¹/₄ cup light-brown sugar

¹/₄ cup light cream or half-and-half, heated

1 tablespoon Cognac, or 1 tablespoon grated orange zest and 1 teaspoon Grand Marnier (optional)

sweetened whipped cream, chocolate ice cream or coffee ice cream

Make the *pâte à chou:* In a small saucepan combine the butter, sugar, salt, and water. Bring the liquid to a boil (all the butter does not have to melt), and immediately add all of the flour at once. Cook the mixture over low heat, beating it briskly and constantly with a wooden spoon until it is smooth, cleanly leaves the sides of the pan, and forms a ball. Remove the pan from the heat, beat in the eggs one at a time, beating until the dough is smooth and glossy.

To form the profiteroles, drop the dough from a teaspoon or tablespoon, or place it in a pastry bag fitted with a 1-inch plain tip, and pipe it onto a parchment-lined baking sheet in mounds about 2 inches apart. Bake the profiteroles in a preheated 425°F. oven for 15 to 18 minutes, reduce the heat to 375°F., and bake them until they are brown and feel light in the hand. If the profiteroles start to brown too quickly, cover them with a sheet of aluminum foil. Cool the profiteroles on a rack.

Make the sauce: In a food processor combine the chocolate and sugar, and with the processor running, pour in the hot light cream or half-and-half, and process the mixture until the chocolate melts. Pour the sauce into a bowl, and when it is cool, stir in the Cognac or Grand Marnier. You will have about 1¼ cups of sauce.

Slit the profiteroles and fill them with the whipped cream or ice cream. Refrigerate or freeze the profiteroles until ready to serve, and serve them covered with the chocolate sauce.   SERVES 12.

Potato Pancakes with Wild Mushroom Ragout

LEMON-SAGE MARINADE
¹/2 cup olive oil

¹/2 teaspoon finely chopped garlic

¹/2 teaspoon finely chopped fresh sage

1 tablespoon fresh lemon juice

salt and pepper to taste

1 pound shiitake mushrooms, cleaned

THE PANCAKES
4 large Idaho potatoes, peeled and washed

1 small onion

a pinch of salt

a pinch of black pepper

¹/2 cup vegetable oil

Mushroom Ragout (recipe follows)

1 tablespoon finely snipped chives

sprigs fresh rosemary and sage for garnish

*M*ake the marinade: In a small bowl combine the oil, garlic, sage, and lemon juice, whisk the mixture until it is blended, and season it with salt and pepper. Clean the shiitake mushrooms, remove the stems and reserve them for another use, and place the mushrooms stem side up in a broiler pan. Brush them with the marinade, and set them aside for at least 2 hours.

Grill the mushrooms: About 30 minutes before serving the potato pancakes, broil or bake the marinated mushrooms under a broiler or in a preheated 500°F. oven for 8 to 10 minutes, or until they are golden brown. Remove the pan from the oven, turn over the mushrooms using a metal spatula, and cook them for 5 minutes longer, or until they are golden brown. Keep the mushrooms warm while making and cooking the potato pancakes.

Grate the potatoes and onion onto a double thickness of paper towels, and squeeze out the water. In a bowl combine the potatoes, onion, salt, and pepper, and mix well. For each pancake, in a large skillet heat the oil over moderately high heat, add one tenth of the potato mixture to the pan, and flatten it into a pancake with a metal spatula. Cook the pancake for 1 minute, or until it is golden, turn it over, and cook it until it is golden brown on the bottom. With a slotted spatula, remove the pancake from the pan, and place it on a paper towel to drain.

Place 1 pancake on each of 10 plates, top each with a few tablespoons of the mushroom ragout and a few of the grilled shiitake mushrooms, sprinkle with the chives, garnish with the rosemary and sage sprigs, and serve immediately. SERVES 10 AS A FIRST COURSE.

Mushroom Ragout

1 pound fresh morels, or 2 ounces dried morels soaked in warm water for 3 hours

1 pound fresh chanterelles, or 2 cups canned tiny chanterelles

1 tablespoon unsalted butter

1 tablespoon olive oil

3 tablespoons finely chopped shallots

¹/2 teaspoon finely chopped garlic

2 cups veal stock

3 cups heavy cream

¹/2 teaspoon finely chopped fresh rosemary

salt and pepper to taste

*C*lean and wash the morels and the chanterelles. In a large heavy saucepan melt the butter in the oil over moderate heat. Add the shallots and the garlic, and sauté them until they are translucent. Add the morels and the chanterelles and sauté them for about 5 minutes, until they are cooked but still firm. With a slotted spoon remove the mushrooms to a sieve placed over a bowl to drain.

To the drippings in the saucepan add the veal stock, bring the liquid to a boil, and boil it until it is reduced to about 1 cup. Add the heavy cream and any liquid drained from the mushrooms, and bring the liquid to a boil. Boil the mixture until it is reduced and thick enough to coat the back of a spoon, and add the mushrooms and the rosemary. Simmer the mixture for 5 minutes, or until it is of sauce consistency, season it with salt and pepper, and keep it warm while preparing the potato pancakes.

SERVES 10.

Acorn Squash with Seafood Ragout

10 medium acorn squash

about ¼ cup vegetable oil

1½ sticks (¾ cup) butter

1 cup all-purpose flour

6 cups court bouillon

½ cup finely chopped shallots

1 large leek, white part only, split, washed, cut into
    julienne slices

1 pound button mushrooms, cleaned, washed, and sliced

1 cup dry white wine

2 pounds red snapper fillets, skin on, cut into 20 equal pieces

2 pounds sea scallops, cleaned, sliced in half horizontally
    if large

3 cups heavy cream

a pinch of saffron

salt and pepper to taste

3 large egg yolks

1 tablespoon finely snipped chives

five 1-pound lobsters, cooked, meat removed from the shells

2 pounds jumbo shrimp, cooked, peeled, and deveined

10 sprigs fresh tarragon

Cut off and discard 1½ inches of stem end of each squash, and remove the seeds and about ¼-inch-thick layer of the flesh. Wash and dry the squash, place them cut side down on a jelly-roll pan, and brush them with the vegetable oil. Bake the squash in a preheated 350°F. oven for 30 minutes, or until they are cooked but still firm enough to hold their shape. Turn the squash cut side up on the pan, and trim a piece from the bottom of each squash so it will not roll over.

In a stockpot melt 1 stick of the butter over low heat, add the flour gradually, whisking until it is blended and the roux thickens, taking care not to let

it brown. Add 4 cups of the court bouillon, ½ cup at a time, whisking well after each addition, until it is blended, before adding more. Cook the sauce for 30 minutes, stirring constantly, until it has thickened and is cooked through.

In a large skillet melt the remaining ½ stick of the butter over moderate heat, add the shallots and sauté them for 1 minute. Add the leek, sauté for 1 minute, and add the mushrooms. Sauté the mixture briefly without allowing it to brown. With a slotted spoon transfer the vegetables to a bowl. To the drippings in the pan add the wine and the remaining 2 cups of court bouillon, bring the liquid to a simmer, add the red snapper pieces, and poach them for a few minutes or until they are just cooked. With a slotted spoon transfer them to a bowl, and repeat with the scallops.

When the scallops are in the bowl, bring the poaching liquid to a boil, and boil it until it is reduced to 1½ cups. Over medium heat add the heavy cream in a slow stream, whisking, then add the saffron. Bring the liquid to a boil, and simmer it until it is reduced by half. Pour the reduced liquid into the white sauce in the stockpot, stirring until blended; pour the mixture through a fine sieve placed over a large saucepan and season the sauce with salt and pepper.

In a small saucepan combine 2 cups of the strained sauce with the egg yolks; whisk until blended. Cook the mixture over low heat, whisking constantly until the sauce is warmed through but does not boil, add the chives, and keep the mixture warm.

Cut the meat from the lobster claws lengthwise and cut the remaining lobster meat in large chunks. Cut each shrimp into 3 pieces. Add the lobster chunks, the shrimp, scallops, and mushroom mixture into the sauce in the large saucepan, and fold the mixture gently until the seafood is coated with the sauce.

Place 1 piece of the red snapper into each of the squash, spoon enough of the sauce and seafood mixture on top to fill the squash three quarters full, and place 1 piece of the remaining red snapper and a piece of lobster claw on top of the mixture in each squash. Spoon some of the chive-sauce mixture on top of each, garnish with a sprig of tarragon, and bake the filled squash in a preheated 450°F. oven for 12 minutes or until golden brown.　　　SERVES 10.

Warm Fruit Compote

2 cups dried apricot halves

2 cups dried figs

2 cups dried pear halves, quartered lengthwise

2 cups sliced dried apples

2 cups pitted prunes

1 cup dark raisins

1 cup golden raisins

3 cups sugar

1 quart water

1 quart white wine

4 cinnamon sticks

6 cloves

1 cup Cognac or bourbon whiskey

In a colander combine the apricots, figs, and pears, rinse them, drain them, and place them in a bowl. In the colander combine the apples, prunes, and raisins, rinse them, drain them, and place them in another bowl. In a Dutch oven or large heavy saucepan combine the sugar, water, the wine, cinnamon sticks, and cloves, and stir the mixture until the sugar is dissolved. Bring the liquid to a boil, add the apricot mixture, and simmer the fruit for 30 minutes, stirring occasionally. Add the apple mixture to the pan, and simmer for 20 minutes, stirring occasionally. Remove the pan from the heat, stir in the Cognac or bourbon, and let the fruit cool. Serve the compôte warm, or store it in the refrigerator for up to 1 month. SERVES 10 TO 12.

Cynthia Peithman's Lemon Cake

Cynthia Peithman is the Pastry Chef at Glorious Food.

1¹/₂ pounds puff pastry

THE LEMON GÉNOISE

5 large eggs, at room temperature

1 large egg yolk

¹/₂ cup plus 2 tablespoons granulated sugar

a pinch of salt

1 teaspoon grated lemon zest

2 teaspoons fresh lemon juice

1 teaspoon vanilla extract

1¹/₄ cups all-purpose flour

3 tablespoons butter, melted and barely warm

THE BUTTERCREAM

2 large eggs, at room temperature

2 large egg yolks

¹/₂ cup granulated sugar

2 teaspoons grated lemon zest

6 tablespoons lemon juice

3 sticks (1¹/₂ cups) butter

THE LEMON SYRUP

³/₄ cup water

¹/₂ cup granulated sugar

1 tablespoon Grand Marnier or to taste

1 tablespoon lemon juice or to taste

THE ALMOND CRUNCH

2 cups blanched sliced almonds

1 large egg white

¹/₂ cup granulated sugar

confectioners' sugar for dusting

Make the puff pastry rounds: Divide the dough into 3 equal pieces and working with one piece at a time, with a floured rolling pin, roll out each piece into a ¹/₈-inch-thick round on a lightly floured surface. Cut out a 10-inch round from each rolled piece of dough and place each round on a baking sheet. With a fork prick each round well. Chill the rounds for at least 20 minutes, and bake them in a preheated 400°F. oven for 15 minutes, or until they are puffed and golden. Bake the pastry at 350°F. for 15 minutes longer, or until it is cooked, and cool the rounds on racks.

Make the génoise: Generously grease a 9-inch

round cake pan. In a large bowl of an electric mixer combine the eggs, egg yolk, sugar, and salt, and whisk the mixture over hot, not boiling, water until it is lukewarm (about 110°F.). With the whisk attachment on the electric mixer or with the beaters, at high speed, beat the warm egg mixture for about 5 minutes, or until it has tripled in volume. Beat in the lemon zest, lemon juice, and vanilla until blended. With a rubber spatula, gently fold in the flour just until it is blended, and fold in the butter. Pour the batter into the prepared pan and bake it in a preheated 350°F. oven for 30 to 40 minutes, or until a cake tester comes out clean. Cool the cake in the pan on a rack for about 30 minutes. Invert the cake onto a rack to cool completely. (The cake can be wrapped in plastic wrap and refrigerated until needed.)

Make the buttercream: In a large heavy saucepan combine the eggs, egg yolks, sugar, lemon zest, lemon juice, and 1 stick of the butter, cut into small pieces. Cook the mixture over moderate heat, stirring constantly with a rubber spatula until the buttercream thickens and registers 160°F. on a candy thermometer. Immediately pour the buttercream into a shallow glass baking dish, and cover it with plastic wrap placed directly on the surface of the butter mixture to prevent a skin from forming. Chill well. (The mixture can keep in the refrigerator for about 2 weeks.) Place the remaining 2 sticks of butter, softened, in a large bowl of an electric mixer with a paddle attachment or the beaters, and beat it at high speed until it is fluffy and almost white. Add 1½ cups of the cold buttercream mixture, about ½ cup at a time, beating well after each addition.

Make the lemon syrup: In a small saucepan combine the sugar and water, and stir until the sugar is dissolved. Bring the syrup to a boil, add the Grand Marnier and lemon juice, and set it aside to cool.

Make the almond crunch: In a bowl combine the almonds and egg white and mix until the nuts are coated. Add the sugar and mix well. Pour the almond mixture onto a jelly-roll pan, bake it in a preheated 350°F. oven for 20 minutes, or until browned, stirring occasionally, and cool it in the pan on a rack. (The crunch will keep for several days stored in an airtight container.)

Assemble the cake: Reserve the best looking puff-pastry round for the top of the cake. Trim the génoise to make it level on the top, and cut it in half horizontally. On a 9-inch cardboard round place one of the remaining puff-pastry rounds, cover the pastry with a thin layer of the buttercream, and place one of the génoise layers on top. Brush the génoise generously with the syrup, spread a thin layer of the buttercream on the top, and repeat the layers with another pastry round, some of the remaining buttercream, and the remaining génoise and syrup. Top the cake with the reserved pastry round but do not spread it with the buttercream. With a sharp knife trim the sides of the cake so they are even, cover the sides with the remaining buttercream, and press the almond crunch into the buttercream. Dust the top of the cake with confectioners' sugar placed in a fine sieve, and chill the cake for 30 minutes before serving. SERVES 12 TO 16.

JANE MONTANT

Curried Zucchini Soup

1 pound zucchini, scrubbed and cut crosswise into thin slices

2 shallots, chopped fine

2 tablespoons butter

½ teaspoon curry powder

1½ to 2 cups chicken broth

salt and pepper to taste

radish, grated, for garnish (optional)

In a saucepan cook the zucchini and shallots in the butter over moderately low heat, stirring, for 3 minutes; add the curry powder, and cook the mixture, stirring, for 1 minute. Add 1½ cups of the broth and simmer the mixture, covered, for 10 to 15 minutes, or until the zucchini is very tender. Season the soup with salt and pepper and puree it in a blender. If desired, thin the soup with the remaining broth and serve the soup warm or chilled. If serving it chilled, garnish it with the radish. SERVES 4.

Marinated Shrimp Salad

THE MARINADE
1 1/2 teaspoons salt

1 teaspoon cracked pepper

1 teaspoon sugar

1/2 teaspoon dried thyme leaves, crushed

1/2 cup white-wine vinegar

3 tablespoons medium-dry sherry

1/3 cup olive oil

1 onion, sliced thin

2 tablespoons capers

1 bay leaf

2 pounds medium shrimp, shelled and deveined

THE DRESSING
3 tablespoons fresh lemon juice

1 tablespoon Dijon-style mustard

salt and pepper to taste

1/3 cup extra-virgin olive oil

1/4 cup finely chopped chives

1 red sweet pepper, cut into julienne strips

1 yellow sweet pepper, cut into julienne strips

2 Belgian endive, trimmed and cut lengthwise into julienne strips

1/4 pound snow peas, trimmed, blanched in boiling water for 5 seconds

Make the marinade: In a bowl whisk the salt, pepper, sugar, thyme, vinegar and sherry until blended, whisk in the oil in a stream, and stir in the onion, capers, and bay leaf. In a kettle of boiling salted water cook the shrimp for 1 minute, or until they are just firm, drain them, and refresh them briefly under running cold water. Toss the shrimp with the marinade, transfer the mixture to a sturdy sealable plastic bag, and let the shrimp marinate, chilled, for at least 8 hours or overnight. Remove the shrimp from the marinade and discard the marinade.

Make the dressing: In a large bowl whisk together the lemon juice and mustard, season with salt and pepper, whisk in the oil in a steady stream, and whisk the dressing until it is emulsified. Stir in the chives, the red and yellow peppers, and shrimp, and arrange the salad on a platter lined decoratively with the endive and the snow peas.   SERVES 4.

Scallion Biscuits with Ham

3/4 cup all-purpose flour

1 teaspoon double-acting baking powder

1/4 teaspoon baking soda

1/4 teaspoon sugar

1/8 teaspoon salt or to taste

fresh ground pepper to taste

1 tablespoon cold unsalted butter, cut into bits, plus extra for pan

1/4 cup minced scallions including the green part

1/4 cup small-curd cottage cheese, drained well in a sieve

2 1/2 tablespoons milk

6 ounces thinly sliced smoked ham

coarse-grain mustard to taste

Into a bowl sift together the flour, baking powder, baking soda, sugar, salt, and pepper. Cut in the butter with a pastry blender until the mixture resembles coarse meal. Add the scallions and cottage cheese, and stir in the milk with a fork, mixing until a soft, sticky dough forms. Turn the dough out onto a lightly floured surface, and knead it gently about 5 times. Pat the dough or roll it lightly with a rolling pin into an 8-x-5-inch rectangle. Cut out 10 rounds with a 2-inch biscuit cutter, rerolling and cutting the scraps, and bake the biscuits on a buttered baking sheet in the middle of a preheated 425°F. oven for 12 to 15 minutes, or until they are golden. Split the biscuits in half horizontally, fill them with the ham slices, and top the ham with dollops of the mustard.
SERVES 10 AS AN HORS D'OEUVRE OR AN ACCOMPANIMENT TO SOUP.

Lemon Cake

THE CAKE
1¹/₂ cups all-purpose flour
1 teaspoon double-acting baking powder
¹/₂ teaspoon salt
1 stick (¹/₂ cup) butter, softened, plus extra for the pan
1 cup sugar
2 large eggs
¹/₂ cup milk

THE LEMON SYRUP
the juice of 1 lemon
¹/₄ cup sugar

Make the cake: Line the bottom and sides of a buttered 8¹/₂-x-4¹/₂-x-2³/₄-inch loaf pan with waxed paper, and butter the paper. Into a bowl sift together the flour, baking powder, and salt. In another bowl with an electric mixer cream the butter with the sugar until the mixture is light and fluffy, and add the eggs, one at a time, beating well after each addition. Add the flour mixture to the butter mixture in batches alternately with the milk, and blend the bat-ter well. Spoon the batter into the loaf pan, spreading it evenly, and bake the cake in the middle of a preheated 325°F. oven for 1 to 1¹/₄ hours, or until a cake tester comes out clean. Transfer the cake in the pan to a rack.

Make the syrup: In a small saucepan combine the lemon juice and sugar, and heat the mixture over low heat, stirring, until the sugar is dissolved. Brush the syrup over the cake and let the cake cool completely before turning it out of the pan. SERVES 8.

Fresh Raspberries with Strawberry Liqueur

3 cups raspberries, picked over
sugar to taste
strawberry liqueur to taste

Arrange the raspberries in a serving bowl and sprinkle them sparingly with the sugar and lavishly with the liqueur. SERVES 8.

MIMI SHERATON

Curried Herring

10 fresh, unmarinated matjes fillets
5 large eggs, hard-boiled, peeled, and chopped
2 tablespoons minced onion
2 teaspoons lemon juice
a pinch of dry mustard
a pinch of turmeric
about ²/₃ cup mayonnaise
3 to 4 teaspoons curry powder or to taste

Rinse the fillets under running cold water, pat them dry with paper towels, and cut each one into about 10 narrow fork-sized slices. In a bowl toss the slices gently with the eggs, onion, lemon juice, mustard, and turmeric; blend in just enough of the mayonnaise to thinly coat the slices, and stir in enough of the curry powder to achieve a mellow gold color and distinct flavor. Adjust the seasonings to taste, and chill the mixture for several hours before serving. SERVES 6.

Beet and Herring Salad

4 large salt herrings, skinned and boned to make 8 fillets
4 cups finely diced canned beets (reserve ¹/₂ cup juice)
6 medium potatoes, boiled, skinned, and diced
3 medium Granny Smith apples, pared, and chopped fine
1 small red onion, minced
2 tablespoons white vinegar
1 tablespoon Dijon-style mustard
2 cups sour cream, beaten until thin
sugar to taste
salt and pepper to taste
3 large eggs, hard-boiled

For the best texture and flavor, the herrings should be soaked whole, but cleaned for 24 hours in several changes of cold water. If you buy the herrings in fillets, soak them for about 8 hours in 3 or 4 changes of cold water. Drain the fillets, and pat them very dry with paper towels. Be sure all the fine bones are removed.

Dice the herrings, place them in a large bowl, and toss them gently with the beets, potatoes, apples, onion, and vinegar. Blend the mustard into the sour cream, and fold it into the herring mixture, trickling in enough of the reserved beet juice to achieve a bright chalky pink color, but not too much or the salad will be too wet. Season the salad with the sugar, and salt, pepper, and more vinegar, sour cream, or mustard, to taste. Chill the salad 8 to 24 hours before serving, stirring it several times.

Separate the egg yolks and egg whites, and rub each separately through a fine sieve over the top of the salad, reserving some yolk and white to decorate the serving bowl as it is refilled.   SERVES 8.

Gravlax with Mustard Sauce

THE GRAVLAX
one 12- to 13-pound fresh salmon

³/4 cup sugar

1¹/2 cups salt

1 teaspoon cracked black pepper

4 tablespoons dried dillseed

1 very large bunch fresh dill (about 25 sprays), washed and patted dry

THE SAUCE
1 cup Swedish or German sweet brown mustard or to taste

1 cup Dijon or Düsseldorf hot yellow mustard or to taste

1 tablespoon sugar or to taste

¹/3 cup white vinegar or to taste

about ¹/2 cup light, mild olive oil

about ²/3 cup minced fresh dill

salt and pepper to taste

Danish-style square rye pumpernickel bread

The salmon should be gutted and scaled but not skinned, so that the 2 fillets are left intact after the large center bones are removed. Working over the flesh of the fish with your fingertips, remove all the small bones, using tweezers if necessary.

Make the gravlax: In a bowl combine the sugar, salt, and pepper. Place one fillet, skin side down, in a large deep glass or ceramic bowl or baking dish. (Do not use a container made of aluminum or any metal other than stainless steel.) Pat one third of the sugar mixture into the flesh of the fish, adding more as it is absorbed, sprinkle it with half of the dillseed, cover it with about two thirds of the dill sprays, and sprinkle the remaining dillseed on top. Work another third of the sugar mixture into the flesh of the remaining fillet, and arrange the fillets flesh sides together, with one thick side of one fillet against the thinner side of the other. Sprinkle the remaining sugar mixture and the remaining dill sprays over and around the fish. Place 2 layers of waxed paper over the fish, cover it with a plate, tile, or board that fits inside the container with the fish, and weight it down firmly and evenly with cans or jars of food. Refrigerate the salmon for at least 2 days but preferably 3. Every 12 hours, remove the weights and waxed paper and turn the fish over without separating the fillets, displacing the dill, or draining off the liquid that accumulates. Replace the paper and weights.

Two to 3 hours before serving, make the sauce: In a bowl whisk the 2 mustards together, whisk in the sugar and half of the vinegar, whisking until the sugar dissolves, then whisk in the remaining vinegar until the mixture is smooth. Add the oil in a stream, whisking until the sauce is emulsified, stir in the dill, and season with salt and pepper and more mustard, sugar, and vinegar to taste.

When the sauce is made, remove the gravlax from the marinade, gently scrape off the spices and herbs, discarding the dill and the liquid, and chill the gravlax until serving time. To slice the gravlax, place one of the fillets, skin side down, on a cutting surface, and with a sharp, thin-bladed stainless-steel knife held almost parallel to the cutting surface, cut the gravlax into paper-thin slices as for smoked salmon.

Cut the bread diagonally into halves or quarters, and serve the bread with the gravlax, with the sauce on the side.   SERVES 10.

Dilled Shrimp and Halibut Salad

5 pounds small shrimp (about 28 to a pound)
4 small celery stalks with leaves
2 small onions, sliced
1 lemon, quartered
2 pinches of salt
16 peppercorns
4 pounds fresh halibut, in 1 or 2 large pieces
THE DRESSING
2 cups mayonnaise or to taste
1¹/2 cups sour cream or to taste
the remaining lemon quarters from above
¹/2 teaspoon salt or to taste
¹/4 teaspoon ground white pepper or to taste
²/3 cup finely chopped fresh dill or to taste

In a large saucepan cover the shrimp with water, add 2 of the celery stalks, 1 of the onions, the juice of a lemon quarter, a pinch of salt, and 8 of the peppercorns. Bring the liquid to a boil over moderately low heat, covered, and without removing the lid let the shrimp stand for 5 minutes, or until one tests done. Drain the shrimp immediately, and douse well with very cold water. Drain, shell, devein and cut the shrimp in half if they are large. Refrigerate the shrimp while cooking the halibut.

In a large saucepan cover the halibut with water, add the remaining 2 stalks of celery, the remaining onion, the juice of another lemon quarter, a pinch of salt, and 8 peppercorns. Bring the liquid to a boil over moderately low heat, covered, and without removing the lid let the halibut stand for 20 minutes, or until the fish falls easily away from the bone and shows no traces of pink. If that does not happen after 20 minutes, bring the liquid to a boil again, turn off the heat, and let the fish stand in the liquid until it tests done. Drain the fish, cool it, and trim away all skin and bones. Break the fish in small pieces and place it in a large bowl. (The fish will break down even more as dressing is added to it.)

Add the shrimp to the halibut, and with a wooden spoon blend in 1 cup of the mayonnaise, 1 cup of the sour cream, 1 tablespoon of lemon juice from a quartered lemon, the salt and white pepper, trying not to mash the fish and adding more mayonnaise, sour cream, and lemon juice as needed until the salad is moist but not too heavily coated. Gently mix in the dill, and adjust the seasoning. Chill the salad for 10 to 24 hours before serving, stirring gently once or twice. SERVES 8 TO 24.

MOIRA HODGSON

Beet and Watercress Salad with Goat's Cheese

4 medium-sized beets
4 heads of Belgian endive, leaves separated
3 bunches watercress, washed, drained, spun dry, tough stems discarded
1 clove garlic, crushed
balsamic vinegar to taste
freshly ground black pepper to taste
coarse kosher salt to taste
²/3 to 1 cup extra-virgin olive oil

8 slices fresh goat's cheese, cut into ¹/2-inch-thick rounds

Cook the beets in their skins in a baking dish in a preheated 375°F. oven for 1 to 2 hours, depending on their size, or until they are tender when tested with a skewer or sharp knife. When they are cool enough to handle, peel and dice them, and place them in a bowl.

Reserve some of the outer endive leaves for decoration, and slice the remainder into thin strips. In a large bowl combine the sliced endive and the watercress.

In a small bowl whisk the garlic, vinegar, pepper, and salt until blended, add the oil in a stream, whisk until the dressing is emulsified, and strain it through a fine sieve into another small bowl, discarding the garlic. Pour some of the dressing over the watercress mixture, toss until the leaves are coated; pour the remaining dressing over the beets, and toss them until coated. Divide the watercress salad among 8 dinner plates. Spoon the beet salad and then a disk of goat cheese on top, and arrange the reserved whole endive leaves around the greens in a fan shape. SERVES 8.

Roast Poussins with Rosemary, Shallots, and Root Vegetables

8 poussins

THE STOCK
4 pounds veal bones

2 pounds chicken necks, bones, and wings

2 carrots, cut into chunks

1 large onion, cut into chunks

3 cloves garlic

2 cups chopped Italian plum tomatoes, with their juice

2 leeks with the green, split, washed

8 sprigs parsley

6 sprigs fresh thyme

1 teaspoon black peppercorns

2¹/₂ quarts water

³/₄ bottle dry white wine, about 2¹/₄ cups

2 tablespoons tomato paste

FOR THE POUSSINS
1 orange, cut into 8 pieces

2 bunches rosemary

¹/₄ cup olive oil

freshly ground pepper to taste

coarse kosher salt to taste

16 large shallots

THE ROOT VEGETABLES
about ¹/₄ cup olive oil

6 large carrots, cut into 1¹/₂-inch pieces

2 large parsnips, cut into 1¹/₂-inch pieces

2 large turnips, cut into 1¹/₂-inch pieces

salt and pepper to taste

2 tablespoons unsalted butter

sprigs rosemary for garnish

The day before serving: Dry the poussins overnight, uncovered, on a rack in the refrigerator.

Make the stock: Roast the veal bones, chicken pieces, carrots, onion, and garlic in a roasting pan in a preheated 375°F. oven until well-browned. Transfer them to a kettle, and add the tomatoes, leeks, parsley, thyme, peppercorns, water, wine, and tomato paste; bring the mixture to a boil, and simmer, uncovered, for 4 hours, adding more water if necessary (cook for 30 minutes after adding extra water).

Strain the stock (you should have at least 10 cups), cool it, and refrigerate it overnight.

Cook the poussins: Put a piece of orange and some rosemary into each poussin, squeeze a piece of orange over each poussin, sprinkle them with some of the oil, season them with the pepper and salt, truss them, place them in a roasting pan with the shallots, and roast them on their sides in a preheated 375°F. oven for 15 minutes. Turn the poussins on their other side, roast them for 15 minutes, turn them breast side up, roast them for 20 minutes, or until they are cooked, transfer them to a serving dish, and keep them warm.

Meanwhile, heat the olive oil in a large roasting pan, add the root vegetables, and cook them with the poussins for about 30 minutes, or until they are lightly browned, turning them occasionally with tongs.

While the poussins and the vegetables cook, remove the stock from the refrigerator, take off the fat, which will be solid, put the stock in a large saucepan, and heat it to simmering. Reserve 6 cups of stock for the rice, and boil the remainder until it is reduced to 1¹/₂ cups.

When the poussins are cooked, transfer them to a large serving platter with the root vegetables, and keep them warm. Skim the fat from the poussins' cooking liquid, add the cooking liquid to the reduced stock, boil it until the liquid is reduced to 1¹/₂ cups, and season it with salt and pepper. Just before serving the poussins, swirl the butter into the mixture, transfer it to a sauceboat, and keep it warm. Garnish the poussins with rosemary sprigs and the shallots, and pass the sauce separately.   SERVES 8.

Wehani Rice Simmered in Chicken Stock

3 cups brown basmati rice

1 onion, chopped fine

1/2 stick (1/4 cup) butter

5 to 6 cups strong chicken stock (or reserved stock from the poussins)

salt and pepper to taste

Rinse the rice thoroughly, place it in a bowl, cover it with cold water. Let it sit for 30 minutes, drain it, and set it aside.

In a large heavy saucepan soften the onion in the butter over moderate heat, stirring frequently with a wooden spoon; add the rice, and fry it, stirring, for about 3 minutes, or until all the grains are well-coated with the butter. Add the stock, and bring it to a boil, season it with salt and pepper, and simmer the mixture, partially covered, for 45 minutes to 1 hour, or until the rice is cooked.   SERVES 8 TO 10.

Sautéed Baby Artichokes

1/2 lemon

4 pounds baby artichokes

6 tablespoons olive oil

2 cloves garlic (green part discarded), minced

freshly ground black pepper to taste

coarse kosher salt to taste

In a bowl squeeze the lemon and add enough water to cover the artichokes. Trim the outer leaves from the artichokes, cut off the stalks and two thirds from the tops, cut each artichoke lengthwise into thirds, and place the artichokes in the lemon-water as you finish each one to keep the cut ends from browning. Drain the artichokes, and spin them dry or dry them in a kitchen towel.

In a large skillet sauté the artichokes in the oil over moderate heat, turning them from time to time, until they are golden. After about 15 minutes, add the garlic, and cook the mixture until the garlic is just golden but not burned. Season the artichokes with the pepper and the salt, and serve them hot.   SERVES 8.

ZACK HANLE

Venison-filled Mini-Brioche with Wild Beach Plum Jelly

1 venison tenderloin

1/4 cup olive oil

1 dozen mini-brioche breads

1 cup wild beach plum jelly or lingonberry jam

In a large skillet lightly brown the venison in the olive oil over moderately high heat for about 5 minutes on each side, and set it aside to cool. Split each brioche in half, and spread each half with some of the jelly. Slice thin the venison and place 2 slices on each of 12 halves of brioche, season with salt and pepper to taste, and top with the remaining halves of brioche.   SERVES 6.

Rose Petal Salad— Three Greens with Rose Dressing

1/2 cup Rose Vinegar (recipe follows)

salt and pepper to taste

1 cup walnut or grape-seed oil

2 heads Boston lettuce, or 3 heads Bibb lettuce, leaves torn into bite-sized pieces, rinsed, and spun dry

1 bunch mâche, trimmed, washed, and spun dry

1 bunch watercress, washed, drained, and spun dry, tough stems discarded

2 cups loosely packed rose petals, washed, drained, and patted dry

In a bowl whisk the rose vinegar, season with salt and pepper, add the oil in a stream, whisking, and whisk the dressing until it is emulsified. In a large crystal bowl toss the lettuce, mâche, watercress, and rose petals with the dressing until the salad is coated.

SERVES 6 TO 8.

Rose Vinegar

1 cup tightly packed fresh rose petals, washed, drained, and patted dry

2 cups white-wine vinegar

Place the rose petals in a jar with a tight-fitting lid, add the vinegar, seal the jar, and place it in a sunny window for 2 to 3 weeks. Strain the vinegar through a hair sieve or a large coffee-filter paper into a clean jar.

Greenshell Mussels and Sauce Mignonette

THE MUSSELS

24 large Greenshell or other large mussels, scrubbed

2 cups Chardonnay

1 cup olive oil

1 tablespoon minced garlic

1 tablespoon grated lemon zest

1 tablespoon minced parsley

1 tablespoon minced shallot

THE SAUCE

1 cup reduced cooking liquid from the mussels

1 small ripe tomato, minced

1/2 teaspoon freshly ground black pepper

1/2 teaspoon salt

Cook the mussels: In a kettle combine the mussels, the Chardonnay, oil, garlic, lemon zest, parsley, and shallot; bring the liquid to a boil, and cook the mussels, covered, over medium heat until the mussels open, about 5 minutes, shaking the pan now and then. Transfer the mussels in their shells to a large bowl, and boil the cooking liquid until it is reduced to about 3 cups.

Make the sauce: In a bowl combine the reduced cooking liquid, the tomato, pepper, and salt; stir the mixture until it is combined, and refrigerate the sauce until it is ready to serve.

Serve the mussels in their shells with the sauce on the side. SERVES 6.

New Zealand Baby Lamb Chops with Fresh Mint Sauce

1 cup cider vinegar

1 large bunch fresh mint, minced

2 trimmed racks of New Zealand baby lamb, cut into individual chops

In a saucepan bring the vinegar to a boil, add the mint, and let it steep while preparing the chops. Arrange the chops on a grill or broiler rack, and brown them on both sides, for approximately 4 minutes on each side. *Do not overcook; the chops should be pink to rare inside.* Place a paper frill on each chop bone, and arrange the chops on a heated serving dish. Keep the chops warm, or if necessary, quickly reheat them at a picnic site over a small portable stove. Serve the chops with the mint sauce. SERVES 6.

Baby Chocolate Cheesecakes

THE CRUSTS

1 1/2 cups graham-cracker crumbs

6 tablespoons butter, melted

2 tablespoons sugar

THE FILLING

one 8-ounce package cream cheese, softened

1 1/2 cups sour cream

1/2 cup sugar

1/2 teaspoon vanilla extract

1 envelope unflavored gelatine

1/4 cup Grand Marnier or Rémy Martin

1 cup semisweet-chocolate morsels, melted and cooled

whipped cream for garnish

Make the crusts: In a bowl combine the graham-cracker crumbs, butter, and sugar, and stir with a fork until the mixture is blended. Press the mixture onto the bottom and sides of six 5-inch tart pans with removable bottoms, and bake the shells in the middle of a preheated 400°F. oven for 8 minutes, or until they are browned lightly. Let the shells cool on a rack.

Make the filling: In a bowl beat the cream cheese

with the sour cream, sugar, and vanilla until blended. In a small saucepan sprinkle the gelatine over the Grand Marnier or Rémy Martin, heat the mixture over moderately low heat until the gelatine dissolves, cool it slightly, and stir it into the cream cheese mixture until blended. Add the chocolate, stir the mixture until it is blended, and spoon it into the shells. Chill the cheesecakes for 2 hours, or until they are firm; carefully remove them from the tart pans, and decorate them with the whipped cream.   SERVES 6.

ROBERT DENNING AND VINCENT FOURCADE

Curried Farm Corn on the Cob

1 stick (¹/₂ cup) butter, softened
2 tablespoons mild curry powder
8 to 10 ears of corn on the cob, silk removed, husks intact

In a small bowl combine the butter with the curry powder, and mix until blended. Turn out the butter mixture onto the butter wrapper, and reshape it into the form of a stick of butter. Refrigerate the butter stick until it is just firm.

Add the corn to a large kettle of boiling water, return the water to a boil, and cook the corn for 5 minutes, or until they are just cooked. Drain the corn, and bring the husks back over each ear to resemble its natural appearance. Serve the corn with the curried butter.   SERVES 8 TO 10.

Tomatoes, Shrimp, and Rice

6 large ripe tomatoes
24 cooked shrimp

THE SAUCE
1 stick (¹/₂ cup) unsalted butter
3 tablespoons mild curry powder
1 tablespoon all-purpose flour
salt and pepper to taste
1 cup heavy cream
ground cumin (optional)
ground turmeric (optional)

3 cups cooked white rice

Add the tomatoes to a large saucepan of boiling water, and when the water returns to a boil, remove the tomatoes, skin them, cut off a slice from the blossom end of each tomato, and scoop out the seeds, leaving enough room for several of the shrimp.

Make the sauce: In a heavy saucepan melt the butter, add the curry powder and flour, mix well, and season with salt and pepper. Over low heat, cook the mixture, stirring it with a wooden spoon until it is bubbly, gradually stirring in the cream until it is blended, and bring the sauce to a boil. Simmer the sauce for 2 minutes, and season it with additional curry powder, the cumin, turmeric, and salt and pepper to taste.

Spoon some of the sauce into each shrimp-stuffed tomato. Arrange the rice on a serving platter, make a pocket in it, and fill it with the sauce.

Serve with Almaden chablis.   SERVES 6.

Poached Bluefish with Curry Sauce

2 cups water
1 cup white wine
3 celery stalks with leaves
2 carrots, sliced thin
1 lemon, cut into wedges; or the zest of 1 lemon, removed with a vegetable peeler
1 small onion, sliced
1 tablespoon capers
1 tablespoon peppercorns
1 tablespoon salt

THE BOUQUET GARNI
3 sprigs fresh chervil
3 sprigs fresh parsley
3 sprigs fresh tarragon
2 sprigs fresh thyme
1 bay leaf

one 3-pound bluefish, scaled and cleaned

THE SAUCE
2 tablespoons butter
2 tablespoons all-purpose flour
2 tablespoons curry powder

In a fish poacher combine the water, wine, celery, carrots, lemon, onion, capers, peppercorns, and salt, and bring the mixture to a boil. Tie the bouquet garni together with kitchen string, and add it and the fish to the poaching liquid. Return the liquid to a boil and simmer the fish, covered, for about 20 minutes, or until it tests done. Remove the fish to a platter, strain the poaching liquid, and reserve it for the sauce.

Make the sauce: In a small saucepan melt the but-ter over low heat, stir in the flour, and cook the roux, stirring, for 3 minutes. Remove the pan from the heat and add 2 cups of the hot fish poaching liquid in a stream, whisking vigorously until the mixture is thick and smooth, and bring the sauce to a boil, stirring. Stir in the curry powder until blended.   SERVES 4.

Nasturtium Sandwiches

good thin-sliced bread, buttered lightly

nasturtium flowers and leaves, rinsed, patted dry, and chopped coarse

Press the buttered side of each bread slice gently into the nasturtium mixture to coat it, and assemble the sandwiches with the coated sides of 2 bread slices together. Remove the crusts with a sharp knife to make an even square of each sandwich, cut sand-wiches diagonally to form triangles, and chill them briefly before serving.

Hazelnut, Chocolate, and Sour Cherry Cake

¹/2 pound hazelnuts

4 ounces unsweetened chocolate

1 cup unbleached all-purpose flour

1¹/2 teaspoons baking powder

a pinch of salt

¹/4 cup dried sour cherries (available at specialty food shops)

1 stick (¹/2 cup) unsalted butter, at room temperature, plus extra for pan

²/3 cup turbinado sugar (pure, unrefined raw sugar available at specialty food shops)

the freshly grated zest of 1 lemon or orange

2 teaspoons rum

¹/2 teaspoon vanilla extract

3 large eggs, at room temperature

Roast the hazelnuts in a single layer in a baking pan in a preheated 350°F. oven or in a skillet over moderately low heat, shaking the pan occasionally, for 10 to 15 minutes, or until they are lightly colored and the skins blister. Wrap the nuts in a kitchen towel to steam for 1 minute, rub them with the towel to remove the skins, let them cool, chop them coarse in a food processor, and transfer them to a bowl. In the food processor chop the chocolate coarse and add it to the nuts.

Make the cake: In a bowl combine well the flour, baking powder, and salt. Stir the flour mixture into the nut mixture, and stir in the cherries. In a large bowl with an electric mixer cream the butter, add the sugar, a little at a time, the lemon or orange zest, rum, and vanilla, and beat the mixture until it is light and fluffy. Beat in the eggs, one at a time, beating well after each addition, and beat the mixture until smooth. With the mixer on low speed, beat in the flour mixture, one third at a time, beating just until combined. Pour the batter into a buttered and floured small loaf pan, spreading it evenly, and bake the cake on the top shelf of a preheated 350°F. oven for 1 hour to 1 hour and 10 minutes, or until a tester comes out clean. Cool the cake in the pan for 10 minutes, invert it onto a rack, and let it cool com-pletely. (*Note:* This cake is best the following day, when it will slice neatly.)   SERVES 6.

Chinoiserie Duck

one 4- to 5-pound Long Island or other duckling

3 large or 5 small cloves garlic, slivered

1 tablespoon Szechuan peppercorns

1 tablespoon coarse salt

about 6 grindings of black pepper

3 firm Bosc pears, peeled, cored and quartered

port

Wash the duck and dry well with paper towels inside and out. With a small sharp knife, make diag-onal incisions into the fat skin at regular intervals and insert a garlic sliver in each cut. In a mortar with a pestle, crush the Szechuan peppercorns with the salt and black pepper until the mixture is medium fine and fragrant; sprinkle a little of the mixture in the duck cavity, rub most of the mixture over the skin, and in a bowl, toss the remaining spice mixture with the pears. Stuff as many pear quarters as will fit into the duck cavity. Place the remaining pears around the duck on a rack over a roasting pan, roast the duck and pears in a preheated 450°F. oven for 1 hour, removing the pears from around the duck after 40 minutes, or when they are tender, and keep them warm. Reduce the oven temperature to 400°F. and roast the duck for another 30 minutes, or until the skin is thin and crisp.

When the duck is done, remove the pears from inside the cavity, place them on the bottom of a serving bowl, cover with the pears that were roasted around the duck, and moisten them with a little port. Serve the pears with the duck. One medium-sized Long Island duckling is ample for 2, but scant for 3, so 2 ducks would serve 5.

Roasted Eggplants

olive oil

fresh or dried rosemary leaves

Chinese eggplants (2 to 3 per person), trimmed, halved lengthwise

coarse salt

Oil a baking sheet with the oil and sprinkle it with the rosemary. Place the eggplants cut side down and close together in a single layer over the rosemary, sprinkle the skin sides with the salt, and bake them in a preheated 400°F. oven for 30 minutes, or until they are tender. (*Note:* If you are serving the eggplant with the duck, bake them with the duck for the last 30 minutes of duck's cooking time.)

Wild Rice with Caramelized Onions, Mushrooms, and Jerusalem Artichokes

1 cup wild rice

2 quarts water

1/2 teaspoon salt

pinch of dried thyme, crumbled

olive oil

1 large or 2 small yellow onions, chopped coarse

3/4 pound mushrooms, the wilder the better (chanterelles are wonderful for this), washed, sliced thin

1 small bay leaf (if only white mushrooms are used)

3 medium Jerusalem artichokes, scrubbed, sliced very thin

fresh parsley, chopped

In a large saucepan combine the rice, water and the salt, bring the water to a boil, and simmer the rice for 30 minutes, or until cooked. While the rice is cooking, in a medium saucepan heat the thyme in enough of the oil to coat the bottom of the pan over moderately low heat until the thyme is fragrant, add the onions, and cook them, stirring, until they are a rich gold color. Add the mushrooms and the bay leaf, and cook the mixture over moderate heat until the mushrooms start to release their liquid. Over moderately low heat cook the mixture, stirring occasionally, until the mushroom liquid has evaporated. Remove the bay leaf. Add the artichokes and more oil, if necessary, and sauté until the artichokes are tender; stir in a generous amount of the parsley.

Drain the rice, stir it into the mushroom mixture, and serve it in a covered dish. This rice will have a complex aromatic flavor that goes very well with the duck. SERVES 4.

Honeydew Melon with Gin and Lime

*1 perfectly ripe honeydew melon, cut into 4 wedges and
 seeded*

lime wedges for garnish

fresh lime juice

gin

Put a melon wedge on each of 4 plates and slip a
lime wedge into a deep cut at one end of each wedge.
Sprinkle the melon wedges generously with the lime
juice and gin. SERVES 4.

Mediterranean Lobster and Fish Stew with Linguine

2 fresh lobsters

¹/₂ cup finely chopped shallots

cloves garlic, crushed, to taste

olive oil

¹/₃ cup Cognac

2 tablespoons tomato paste

1 cup good red wine

salt to taste

crushed red-pepper flakes to taste

fish stock

2 pounds monkfish (or use halibut or cod), cut into 8 pieces

THE GARNISH

1 large green sweet pepper, cut into julienne strips

1 large red sweet pepper, cut into julienne strips

1 large yellow sweet pepper, cut into julienne strips

1 large red onion, sliced thin

olive oil

fresh basil leaves, chopped

cloves garlic, crushed

2 large ripe tomatoes, peeled, seeded, and diced

salt and pepper to taste

1 pound linguine

grated Romano cheese

grated Parmesan cheese

additional fresh basil, chopped

Cut the lobsters in their shells into pieces, remove
the claws, and in a large deep skillet sauté all the
lobster parts, the shallots and garlic in the oil. When
the lobster turns red, add the Cognac, and when it
boils, carefully ignite it. When the flame dies, add
the tomato paste and wine, mixed together, season
with salt and pepper flakes, add enough of the stock
to cover the lobster, bring the liquid to a boil, and
simmer it for 20 minutes. Remove the lobster from
the skillet, discard the body pieces, transfer the tail
and claw pieces to a bowl, and keep them warm. In
the hot liquid in the skillet poach the monkfish just
until it is firm, and remove it to the bowl with the
reserved lobster, and keep it warm. Bring the liquid
in the skillet to a boil, and boil it until it is reduced to
the desired sauce consistency.

Make the garnish: In a skillet sauté the green,
red, and yellow peppers and the onion in the oil with
the basil and garlic to taste over moderately high
heat until the vegetables are tender-crisp. Stir in the
tomatoes, season with salt and pepper, and cook the
mixture, stirring, for a few minutes.

Meanwhile, in a kettle of boiling salted water,
boil the linguine until it is *al dente,* drain it, and
arrange it on a large platter with a lobster tail at each
end of the platter, the claws around the edge, and the
pepper mixture in between. Make a well in the center
of the pasta, add the monkfish, coat with the sauce,
and sprinkle with the cheeses and basil.

Serve with Luna dei Feldi, Santa Margherita,
1989, which is dry, crisp, and light. SERVES 4.

Tart of Figs with Blackberry and Cassis Glaze

THE PASTRY

1¹/₄ cups all-purpose flour

1 teaspoon salt

1 stick (¹/₂ cup) unsalted margarine (do not use butter)

1 cup (4 ounces) grated Cheddar cheese

THE FILLING

¹/₂ cup nonfat dry milk

¹/₂ cup brown sugar

¹/₂ cup granulated sugar

¹/₃ cup all-purpose flour

a pinch of ground cinnamon

a pinch of salt

figs, halved

THE GLAZE

about ¹/₂ cup blackberry jelly or jam or strained preserves

cassis

Make the pastry: In a bowl combine the flour and salt, cut in the margarine with a pastry blender until the mixture resembles coarse crumbs, stir in the cheese with a fork, and add ice water, a tablespoon at a time, stirring until the mixture forms a dough. Shape the pastry into a ball, flatten it slightly, wrap it in plastic wrap, and refrigerate it for 30 minutes. Roll out the chilled pastry onto a lightly floured surface into a 15-inch round, and transfer it to a baking sheet. Press the edges to form a ¹/₂-inch-high border on the pastry round. Chill the pastry shell while preparing the filling.

Make the filling: In a bowl combine the dry milk, brown sugar, granulated sugar, flour, cinnamon, and salt, and mix until blended.

Remove the pastry shell from the refrigerator, sprinkle the filling mixture over the bottom of the shell, and arrange the figs, cut side down, in a pretty design over the mixture. Bake in a preheated 450°F. oven for 10 to 12 minutes, reduce the oven temperature to 350°F., and bake the tart for 20 minutes longer, or until the crust is browned.

Make the glaze: In a small saucepan combine the jelly with the cassis to taste, and heat the mixture, stirring, until the jelly melts and the mixture is thick and clear. When the tart is baked, cool it slightly, and pour the glaze over the figs.   SERVES 8.

MAI HALLINGBY

Crayfish in Dill

20 to 30 crayfish per person

5 to 6 tablespoons salt

1 bunch fresh dill, some reserved for garnish

lemon wedges for garnish

sliced French bread or thinly sliced white bread, toasted

butter, softened

Wash the crayfish thoroughly and place in a bowl of cold water until ready to cook. In a large saucepan or kettle three quarters filled with water, combine the salt and most of the dill, bring the liquid to a boil, and simmer it for 10 minutes to infuse the dill. Taste the water to make sure it has enough salt and dill flavor, add the crayfish all at once, return the liquid to a boil, and simmer the crayfish for 8 to 10 minutes. Turn off the heat, and let the crayfish sit for 2 min-utes. With a sieve or slotted spoon, remove the crayfish from the water to a colander, reserving the water, and cool them to room temperature. When the cooking liquid is cool, pour it over the crayfish (reserve it—it makes an excellent bisque), and set them aside until ready to serve.

On a large plate arrange the crayfish in layers on top of each other in a circular design, and garnish them with the reserved dill and lemon wedges. Serve them with the toast and butter, and provide small forks or picks for extracting the meat.

Anchovy Cocktail Sandwiches

eggs, hard-boiled, peeled, and halved or sliced

butter, softened

sliced rye or pumpernickel bread

canned anchovy fillets or Swedish herring fillets in white-wine sauce, drained

Place the egg yolks and the egg whites from the halved eggs in separate bowls, and mash each with a fork until they are finely chopped. If egg slices are preferred, leave them intact. Butter one side of each bread slice, quarter the bread diagonally into triangles or crosswise into small squares, decorate each buttered side with the chopped egg yolks and egg whites or the egg slices, and top each with an anchovy or herring fillet.

Roosamanna (Cream-of-Wheat Fruit Mousse)

1/2 cup water

1 cup freshly squeezed cranberry, raspberry, or red-currant juice

2 to 3 tablespoons sugar or honey

1/2 cinnamon stick

1/4 cup farina (cream of wheat)

fresh blackberries, raspberries and red currants for garnish

Crème à la Vanille (recipe follows)

In a deep saucepan combine the water, fruit juice, sugar or honey, and cinnamon stick; bring the liquid to a boil, stirring until the sugar is dissolved, and boil the mixture for 5 minutes. Slowly stir in the farina, and boil it for 5 minutes, stirring. Remove the pan from the heat, discard the cinnamon stick, pour the mixture into a glass mixing bowl, and cool it until it is lukewarm. With a whisk or an electric mixer, beat the mixture until it is light in color and fluffy. The mousse is ready to serve, and can be held at room temperature if it is served within a few hours.

To serve the mousse, pour it into a large crystal bowl or individual small bowls, garnish it with the fresh berries, and serve the sauce on the side.

SERVES 4.

Crème à la Vanille

2 large egg yolks

1 1/4 cups milk

1 tablespoon sugar

1/2 vanilla bean, split

In a small bowl mix the egg yolks with a fork. In a small saucepan heat the milk, sugar, and vanilla bean until almost to a boil, and pour some of the mixture into the egg yolks. Mix the egg yolks until blended, pour the mixture into the saucepan with the remaining milk mixture, and cook the sauce over low heat until it coats the back of a spoon, stirring constantly. Pour the sauce through a sieve into a bowl, discard the vanilla bean, cover the sauce with plastic wrap placed directly on the surface to keep a skin from forming, and refrigerate the sauce until cold. MAKES ABOUT 1 1/2 CUPS.

Chicken Salad with Walnuts

4 pounds skinless boneless chicken breasts

1/4 cup dried tarragon leaves

4 whole hearts of celery (2 packages), chopped fine

2 cups chopped walnuts

2 cups mayonnaise

1 cup sour cream

salt and pepper to taste

In a large saucepan cover the chicken with water, add the tarragon, bring the water to a boil, and simmer the chicken, covered, for 15 to 20 minutes, or until it is just cooked through. Drain off the broth, reserving it for another use, if desired, and cool the chicken completely. Cut the chicken breasts into small chunks, place them in a large bowl, add the celery, walnuts, mayonnaise, sour cream, and salt and pepper, and combine the mixture well.

SERVES 12 TO 16.

NOTE: *For a variation, 2 tablespoons mild curry powder may be added to this recipe along with 2 cups halved seedless grapes.*

Pasta Primavera

8 cups cooked rotelli pasta, mixed with 1 cup Italian olive oil to prevent sticking, cooled to room temperature

2 cups fresh or frozen cooked peas

2 cups blanched, diced very small zucchini

1 cup finely sliced white mushrooms

1 cup blanched, diced green bell pepper

1 cup blanched, diced orange, red, or yellow sweet pepper

1/2 cup coarsely chopped fresh basil leaves

1/2 cup coarsely chopped Italian parsley

1/2 cup finely chopped scallion (including the green tops)

1/4 cup salt or to taste

1 tablespoon coarse ground black pepper

1/4 cup Italian red-wine vinegar

1 cup olive oil

California red-leaf lettuce

oil-cured Italian black olives for garnish

In a large bowl, combine the pasta, peas, zucchini, mushrooms, bell pepper, sweet pepper, basil, parsley, and scallion. In a bowl, whisk together the salt, pepper, and vinegar, adding the oil in a stream, whisking until the dressing is emulsified. Pour the dressing over the pasta mixture, and toss the mixture well. Serve the salad on a bed of the lettuce, and garnish with the olives. SERVES 8 TO 12.

Watercress Sandwiches

1/2 cup sour cream

one 3-ounce package cream cheese, softened

1 tablespoon lemon juice

1 teaspoon finely snipped chives

dash of Worcestershire sauce

1 cup lightly packed chopped watercress

salt and cayenne pepper to taste

18 slices white bread, crusts trimmed

2 tablespoons butter, softened

watercress sprig for garnish

In a bowl combine the sour cream, cream cheese, lemon juice, chives, and Worcestershire, and mix until blended. Stir in the chopped watercress, salt and cayenne. Flatten each bread slice with a rolling pin, spread one side of each slice with some of the butter, and spread the buttered sides with the watercress mixture. Roll up each bread slice jelly-roll fashion, arrange the sandwiches seam side down on a serving plate, and garnish with the watercress sprig. The sandwiches may be made a day ahead of serving. MAKES 36 SMALL SANDWICHES.

Black Walnut Chocolate Cake

THE CAKE

1 stick (¹/2 cup) butter

2 cups granulated sugar

2 cups cake flour

2 teaspoons baking powder

¹/2 teaspoon salt

1¹/2 cups milk

2 large eggs

six 1-ounce squares unsweetened chocolate, melted and cooled

2 teaspoons vanilla extract

1 cup chopped black walnuts

THE FROSTING

1 stick (¹/2 cup) butter, softened

1¹/2 pounds confectioners' sugar

four 1-ounce squares unsweetened chocolate, melted and cooled

2 large eggs

1 teaspoon vanilla extract

1 cup chopped black walnuts

strong coffee or coffee essence for thinning the icing

Make the cake: Grease three 8-inch round cake pans, line the bottom of each with a waxed-paper round, and grease the paper. In a bowl with an electric mixer cream the butter with the sugar at high speed until the mixture is light and fluffy. Into another bowl sift the flour, baking powder, and salt, and at medium speed add a quarter of the flour mixture at a time to the butter mixture alternately with the milk, beginning and ending with the flour mixture and beating each addition just until it is blended before adding the next one. Beat in the eggs, one at a time, until blended; gradually blend in the chocolate, add the vanilla, and fold in the walnuts. Divide the batter among the prepared pans, and bake the cake layers in a preheated 350°F. oven for 35 minutes until cake is done. Cool the layers in the pans for 10 minutes, and then invert them to cool completely on a wire rack.

Make the frosting: In a bowl with an electric mixer beat the butter with the confectioners' sugar until the mixture is light and fluffy. Beat in the chocolate, add the eggs and vanilla, beat until blended, and fold in the walnuts. Stir in enough of the coffee to make the frosting of spreading consistency.

Place 1 cake layer on a serving plate, and sandwich all the layers together with frosting. Cover the cake with the remaining frosting.   SERVES 12.

Pecan Puffs

1 stick (¹/2 cup) butter, softened

2 tablespoons granulated sugar

1 cup pecan pieces, ground

1 cup sifted cake flour

confectioners' sugar for coating

In a bowl beat the butter with the sugar until the mixture is fluffy, and stir in the pecans and flour until blended. Roll the dough into small balls, and place them on a greased baking sheet. Bake the puffs in a preheated 300°F. oven for 45 minutes, or until they are golden, checking them frequently because they burn easily. While the puffs are hot, roll them in confectioners' sugar, and cool them on a rack. When the puffs are cool, roll them again in confectioners' sugar.   MAKES ABOUT TWO DOZEN.

Nilma's Sorrel Soup

1 cup chopped onions
3 tablespoons butter
5 cups chicken broth
6 medium potatoes, peeled and diced
1 pound sorrel leaves, washed well and stems discarded
1 teaspoon sugar
1 cup heavy cream
salt and pepper to taste
Melba Toast

In a heavy saucepan cook the onions in the butter over moderately low heat, stirring occasionally, until they are transparent. Add the broth, potatoes, and all but 1 cup of the sorrel. Bring the liquid to a boil, simmer for 20 minutes, or until the potatoes are tender, and stir in the sugar. In a blender puree the potato mixture in batches until it is smooth, pour the mixture into a bowl, stir in the heavy cream and the reserved sorrel leaves, chopped coarse, and season with salt and pepper. Let the soup cool and chill it, covered, for 2 hours, or overnight. Serve the soup ice cold with the Melba toast.   SERVES 8.

Leek and Ham Quiche

4 leeks, white part only, washed well, sliced
2 tablespoons butter
1/2 cup milk
1 cup diced Virginia ham
one 9-inch pastry shell, baked
1 cup grated Gruyère cheese
1 cup heavy cream, scalded
2 large eggs, beaten lightly
1 large egg yolk
1/4 teaspoon salt
freshly grated nutmeg to taste
freshly ground pepper to taste

In a large heavy skillet sauté the leeks in the butter over moderately high heat, stirring, for about 2 minutes. Add the milk and simmer the mixture until the milk evaporates. Remove the skillet from the heat and stir in the ham. Spread the leek mixture over the bottom of the pastry shell and sprinkle it evenly with the Gruyère. In a bowl, whisk together the heavy cream, eggs, egg yolk, salt, nutmeg, and black pepper, and pour the mixture over the Gruyère. Bake the quiche on a baking sheet in the middle of a preheated 350°F. oven for 30 minutes, or until it is set. Serve the quiche warm or cold.   SERVES 8.

Vegetable Terrine

THE CELERY ROOT AND POTATO LAYER
2 pounds (2 medium) celery root (celeriac)
2 pounds potatoes
1½ sticks (12 tablespoons) butter
¼ cup heavy cream
salt and pepper to taste

THE CARROT LAYER
2 pounds carrots, peeled and cut into pieces
3 tablespoons butter
⅛ teaspoon freshly grated nutmeg
salt and pepper to taste

THE BROCCOLI LAYER
2 bunches broccoli, cut into flowerets, stems discarded
½ stick (¼ cup) butter
⅛ teaspoon freshly grated nutmeg
salt and pepper to taste

Make the celery root and potato layer: Peel the celery root and the potatoes, cut them into 1-inch pieces, and put each vegetable in a separate pan with enough cold salted water to cover. Bring the water to a boil, and simmer the vegetables, covered, for 30 minutes, or until they are tender. Drain, mash, and sieve the celery root into a bowl with 6 tablespoons of the butter and all the heavy cream. Drain and mash the potatoes with the remaining 6 tablespoons of butter, stir the potato mixture into the celery-root mixture, and season with salt and pepper. Spread the mixture in a 7-inch round baking dish preferably made of glass so the layers will show.

Make the carrot layer: In a large saucepan cover the carrots with cold salted water, bring the water to a boil, and simmer the carrots, covered, for 10 minutes, or until they are tender. Drain the carrots, and mash them with the butter, nutmeg, and salt and pepper. Spread the carrot mixture over the celery-root layer.

Make the broccoli layer: In a large saucepan of boiling salted water cook the broccoli for 4 to 5 minutes, or until it is tender, drain it, place it in a food processor, and puree it with the butter, nutmeg, and salt and pepper. Spread the broccoli mixture over the carrot layer.

Bake the terrine in a preheated 300°F. oven for 20 minutes, or until hot.   SERVES 10 TO 12.

Bill Blass Meat Loaf

2 pounds chopped sirloin
½ pound pork
½ pound veal
1 cup chopped celery
1 cup chopped onion
about ½ stick (¼ cup) butter
1½ cups fine fresh bread crumbs
½ cup chopped parsley
⅓ cup sour cream
1 large egg, beaten with 1 tablespoon Worcestershire sauce
dried marjoram crumbled, to taste
dried thyme crumbled, to taste
salt and pepper to taste
1 12 oz. bottle chili sauce

In a food processor coarsely grind the sirloin, pork and veal, and place the meats in a large bowl. In a large skillet sauté the celery and onion in the butter until tender, and place the vegetables in the bowl with the sirloin mixture. Add the bread crumbs, parsley, sour cream and egg beaten with Worcestershire. Season the mixture with the marjoram, thyme, and salt and pepper. Form the mixture into a loaf in an aluminum-foil–lined roasting pan, pour the chili sauce over the loaf, and bake in a preheated 350°F. oven for 1 hour.   SERVES 6.

Potato Skins

6 russet (baking) potatoes, scrubbed
olive oil

Prick the potatoes a few times with a fork and bake them in a preheated 350°F. oven for 1 hour, or until tender. Cut the potatoes in half lengthwise and scoop them out, leaving a ½- to ¼-inch-thick shell. Reserve the pulp for another use. Place the potato shells on a baking sheet, brush the cut sides with oil, and season with salt and pepper. Bake in a preheated 400°F. oven for 30 minutes or until they are crisp.   SERVES 6.

Salmon and Sole Mousse with Red-Pepper Mayonnaise and Watercress Mayonnaise

1 quart water

2 carrots, peeled and sliced

2 celery stalks, sliced

1 small onion, sliced

1¹/₂ pounds yellowtail sole fillets

1¹/₂ pounds salmon fillets, skinned

4 envelopes unflavored gelatine

1 cup dry vermouth

2 cups heavy cream

2 teaspoons Worcestershire sauce or to taste

salt and pepper to taste

1 pound medium shrimp, poached, peeled, deveined, and halved lengthwise, for garnish

1 seedless cucumber, peeled and diced, for garnish

Red-Pepper Mayonnaise (recipe follows)

Watercress Mayonnaise (recipe follows)

In a large saucepan combine the water, carrots, celery and onion, bring the liquid to a boil, and simmer it, covered, for 20 minutes. Strain the broth into a bowl, discard the vegetables, and return the broth to the pan. Add the sole fillets to the broth, bring the liquid to a boil, and simmer the fillets, covered, for 5 minutes, or until they are cooked. With a slotted spatula transfer the fillets to a food processor, strain the broth into a bowl, and return it to the saucepan, cleaned. Add the salmon fillets to the broth, bring the liquid to a boil, and simmer the fillets, covered, for 5 minutes or until they are cooked. Transfer the fillets to a plate, strain the broth into a bowl and then back into the saucepan, cleaned. Bring the broth to a boil and boil it until it is reduced by half.

In a small bowl sprinkle the gelatine over the vermouth and let the gelatine stand for 5 minutes, or until it is softened. Pour the gelatine into the broth, heat the mixture over moderate heat until the gel-atine is dissolved, and add the cream and the Worcestershire.

Puree the sole fillets, and with the machine running, pour in half the gelatine mixture, processing it until it is blended. Transfer the mixture to a bowl and season with salt and pepper. In the processor, cleaned, puree the salmon fillets, and with the machine running, pour in the remaining gelatine mixture, processing it until it is blended, and season with salt and pepper to taste.

Spread 1¹/₂ cups of the salmon mixture over the bottom of a 9-x-4-inch loaf pan, and freeze it for 10 minutes or until it is set. Spread 1¹/₂ cups of the sole mixture over the set salmon mixture, and freeze it for 10 minutes or until it is set. Layer the remaining salmon and sole mixtures over the set mixtures, allowing each layer to set before adding the next layer. Cover the mousse with plastic wrap and re-frigerate it for 2 hours to set it completely.

To serve the mousse, dip the pan into a bowl of warm water for a few seconds, dry the pan with a towel, and invert the mousse onto a cutting board. Slice the mousse crosswise into ³/₈-inch-thick slices, arrange them on a serving dish, and garnish them with the shrimp and cucumber. Pass the red-pepper mayonnaise and watercress mayonnaise separately.

Serve with Puligny Montrachet.   SERVES 8.

Red-Pepper Mayonnaise

2 sweet red peppers

4 large egg yolks

1 teaspoon Dijon mustard

2 cups olive oil

the juice of ¹/₂ lemon

about 1 cup heavy cream

hot red-pepper sauce to taste

salt and pepper to taste

Broil the peppers on the oven rack placed 4 to 6 inches away from the coils until the peppers are blackened on all sides, remove them with tongs to a plastic bag, seal the bag, and let the peppers stand until they are cool enough to handle. Remove the skin, stems and seeds, place the peppers in a food processor, and puree them. Add the egg yolks and mustard, and process the mixture until it is blended. With the machine running, pour in the oil in a stream, process until the sauce is emulsified, pour in the lemon juice, and process until it is blended. With the machine running, pour in enough of the heavy cream to make the mayonnaise of coating consistency, and season it with the hot-pepper sauce and salt and pepper.   MAKES ABOUT 4 CUPS.

Watercress Mayonnaise

1 bunch watercress, stems removed, leaves washed and drained

4 large egg yolks

1 teaspoon Dijon mustard

2 cups olive oil

the juice of 1/2 to 1 lemon

about 1 cup heavy cream

hot red-pepper sauce to taste

salt and pepper to taste

Place the watercress leaves in a food processor, and puree them. Add the egg yolks and mustard, and process the mixture until it is blended. With the machine running, pour in the oil in a stream, process until the sauce is emulsified, and pour in enough of the lemon juice to thin the mayonnaise slightly. With the machine running, pour in enough of the heavy cream to make the mayonnaise of coating consistency, and season it with the hot-pepper sauce and salt and pepper.   MAKES ABOUT 4 CUPS.

Croquembouche Stonor Lodge

THE PÂTE À CHOU

2 cups milk

1 stick (1/2 cup) butter

1/2 cup sugar

1 teaspoon salt

2 cups all-purpose flour

8 eggs

THE FILLING

1 teaspoon unflavored gelatine

1 cup light cream

6 large egg yolks

3/4 cup sugar

8 ounces white chocolate, melted and cooled

1 cup triple-strength coffee

3 cups heavy cream, whipped

THE CHOCOLATE SAUCE

6 ounces unsweetened chocolate, grated

6 ounces semisweet chocolate, grated

3 cups heavy cream

raspberries for garnish

sprigs of fresh mint for garnish

Make the pâte à chou for the profiteroles: In a large saucepan combine the milk, butter, sugar, and salt, bring the liquid to a boil, and immediately add all of the flour. Beat the mixture vigorously over moderate heat until it is blended and the dough leaves the sides of the pan. Remove the pan from the heat, and beat in the eggs, one at a time, making sure each egg is blended before adding another one. Spoon the mixture into 12 mounds onto each of 2 baking sheets, leaving 2 inches between each mound, and bake them in a preheated 425°F. oven for 18 to 20 minutes, or until they are golden and dry inside. Cool the profiteroles on a rack.

Make the filling: In a small saucepan sprinkle the gelatine over 1/4 cup of the light cream, let it stand 5 minutes, or until the gelatine is softened, and heat it over low heat until the gelatine is dissolved. In a large bowl with an electric mixer beat the egg yolks with the sugar at high speed for 10 minutes or until the sugar is dissolved, add the remaining 3/4 cup of light cream, the white chocolate, and coffee, and beat the mixture until it is blended. Add the gelatine mixture, beat the mixture until it is blended, and fold in the whipped cream. Refrigerate the filling, covered, until it is set.

Make the sauce: In a medium saucepan combine the unsweetened chocolate, semisweet chocolate, and heavy cream, and heat the mixture over moderate heat, stirring until the chocolate melts and the mixture is blended. Remove the pan from the heat, and cool it to room temperature.

To serve: Split the profiteroles and fill them with the white-chocolate filling. Spoon some chocolate sauce over each of 8 chilled dessert plates, arrange 3 profiteroles on each plate, and garnish the plates with the raspberries and mint sprigs.

Serve with Dom Ruinart Rosé.　　　SERVES 8.

MRS. JOHN G. WINSLOW

Seafood Bisque

two 1-pound lobsters in the shell

10 tablespoons butter

12 shrimp, unshelled

¹/₄ pound scallops

1 cup crushed tomatoes

1 cup heavy cream

3 ounces sherry

¹/₄ teaspoon paprika

a pinch of cayenne

Plunge the lobsters, head first, into a kettle of boiling salted water, and boil them, covered, for 15 minutes. Remove them from the pan, and cool them, reserving the cooking liquid. Remove the meat from the shells, and place it in a bowl. Place the shells in a food processor, chop them, and add them to the kettle with the lobster cooking liquid.

In a large skillet melt 4 tablespoons of the butter over moderately high heat and sauté the shrimp for 2 minutes or just until they are pink. Remove the pan from the heat, and set aside. Shell the shrimp, add them to the lobster meat, and add the shells to the mixture in the kettle.

Add 4 tablespoons of butter to the shrimp drippings in the skillet, sauté the scallops just until they are opaque, and add them to the bowl with the lobster. Pour the scallop drippings and the tomatoes into the kettle, bring the mixture to a boil, and simmer over moderate heat, uncovered, for 30 minutes.

Strain 6 cups of the tomato mixture into a large saucepan, add the heavy cream, bring the liquid to a boil, and simmer for 5 minutes. Add the sherry, and simmer the liquid for 5 minutes. Add the lobster, shrimp, and scallops, remove the pan from the heat, add the remaining 2 tablespoons of butter, and stir

until the butter melts. Season the bisque with the paprika and cayenne.

Suggested wine: Olivier Leflaive Corton-Charlemagne '85.　　　SERVES 4.

Roasted Rack of Lamb

hotel rack of lamb (8 chops), split, chine bones removed, and the ends of rib bones trimmed and cleaned

1 clove garlic, split

salt and pepper to taste

1 cup Dijon mustard

1 tablespoon fresh rosemary leaves

1 cup fresh bread crumbs

¹/₂ stick (¹/₄ cup) butter, melted

Rub the meat with the garlic, and season it with salt and pepper. In a bowl mix the mustard with the rosemary, and spread the mixture over the meat. In another bowl mix the bread crumbs with the butter, and cover the meat with the mixture. Cover the exposed bones with aluminum foil, place the meat in a roasting pan, and roast it in a preheated 400°F. oven for 35 to 45 minutes for medium-rare.

Suggested wine: Château Cheval Blanc '82.

SERVES 4.

Madeleines

1 1/2 sticks (3/4 cup) butter, melted and cooled, plus additional
    for greasing the pans

fine dry bread crumbs for coating the pans

2 large eggs

1/3 cup granulated sugar

1/2 teaspoon vanilla extract

1 cup all-purpose flour

1 teaspoon grated lemon zest

3 tablespoons vegetable oil

confectioners' sugar for dusting

Grease the shells of a madeleine pan with melted butter, and sprinkle them with bread crumbs. In a bowl with an electric mixer beat the eggs with the granulated sugar and vanilla until the mixture is thick and lemon-colored. Fold in the flour, lemon zest, 3/4 cup butter, and the oil, and mix just until blended. Fill the shells three quarters full with the batter, and bake the madeleines in a preheated 425°F. oven for 8 minutes. Remove the madeleines from the pan immediately, and cool them on a wire rack. Clean, grease, and crumb the pan and repeat with the remaining batter. Sprinkle the madeleines with confectioners' sugar before serving.

MAKES 30 COOKIES.

NOTE: *This batter will not hold long, so you must make your cookies right away.*

LADY MARY ROTHERMERE

Smoked Salmon Marie

1/4 pound mushrooms, cleaned and trimmed

1 pound thinly sliced smoked Scottish salmon, cut into
    5-inch-long julienne strips

2 small jars sliced pimientos, drained, patted dry

about 1 cup mayonnaise

about 3 drops hot-red-pepper sauce

3 large eggs, hard-boiled

fresh parsley, chopped fine, for garnish

brown bread slices, cut into triangles, buttered

In a small saucepan boil the mushrooms in salted water for 4 minutes, drain them, pat them dry with paper towels, slice them thin, and place them in a large bowl. Add the salmon, pimientos, and enough mayonnaise to coat the mixture lightly, and season with the hot-pepper sauce. Spoon the mixture onto the center of a platter. Chop the egg whites, sprinkle them around the salmon, sieve the egg yolks, and sprinkle them around the egg whites. Garnish the salmon with the parsley, and serve it with the bread triangles.

SERVES 12.

English Summer Fruit Salad with Mint

1 pint blueberries

1 pint raspberries

1 pint strawberries

2 to 3 very ripe peaches

sugar to taste

lemon juice to taste

poppy seeds (optional)

fresh mint leaves, chopped (optional), plus large mint leaves
    for garnish

Wash and drain the blueberries, raspberries, and strawberries. Hull the strawberries, peel, pit, and slice the peaches, and combine all the fruits in a bowl. Sweeten the fruit mixture with the sugar, sprinkle with lemon juice to keep the peaches from turning brown, and toss the fruit to mix well. Sprinkle the fruit with the poppy seeds and chopped mint, if desired, and garnish with the mint leaves.

SERVES 12.

Brie and Chutney Tarts

2-inch pastry shells, baked, made from your favorite pastry

Brie

bottled chutney

slivered almonds

Arrange the pastry shells on a jelly-roll pan. Pinch or cut small pieces of Brie, place a piece in each pastry shell, spoon a little chutney over each piece of cheese, and top the cheese with an almond sliver. Bake the tartlets in a preheated 350°F. oven for 2 minutes, watching carefully, as the almonds burn quickly.

Tomato Bouillon

2 quarts canned Italian tomatoes

6 celery stalks, chopped

3 carrots, peeled and chopped

1 small sweet green pepper, seeded and chopped

1 small sweet red pepper, seeded and chopped

2 whole cloves

1 tablespoon chopped parsley

1 teaspoon dried basil leaves, crushed

1 bay leaf

¼ cup fresh lemon juice

salt and pepper to taste

In a kettle combine the tomatoes, celery, carrots, green pepper, red pepper, cloves, parsley, basil, and bay leaf. Bring the mixture to a boil, and simmer it for 25 minutes. Pour the mixture through a sieve into a tureen or another saucepan, discard the vegetables, stir in the lemon juice, and season with salt and pepper. SERVES 6 TO 8.

Roast Quail with Apricot-Rice Stuffing and Sauce Bigarade

THE STUFFING

⅓ cup chopped dried apricots

3 tablespoons golden raisins

2 tablespoons Grand Marnier or other orange-flavored liqueur

2 cups cooked long-grain white rice

2 cups cooked wild rice

¼ teaspoon ground cinnamon

1 teaspoon chopped fresh thyme; or ¼ teaspoon dried thyme leaves, crushed

ground white pepper to taste

salt to taste

12 fresh quail, cleaned, breastbones removed

1 stick (½ cup) butter, melted

seasoned salt to taste

THE SAUCE

4 teaspoons sugar

1 tablespoon wine vinegar

1 cup Brown Sauce (Sauce Espagnole, recipe follows)

the juice of 1 orange

fresh lemon juice to taste

1 tablespoon julienned orange zest

1 tablespoon Grand Marnier or other orange-flavored liqueur

freshly ground white pepper to taste

White and Wild Rice Pilaf (recipe follows)

1 orange, sliced crosswise, for garnish

fresh herbs for garnish

Make the stuffing: In a large bowl combine the apricots, raisins, and liqueur, mix well, and marinate the mixture for several hours. Add the white rice, wild rice, cinnamon, thyme, and pepper; season with salt and mix well. If the mixture is hot, cool it completely.

Spoon some stuffing into each quail, and use skewers and kitchen string to close the cavity, tie the legs together, and hold the wings in place on each bird. Place the quails, breast side up, on a rack in a shallow roasting pan or two, brush the birds with the butter, sprinkle them with the seasoned salt, and roast them in a preheated 450°F. oven for 15 to 20 minutes, or until a drumstick moves easily in its socket and the juices run clear when the breast is pierced. Broil the birds for a few minutes for more even browning, transfer them to a platter, remove the skewers and strings, and keep the quail warm while making the sauce.

Make the sauce: If more than one roasting pan was used, pour the juices and browned bits from the second roasting pan into one pan, and set it aside. In a small saucepan dissolve the sugar in the vinegar, cook the mixture over low heat until the sugar dissolves and caramelizes, add the brown sauce, stirring until blended, and pour the mixture into the pan juices in the roasting pan. With the roasting pan on the stove top over moderately high heat, bring the juice mixture to a boil, stirring until blended, and simmer it for 5 minutes. Just before serving add the orange juice, lemon juice, orange zest, and liqueur, and season with the salt and pepper. Pour the mixture into a warm sauceboat, and serve with the quail, arranged on the pilaf. Garnish with the orange slices and fresh herbs. SERVES 8.

Lennie's Rolls

3 envelopes fast-acting or regular dry yeast

1 cup lukewarm water

1 cup vegetable shortening

one cup boiling water

2/3 cup sugar

1 tablespoon salt

2 large eggs, at room temperature

about 6 cups all-purpose flour

about 1 stick (1/2 cup) butter, melted

In a small bowl sprinkle the yeast over the lukewarm water and stir until the yeast is dissolved. In a large bowl combine the shortening and boiling water and stir until the shortening melts. Add the sugar, salt, and yeast mixture and mix well. Add the eggs, stir until mixed, and add the flour gradually, beating until the dough is smooth, not sticky. Cover the dough with plastic wrap, and set it aside in a warm place free from drafts until it is doubled, about

45 minutes. Punch down the dough, turn it out onto a lightly floured surface, and knead it a few times. Break the dough in half, and working with one half at a time, roll out the dough to 1/2-inch thickness, cut it with a 2- to 2 1/2-inch round cutter, dip each round into the butter to coat lightly, fold each round in half, and place the rolls touching each other but not packed together in a greased jelly-roll pan or in several greased baking pans. Reserve the remaining butter. Cover the rolls with plastic wrap or a clean kitchen towel, and let them rise in a warm place free from drafts for about 30 minutes, until doubled. Bake the rolls in a preheated 400°F. oven for 25 to 30 minutes, or until they are done, and brush them with the remaining butter. MAKES ABOUT 3 DOZEN ROLLS.

Brook House Apples

THE APPLES

2 cups sieved pureed raspberries

8 red Delicious apples, peeled, cored, and brushed
    with lemon juice

THE FILLING

2 cups heavy cream

1 pound white chocolate, grated

1/2 cup finely chopped pistachio nuts

THE SAUCE

6 large egg yolks

1/2 cup sugar

2 cups milk, scalded

Calvados to taste

fresh mint leaves for garnish

marzipan, crumbled, for garnish

chocolate, grated, for garnish

Poach the apples: In a large deep skillet bring the raspberry puree almost to a boil, add the apples, and cook them over moderate heat, covered, for 20 minutes, or until they are soft but not mushy, turning them every 5 minutes and basting them with the puree to distribute the color evenly. Test for doneness by inserting a wooden pick or cake tester into the apples. With a slotted spoon transfer the apples to a plate to drain, let them cool, and refrigerate them, covered with plastic wrap, until they are cold.

Make the filling: In a medium heavy saucepan heat the heavy cream until it is almost to a boil, remove the pan from the heat, add the chocolate, and stir until the chocolate melts and the mixture is smooth and thick. Stir in the pistachios, cool the mixture slightly, and refrigerate it until it is completely cooled. Place the filling in a pastry bag fitted with a 1/2-inch plain tip, fill the apples with the mixture, and refrigerate them until serving.

Make the sauce: In the top of a double boiler, beat the egg yolks with the sugar until blended, pour in the scalded milk, in a stream, whisking constantly, and cook the mixture over hot, not boiling, water until it is thick enough to coat the back of a spoon. Remove the pan from the heat, pour the sauce into a bowl, and add the Calvados. Place the bowl in a larger bowl of ice and water until the sauce is cool, stirring it frequently. Cover the sauce with plastic wrap placed directly on the surface to prevent a skin from forming, and refrigerate it until serving.

To serve, spoon some sauce over each of 8 dessert plates, place an apple on top, and garnish with the mint leaves, marzipan, and chocolate. Pass the remaining sauce.   SERVES 8.

NANCY GOLDBERG

New Orleans Gumbo

1/2 pound bacon, chopped into 1/4-inch pieces

2 large onions, chopped

3 pounds fresh okra, cut into 1/2-inch pieces

four 28-ounce cans Italian plum tomatoes

1 cup homemade chicken broth

1 ham hock

2 teaspoons chopped fresh thyme

2 pounds shrimp, peeled and deveined

2 pounds shucked oysters and their liquor

1 pound lump crabmeat, free of shells

hot red-pepper sauce to taste

salt and pepper to taste

2 tablespoons gumbo filé powder

boiled white rice

In a large Dutch oven sauté the bacon over moderate heat until it is crisp, add the onions and sauté them until they are tender. Add the okra, and sauté it a few minutes, stirring so the okra does not burn. Add the tomatoes and their juice, the chicken broth, ham hock, and thyme; bring the mixture to a boil, stirring frequently, and simmer it, covered, for at least 3 hours, until the okra has fallen apart. If there is too much liquid, simmer the mixture uncovered until it reaches the desired consistency. Add the shrimp and oysters, simmer the mixture until the shrimp are opaque and the oysters begin to curl, add the crabmeat, heat through, season with the hot-pepper sauce and salt and pepper, and stir in the filé powder. *Do not let the gumbo boil after you have added the filé powder or it will become bitter.*

This is really better if made a day ahead, refrigerated, and carefully reheated. Serve the gumbo in large bowls with the rice.   SERVES 10 TO 12
(NEVER MAKE LESS, AS IT IS A WONDERFUL LEFTOVER).

Doves Braised in Port

⅓ stick butter
3 tablespoons olive oil
1 cup diced onions
12 doves, cleaned
2 tablespoons brandy
2 tablespoons all-purpose flour
1 quart chicken broth
1 cup port or red Burgundy
1 teaspoon chopped fresh thyme
BOUQUET GARNI
1 sprig of parsley
1 bay leaf

In a large Dutch oven melt the butter in the oil over moderate heat, add the onions, and sauté until they are tender. Brown the doves over moderately high heat, add the brandy, and carefully ignite it. When the flames subside, remove the doves to a platter, and set them aside. Add the flour to the pan, stir until the roux is bubbly and walnut-colored, gradually stir in the chicken broth and port or Burgundy, bring the sauce to a boil, stirring, and boil it for 3 minutes, until it is thickened and smooth. Add the thyme, tie the parsley and bay leaf together with kitchen string to make the bouquet garni, add it to the sauce, and simmer the sauce until it is reduced by half. Return the doves to the pan, and simmer them slowly for 15 minutes or until they are cooked. Remove the doves to a platter, season the sauce with salt and pepper, and ladle it through a sieve over the doves.

SERVES 3 TO 4.

Artichoke Bottoms Stuffed with Artichokes

large artichokes, boiled, hot or cold
hollandaise sauce for hot artichokes
mayonnaise for cold artichokes
salt and pepper to taste

Remove the leaves from the artichokes, and with a metal teaspoon, scrape off the edible part into a bowl. Mix in enough hollandaise sauce or mayonnaise to coat, and season with salt and pepper. Remove and discard the fuzzy chokes from the remaining artichokes, set the bottoms on a plate, and fill them with the leaf mixture.

Crème Brûlée

2 cups heavy cream
one 1-inch piece of vanilla bean
4 large egg yolks
2 tablespoons granulated sugar
brown sugar
strawberries or other fresh fruit

In a medium heavy saucepan combine the heavy cream and the vanilla bean, and heat the mixture over moderately low heat until it is hot but not boiling. In a bowl combine the egg yolks with the granulated sugar, beat until blended, and pour in the hot cream mixture in a slow stream, whisking until blended. Pour the mixture back into the saucepan, cleaned. Heat the mixture over low heat until it is thickened and coats the back of a spoon. If it should begin to curdle, immediately remove the pan from the heat, and whisk the mixture vigorously. Pour the custard into a shallow glass oven-safe dish not more than 2 inches deep, cover it with plastic wrap placed directly on the surface of the custard to prevent a skin from forming, and refrigerate it overnight. The next day, sprinkle the custard with a ¼-inch-thick layer of brown sugar, sieving the sugar if it is lumpy. Place the dish under the broiler, and heat it until the sugar caramelizes, watching carefully so the sugar does not burn. Refrigerate the custard until serving, and serve with the strawberries. SERVES 4 TO 6.

NOTE: The recipe may be doubled or tripled without a problem.

Erlinda's Roast Boned and Stuffed Chicken

THE STUFFING
1 pound ground white chicken meat
1 pound ground dark chicken meat
2 large eggs
2 tablespoons heavy cream
1 teaspoon ground cumin
salt and pepper to taste
1 black truffle, cut into thin julienne strips

one 3¹/₂-pound chicken, boned

In a bowl combine the ground chicken, eggs, heavy cream, and cumin, season with salt and pepper, and gently mix in the truffle. Pack the chicken with the stuffing mixture, and wrap it in aluminum foil. Set the chicken on a rack over boiling water in a large saucepan and steam it, covered, for 1 hour, or until it is cooked, adding more boiling water to the pan if necessary during cooking. Set the chicken and the rack in a roasting pan, carefully fold back the foil, and brown the chicken in a preheated 400°F. oven. Serve the chicken sliced.   SERVES 6 TO 8.

Fresh Pear Ice Cream with Chocolate Leaves and Poached Pears

1 large egg
¹/₃ cup sugar
3 large firm Bartlett pears, peeled, cored, cut into chunks, and pureed until smooth in a food processor
1 cup heavy cream, well-chilled
1 teaspoon pear brandy or ¹/₂ teaspoon vanilla and ¹/₂ teaspoon almond extract
Poached Pears (recipe follows)
Chocolate Leaves (recipe follows) for garnish

In a large bowl whisk the egg and sugar until thick and creamy. Whisk in the pear puree, heavy cream, and the brandy or extracts, and freeze the mixture in

an ice-cream freezer as the manufacturer directs. Serve the ice cream with the poached pears and chocolate leaves.   MAKES 1 PINT.

Poached Pears

¹/₄ to ¹/₂ cup sugar to taste
1 cup water
the zest of a lemon removed with a vegetable peeler; or fresh gingerroot, peeled and sliced
the juice of ¹/₂ lemon
4 pears with stems intact

In a deep saucepan combine the sugar, water, lemon zest or ginger, and lemon juice; bring the liquid to a boil, stirring until the sugar is dissolved, and simmer the syrup for 5 to 10 minutes. Peel the pears, leaving the stem intact, add them to the syrup, and simmer them, covered, for 45 minutes, or until they are tender. Cool and then chill the pears.
                    SERVES 4.

Chocolate Leaves

semisweet-chocolate pieces
assorted small leaves, rinsed and patted dry

In the top of a double boiler set over hot, not boiling, water, melt the chocolate, stirring it until smooth. Remove the pan from the heat and let the chocolate cool slightly, stirring it occasionally. With a table knife, spread the chocolate thickly over the back of each leaf, and place the leaves, chocolate side up, on a plate. Refrigerate the leaves until the chocolate hardens, and then carefully peel away the real leaves from the chocolate.

Postrio Lamb and Eggplant Crépinettes

THE FILLING

1 medium yellow onion, cut into ¹/₄-inch cubes

1 sweet red pepper, seeded and cut into ¹/₄-inch cubes

1 large clove garlic, crushed

about ¹/₄ cup olive oil

1 medium globe eggplant, or 2 large Japanese eggplants, cut into ¹/₄-inch cubes

salt and pepper to taste

THE SAUSAGE

5 pounds ground lamb or cubed lamb shoulder if grinding your own

1¹/₄ ounces salt

¹/₂ ounce coarsely ground black pepper

¹/₄ ounce ground coriander

1 head (3 ounces) of garlic, peeled, minced fine

1 bunch Italian parsley, chopped

1 cup chicken broth, chilled

1 pound caul fat

additional olive oil for frying

eggs, cooked the way you like them

Make the filling: In a large skillet sauté the onion, pepper, and garlic in some of the oil, cooking the mixture until the onion begins to soften. With a slotted spoon, transfer the vegetables to a bowl, and set aside. To the hot drippings in the pan add more oil, and when it is hot, add the eggplant, and cook it, stirring, until it begins to soften and brown. Return the onion mixture to the pan, and cook it over moderately high heat, stirring to mix well. Season with salt and black pepper, transfer the mixture to a baking sheet, and refrigerate it until ready to assemble the crépinettes.

Make the sausage: Spread the ground lamb or lamb cubes over a baking sheet and refrigerate until well-chilled. In a small bowl combine the salt, pepper, coriander, garlic, and parsley; mix well, and evenly sprinkle the mixture over the lamb. If using cubed lamb, at this point grind it through a medium plate. Place the seasoned ground lamb in a mixing bowl and with an electric mixer mix it for 1 minute, adding the broth slowly during the first 30 seconds. Refrigerate the sausage until ready to assemble the

crépinettes, or refrigerate it overnight for a better flavor.

Assemble the crépinettes: Cut the caul fat into 4-inch squares (approximately 20). Divide the sausage into 4-ounce balls, and flatten each into a pancake. Spoon 1 teaspoon of the eggplant filling into the center of each sausage pancake, fold the meat around the filling, and flatten each ball into a pancake, keeping the filling inside the sausage. Wrap each patty in a caul-fat square, making sure that the skin overlaps slightly on the underside.

Cook the crépinettes: Heat a skillet over medium heat, add a few drops of the oil, fry the crépinettes, seam side down, until lightly browned, turn them and cook on the second side, about a minute altogether. Serve the crépinettes with the eggs.

MAKES 20 PATTIES.

Postrio Olive Thyme Bread

3 cups unbleached all-purpose flour

³/₄ cup whole-wheat flour

2 tablespoons minced fresh thyme leaves

1 tablespoon fresh yeast (1 cake)

1¹/₂ teaspoons salt

1 cup warm water

¹/₄ cup olive oil

1 cup pitted niçoise olives, sliced

In a large bowl of an electric mixer combine the all-purpose flour, whole-wheat flour, thyme, yeast, salt, and warm water. Mix at low speed for 2 minutes with the dough hook. At one higher speed add the oil and olives, and mix for 4 to 5 minutes, adding additional water as needed to make a stiff but cohesive dough. Turn out the dough on a lightly floured surface, and knead briefly just until the dough feels soft but is not smooth. Place the dough on a lightly floured surface, cover it with a slightly damp clean kitchen towel, and let the dough rise in a warm place free from drafts for about 45 minutes, or until doubled.

Cut the dough in half, and working with half of the dough at a time, punch the dough down to flatten it, stretch it into a rectangle, and fold it lengthwise into thirds, then fold it in half, closing the seam by hitting it firmly with the heel of your hand. Roll the resulting cylinder lightly across the table to round it.

Place the loaves in a warm place with the seam sides up, covered with a clean kitchen towel, and let them rise for about 30 minutes.

Heat the oven to 450°F. and place a baking stone on the upper rack. When the stone is hot and the bread is ready, turn the loaves over and make a shallow lengthwise cut across the tops. Slide the dough onto the stone and bake them for 35 to 40 minutes, or until the desired color is attained. Cool the breads completely before serving.   MAKES 2 LOAVES.

Postrio Deep-fried Whole Fish with Cucumber Salad and Ponzu

THE SALAD
1 hothouse cucumber, sliced very thin crosswise

one 2-inch piece daikon (Japanese radish, available at specialty produce markets), peeled and sliced thin crosswise

$^1/_2$ teaspoon of salt, plus extra to taste

1 small red onion, sliced thin crosswise

1 bunch fresh mint, leaves only, chopped fine

$^1/_2$ cup chili oil or olive oil

$^1/_4$ cup lime juice (fresh only)

$^1/_4$ cup rice-wine vinegar

salt and pepper to taste

THE PONZU SAUCE
$^1/_2$ cup Japanese soy sauce or tamari

$^1/_4$ cup lime juice (fresh only)

$^1/_4$ cup rice-wine vinegar

1 jalapeño pepper, seeded and sliced into rings

1 scallion, sliced

1 teaspoon finely chopped cilantro (fresh coriander)

THE BATTER
1 cup all-purpose flour

1 tablespoon baking powder

1 tablespoon chopped cilantro (fresh coriander) and chives

$1^1/_4$ cups water

salt and pepper to taste

one 1- to $1^1/_2$-pound whole fish such as American red snapper or striped bass, scaled and cleaned

peanut oil for deep-frying

flour for dredging

salt and pepper to taste

Make the salad: In a colander or strainer combine the cucumber, the daikon, and $^1/_2$ teaspoon salt, and toss the mixture to coat the vegetables with the salt. Let the mixture stand to drain for 30 minutes. Transfer the mixture to a bowl, add the onion, mint, oil, lime juice, and vinegar, mix well, and season with salt and pepper. The mixture should be crunchy and have enough liquid in it to dip the cooked fish in.

Make the sauce: In a bowl combine the soy sauce or tamari, lime juice, and vinegar; mix well, and let the sauce sit for 1 hour or so for the flavors to combine. No salt or pepper should be needed.

Make the batter: In a bowl combine the flour, baking powder, cilantro and chives, and cups water; mix well to eliminate lumps, and season to taste with salt and pepper. Let the batter sit for a few minutes while preparing the fish to relax and form a lighter coating.

Prepare the fish: With a sharp knife cut the fillets from the carcass of the fish, remove all the small bones using a tweezers or needle-nose pliers, and remove the skin. The carcass may be fried before the fillets and kept warm for a few minutes in a 350°F. oven. Sprinkle the carcass with salt and pepper, dip it into flour to coat completely, shaking off the excess, lower into a wok or deep skillet of 350°F. oil, and fry it until crisp and golden brown. Much of the meat remaining on the bones can be eaten. Dip the fillets into the batter to coat evenly and fry them in the same manner.

To serve, place the fish carcass on a plate with the fillets alongside. Serve the cucumber salad and ponzu sauce in separate bowls on the side.

SERVES 2 TO 4.

Three-Layer Chocolate Mousse

Each layer of the mousse is made separately but exactly the same way. Chill one layer while making the next one. The mousse can be layered in wineglasses or parfait glasses for individual servings, or as one large mousse in an 8-inch springform pan, and if using the springform pan, chill it completely in the freezer for 1 hour before unmolding.

THE SEMISWEET-CHOCOLATE LAYER

4^1/2 *ounces semisweet chocolate, grated*

1 *tablespoon brewed espresso*

1 *tablespoon Grand Marnier*

^{1}/3 *cup heavy cream*

^{1}/3 *cup crème fraîche*

THE MILK-CHOCOLATE LAYER

4^1/2 *ounces milk chocolate, grated*

1 *tablespoon brewed espresso*

1 *tablespoon Grand Marnier*

^{1}/3 *cup heavy cream*

^{1}/3 *cup crème fraîche*

THE WHITE-CHOCOLATE LAYER

4^1/2 *ounces white chocolate, grated*

1 *tablespoon Grand Marnier*

^{1}/3 *cup heavy cream*

^{1}/3 *cup crème fraîche*

Make the semisweet-chocolate layer first: In a stainless-steel bowl set over a pan of hot—not boiling—water, combine the chocolate, espresso, and Grand Marnier. Heat the mixture, stirring, until the chocolate melts and the mixture is smooth. Remove the bowl from the heat, and let the mixture cool. In a small bowl with an electric mixer combine the heavy cream and crème fraîche, beat the mixture at high speed until it holds medium peaks (do not overbeat), and with a rubber spatula, fold the cream mixture into the chocolate mixture. Pour or pipe the mixture into the desired container, and chill it until it is set.

In the meantime, make the milk-chocolate layer: Make the mousse following the directions for the semisweet-chocolate layer, pour or pipe it over the semisweet-chocolate mousse, and chill it until it is set.

Make the white-chocolate layer: Make the mousse following the directions for the semisweet-chocolate layer, without the espresso. Pour or pipe the white-chocolate mousse over the milk-chocolate mousse, and chill it until it is set.

To unmold the mousse in a springform pan: Wrap a warm kitchen towel around the outside of the pan to slightly melt the mousse, and remove the side of the pan.   SERVES 6.

JEREMIAH TOWER WITH MRS. PRENTICE COBB HALE

Lobster and Asparagus Ragout

two 1-pound lobsters

4 sprigs fresh tarragon

^{1}/2 *cup rich fish-shellfish stock*

^{1}/2 *cup heavy cream*

^{1}/2 *stick (^{1}/4 cup) unsalted butter*

1 bunch asparagus, tips only

salt and pepper to taste

one large brioche bread, hollowed-out, buttered on the inside and heated

Plunge the lobsters, head first, into a kettle of boiling salted water, return the water to a boil, and cook them, covered, for 5 minutes. Transfer the lobsters to a large basin of ice and water to cool for 5 minutes, drain them, remove the meat, place the green roe in a small bowl, and cut the meat into ^{1}/2-inch chunks.

In a small saucepan boil the tarragon in the fish stock for 3 minutes, strain the liquid into a sauté pan (discard the tarragon), add the heavy cream, bring the liquid to a boil, and simmer it for 10 minutes. Remove the pan from the heat and whisk the butter into the stock until it is melted. Add the lobster meat, and let it warm through.

In the meantime cook the asparagus tips in boiling salted water for 5 minutes, or until they are tender; drain them and stir them into the cream mixture. Remove 1/2 cup of the warm ragout liquid to the bowl with the roe, whisk until blended, and add the mixture to the ragout. Reheat the ragout very quickly until it is hot but not near a boil, stirring constantly, season it with salt and pepper, and serve it in the brioche.   SERVES 4.

ANITA   MARDIKIAN   PICHLER

Lamb Shish Kebab

one 5- to 6-pound leg of lamb, trimmed, boned, and cut into
    1-inch squares
1/2 pound onions, sliced
1 tablespoon salt
1 teaspoon dried oregano, crumbled
1/3 cup sherry
2 tablespoons olive oil

In a large bowl combine the lamb, onions, salt, oregano, sherry, and oil, mix well, and marinate the lamb, covered, at room temperature for at least 1 hour, or overnight in the refrigerator. Arrange the meat on skewers, and broil the shish kebab over a charcoal fire until browned and crisp on all sides.
SERVES 6 TO 8.

Bulgur Pilaf

1 small onion, chopped fine
1 stick (1/2 cup) butter
3 cups bulgur
6 cups chicken, lamb or beef broth
salt and pepper to taste

In a large skillet sauté the onion in 1 tablespoon of the butter for 2 minutes, or until the onion is tender, and transfer it to a bowl. In the same skillet melt the remaining butter over moderate heat, add the bulgur, and cook the mixture, stirring, until the butter begins to bubble. Stir in the onion and the broth, season with salt and pepper, bring the liquid to a boil, and transfer the mixture to a baking dish. Bake the bulgur mixture in a preheated 375°F. to 400°F. oven for 30 minutes, remove the dish from the oven and stir the mixture, and bake for 10 minutes longer.
SERVES 12.

Rose Petal Preserves

2 cups rose petals
2 tablespoons lemon juice
2 cups sugar
1 1/2 cups water

Wash the petals, pluck off the white part at the end of each one, and in a medium saucepan combine the petals and the lemon juice. Stir the petals over low heat with a wooden spoon until the petals disintegrate, and transfer them to a bowl of cold water—this will help keep the color bright. In a small saucepan combine the sugar with the water, stirring until the sugar dissolves; bring the syrup to a boil over high heat, and add the petals, drained. Simmer the mixture over low heat for 10 to 12 minutes, stirring, until the syrup thickens, remove the mixture from the heat, and let it cool.   MAKES ABOUT 2 CUPS.

Squash, Chicken, and Sausage Soup

*1 winter squash (acorn, hubbard, etc.) large enough to serve
  as a tureen*

1 small chicken

1 tablespoon salt

cayenne to taste

2 carrots, chopped

2 celery stalks, chopped

2 scallions, chopped

1 pound cooked chorizo, sliced

Cut off the stem end of the squash, remove the seeds, and scoop out 1 pound of the flesh, leaving the squash shell to serve as a tureen to hold the soup. Put the squash shell on a baking sheet, and set it aside.

In a kettle cover the chicken with water, add the salt and 2 dashes of the cayenne, bring the liquid to a boil, and simmer the chicken, covered, for 30 minutes. Remove the chicken from the liquid, discard the skin and bones, and remove the meat. Cut the meat into pieces and return it to the cooking liquid in the kettle, add the carrots, the celery, the scallions, and the chorizo, and simmer the mixture for 12 to 15 minutes, or until the vegetables are cooked. Meanwhile, bake the squash shell in a preheated 325°F. oven until it is warm. Ladle the soup into the squash shell, and serve the soup from the "tureen."

SERVES 4.

Sautéed Spinach and Radishes

*1 pound radishes, scrubbed, trimmed, and quartered
  lengthwise*

1 stick (¹/₂ cup) butter

1 teaspoon salt

*1 pound spinach leaves, washed well, spun dry, and stems
  removed*

In a skillet sauté the radishes in half the butter with ¹/₂ teaspoon of salt. In another skillet sauté the spinach in the remaining butter with the remaining salt

for 3 to 4 minutes, or until the spinach is tender. While the radishes finish cooking, arrange the spinach in a "nest" on a serving dish, and fill the nest with the radishes. SERVES 4 TO 6.

Braised Pork with Fragrant Purslane
(PORTULACA OLERACEA)

*2 pounds not-too-lean roasting pork cut into 1-by-1¹/₂-inch
  chunks*

¹/₂ cup light olive oil

4 cloves garlic, mashed to a paste

1 teaspoon coarsely ground black pepper

about 2 cups chicken broth

¹/₂ pound fresh purslane sprigs

2 teaspoons salt

Brown the pork on all sides in the oil in a Dutch oven over moderate heat, stir in the garlic and pepper, add the broth, and braise the pork in a preheated 375°F. oven for 1¹/₄ hours, adding more broth or water if needed. Add the purslane and the salt, and cook the mixture for 15 minutes. Pile the purslane in the center of a serving dish, and surround it with the pork. SERVES 4 TO 6.

Mexican Chicken, Pork, and Hominy Stew
(POZOLE)

1 pig's foot or hock (not smoked)

salt and pepper to taste

1 tender whole chicken

2 pounds boneless pork shoulder, cut into small pieces

2 pounds maíz cacahuazinthle (special white corn, available in Mexican food stores as "maíz for pozole," or use canned hominy), washed well in cold water

2 medium onions, minced, plus additional

6 ancho chiles (mild, dried poblanos), toasted, deveined, seeded and minced

4 fresh jalapeño chiles, seeded and minced (wear rubber gloves), or a sauce of green chiles, boiled, seeded, and pureed

2 cloves garlic, minced

vegetable oil

1 pequín chile, minced

1 head of romaine lettuce, minced

dried oregano leaves

6 limes, halved

radishes, minced

hard pieces of tortilla, refried

In a kettle cover the pig's foot with water, season with salt and pepper, bring the liquid to a boil, simmer the mixture for 1 hour, adding more water if necessary, add the chicken and the pork and more water if necessary to cover the meats, cook the mixture for 1 hour, add the corn, and cook for 1 hour, or until the meats and the corn are tender. Remove the meats from the bones, discard the skin and bones, and return the meats to the cooking liquid in the kettle.

In a large heavy skillet cook the 2 minced onions, the *ancho* and jalapeño chiles, and the garlic in the oil over moderately high heat until the onions are tender. Transfer the mixture to the kettle, and add enough water to the mixture so it has a souplike consistency. Bring the mixture to a simmer, and simmer it for 30 minutes, but be careful that the corn does not disintegrate (it should be soft, with the kernels whole).

Serve the soup very hot in bowls, and accompany it with little side dishes of the *pequín*, lettuce, minced onion, oregano, limes, radishes, and tortilla pieces. SERVES 8 TO 10.

Papas Chicas (Baby Potatoes) with Sole, Artichokes, and Onions

1 pound very small new potatoes, scrubbed

4 large or 6 medium artichokes

1 pound small green onions, peeled

6 tablespoons olive oil

6 tablespoons butter

$^{1}/_{2}$ teaspoon dried rosemary, crushed

2 pounds sole fillets, rinsed, patted dry, and cut into 1-inch squares

$^{1}/_{4}$ cup chopped Italian parsley

salt to taste

In a saucepan cook the potatoes in boiling salted water for 15 to 20 minutes, or until they are cooked but still firm, and drain them. In a large saucepan of boiling salted water cook the artichokes for 25 to 30 minutes, or until they are cooked but still firm. Drain the artichokes, discard the leaves and the "chokes," and cut each artichoke heart into eighths. In a saucepan cover the onions with salted water, bring the water to a boil, cook the onions, covered, for 7 to 8 minutes, or until they are cooked but firm, and drain them.

In a large deep skillet heat the oil and butter over moderate heat until the butter is bubbling, add the vegetables and rosemary, and fry gently for 3 to 4 minutes. Add the fish and parsley, and fry gently for 3 to 4 minutes longer, or until the fish is barely cooked through. Season with salt, and serve immediately in hot soup plates. SERVES 6 TO 8.

Broccoli Pie

THE PASTRY
2 cups all-purpose flour

2 teaspoons baking powder

1 teaspoon salt

2 sticks (1 cup) butter

6 to 8 tablespoons ice water

THE FILLING
2 pounds broccoli cut into flowerets, cooked and cooled

1 stick (¹/₂ cup) butter, melted

3 medium carrots, cut into 2-inch sticks, cooked, and cooled

*M*ake the pastry: In a bowl combine the flour, baking powder, and salt, and cut the butter into the mixture until it is the consistency of dry oatmeal. Stir in ice water with a fork, mixing the dough until it is a firm dough, but mixing as little as possible. Form the dough into 2 balls, flatten each into a disk, wrap each in plastic wrap, and refrigerate for 2 minutes.

Roll out each disk into a 14-inch round onto a lightly floured surface. Line a deep 12-inch pie plate with 1 round of pastry, fill it with the broccoli, and drizzle the broccoli with the melted butter. Cut the second round into ³/₄-inch-wide strips, weave the strips into a lattice pattern over the broccoli, cut off the excess at the ends, and pinch the ends into the crust lining the pie plate. Insert the carrot sticks upright to fill the openings in the lattice, and bake the pie in a preheated 375°F. oven for 30 minutes.

SERVES 8.

BARONESS SANDRA DI PORTANOVA

Eggs with Chorizo

3 ounces chorizo, crumbled

1 tablespoon vegetable oil

2 large eggs, beaten

*I*n a small skillet fry the chorizo in the oil over moderate heat, stirring. Add the eggs, and cook them, mixing them with the chorizo, until they are done to taste.

SERVES 1.

Sunset Shrimp Surrealist

¹/₄ cup finely chopped onion

1 clove garlic, minced

1¹/₂ teaspoons chili powder

¹/₂ teaspoon paprika

1 cup lemon or lime juice

2 tablespoons Worcestershire sauce

3 dashes hot red-pepper sauce

12 jumbo shrimp, shelled and deveined, heads and tails intact

butter, melted

*I*n a bowl combine the onion, garlic, chili powder, paprika, lemon or lime juice, Worcestershire, and hot-pepper sauce, and blend well. Add the shrimp, cover, and marinate them overnight in the refrigerator. To cook, arrange the shrimp on skewers and barbecue them, basting with the melted butter, until they are done. Serve the shrimp on the skewers at sunset with chilled dry white wine or champagne.

SERVES 2.

Coconut Ice

the milk from 1 coconut

1 cup heavy cream

14 ounces cream of coconut

14 ounces condensed milk

4 ounces shredded coconut

six coconut half shells

*I*n a bowl combine the coconut milk, heavy cream, cream of coconut, condensed milk, and shredded coconut, and pour the mixture into an ice-cream freezer. Freeze the mixture according to the freezer manufacturer's instructions. Serve the ice sprinkled with grated coconut in coconut shell halves.

SERVES 6.

NOTE: *For pineapple ice, substitute 2 cups pineapple juice for the coconut milk and 4 ounces crushed pineapple for the shredded coconut. Serve the ice in hollowed-out mini-pineapple halves.*

Salmon Surprise (Baked Mozzarella with Smoked Salmon)

2 mozzarella cheeses, or 8 bocconcini (small mozzarellas)

¹/₂ pound thinly sliced smoked salmon

THE SAUCE
2 cups heavy cream

¹/₂ cup chopped parsley, plus additional for garnish

1 clove garlic

¹/₄ teaspoon ground white pepper

¹/₄ teaspoon salt

capers for garnish

pitted black olives for garnish

Slice the mozzarella into twelve 3-x-2-x-1-inch pieces, wrap each piece in 1 or 2 slices of the salmon, and place them in an aluminum foil–lined baking dish.

Make the sauce: In a blender combine the heavy cream, ¹/₂ cup parsley, the garlic, pepper, and salt; mix the sauce for several seconds, or until it is blended well, and pour it into the top of a double boiler. Heat the sauce until it is warm but do not let it boil, and bake the mozzarella pieces in a preheated 350°F. oven for about 5 minutes, or until the mozzarella is soft but not runny. (Do not start to bake the mozzarella until the sauce is warm.) Place 2 of the baked mozzarella pieces on each of 6 warm plates, top the pieces with 5 to 6 tablespoons of the warm sauce, and garnish them with parsley, a few of the capers, and the olives. Serve immediately.

SERVES 6.

Pasta Arabesque

1 pound cooked spinach, well drained

2 cups heavy cream

1 clove garlic

the juice of 1 lemon

¹/₂ teaspoon pepper

salt to taste

2 pounds macaroni

warm milk (optional)

grated Parmesan cheese

In a food processor or blender combine the spinach, heavy cream, garlic, lemon juice, pepper, and salt. Puree the mixture until smooth, transfer it to the top of a double boiler, and heat it well but do not let it boil. In a kettle of boiling salted water boil the macaroni until it is *al dente,* and drain it. In a large bowl combine the hot puree and the macaroni, and toss the mixture well, stirring in a little of the warm milk if the sauce is too thick. Serve the pasta on prewarmed plates, and pass the Parmesan separately.

SERVES 8 TO 10.

Pasta Jada (Jade) or Acapulco

4 to 6 large ripe avocados, pitted and skinned

1 cup heavy cream

2 cloves garlic

2 pounds rigatoni

grated Parmesan cheese to taste

pitted black olives to taste

warm milk (optional)

In a food processor or blender combine the avocados, cream, and garlic, and puree the mixture until smooth. Transfer it to the top of a double boiler, and warm it for a short while. In a kettle of boiling salted water boil the rigatoni until it is *al dente,* and drain it. In a large bowl combine the warm puree, the rigatoni, Parmesan, and olives, and toss the mixture well, stirring in a little warm milk if the sauce is too thick. Serve immediately.

SERVES 10 TO 12.

NOTE: *This dish is also excellent served cold.*

Pasta di Portanova with Caviar

3 cups heavy cream

1 cup (4 ounces) grated imported Swiss cheese

1/2 teaspoon ground white pepper

2 pounds tagliolini or fettuccine, preferably homemade

1 pound caviar

In the top of a double boiler heat the cream until it is hot but not boiling, add the cheese, stirring until it is melted, and the pepper (do not add salt). Meanwhile, in a kettle of boiling salted water cook the tagliolini or fettuccine until it is cooked a little more than al dente, and drain it. In a large bowl combine the pasta, cheese sauce, and 2 tablespoons of the caviar, and toss the mixture gently, trying not to break the caviar eggs. Arrange the pasta on pre-warmed plates, make a neat hole in the center of the pasta on each plate, and fill the hole with a large tablespoonful of the remaining caviar. Serve immediately. SERVES 10 TO 12.

Index

PHOTOGRAPHY CREDITS

Frontispiece: Billy Cunningham. Pages ii–iii: Billy Cunningham. Pages 2–9: Billy Cunningham. Page 10 (l): Billy Cunningham. Page 10 (r): Eric Boman. Page 13: Eric Boman. Page 14: Eric Boman. Page 16: Eric Boman. Pages 18–27: Pascal Hinous. Pages 28–31: Marina Faust. Pages 32–33: Pascal Hinous. Pages 34–35: Pascal Hinous. Page 35: Ricardo Vidargas. Pages 36–41: Pascal Hinous. Pages 42–57: Manfredi Bellati. Pages 58–59: Isidoro Genovese. Pages 60–61: Manfredi Bellati. Pages 62–97: Billy Cunningham. Pages 98–101: Peter Vitale. Pages 102–119: Billy Cunningham. Pages 120–121: Edgar de Evia. Pages 122–125: Eric Boman. Pages 126–167: Billy Cunningham. Pages 168–183: Peter Vitale.